THE DESERT AIR WAR

In the face of the massive publicity accorded to General Montgomery and his adversary, General Erwin Rommel, and bearing in mind the endless controversy that has raged over the dismissal by Mr Churchill of Generals Wavell and Auchinleck, it is easy to forget that the war in North Africa would have run a very different course had it not been for the part played by the Royal Air Force. During those long months when the men on the ground went back and forth across the desert in a dizzying succession of triumphs and reverses the men of the Royal Air Force, often woefully underequipped, struggled valiantly to keep possession of the skies under which the troops were fighting.

Richard Bickers, author of several books on the history of the aerial warfare, saw the war in North Africa and Italy from both the ground and the air, and uses his own experiences, interwoven with the recollections of numerous contemporaries, to create a vivid picture of what it was like to fly, to fight and to control operations over the desert at that time. He also gives the usually ignored ground crews the full measure of the recognition due to them — ground gunners, armourers, motor transport drivers and others.

In view of the fact that death was never very far away, the impression he creates of life in the Desert Air Force is surprisingly light-hearted. But, as he says, they were all very young at the time, morale was also high and nothing was to be gained by going around with a long face. An unending diet of sand and flies found compensation in the thrill of flying and the re-emergence of a kind of chivalry conjured up by this new and sophisticated form of combat.

In Richard Bickers the men of the Desert Air Force have found a talent worthy of their exploits and their indomitably cheerful spirit.

By the same author:

GINGER LACEY, FIGHTER PILOT
(Robert Hale, 1962)

THE FIRST GREAT AIR WAR
(Hodder & Stoughton, 1988)

THE BATTLE OF BRITAIN
(Salamander, 1990)

THE
DESERT AIR WAR
1939-1945

by

Richard Townshend Bickers

LEO COOPER · LONDON

First published in Great Britain in 1991 by
LEO COOPER
190 Shaftesbury Avenue, London, WC2H 8JL
an imprint of Pen & Sword Books Ltd.
47 Church Street, Barnsley, S. Yorks., S70 2AS.

Copyright © Richard Townshend Bickers, 1991
A CIP catalogue record for this book is available from
The British Library
ISBN: 0–85052–216–1

Printed and bound in Great Britain by
Redwood Press Limited
Melksham, Wiltshire

NI 940.544

CONTENTS

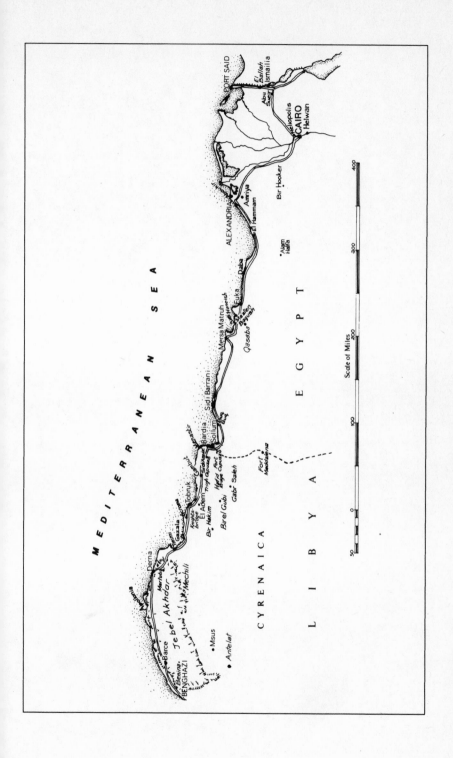

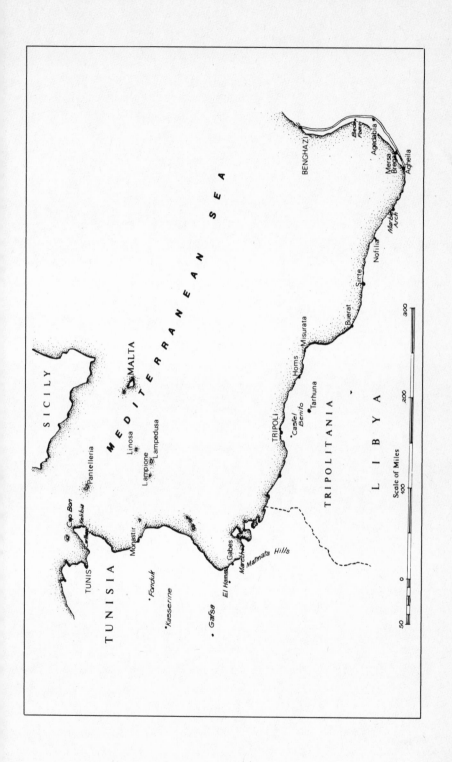

MEDITERRANEAN SEA

SICILY

MALTA

Linosa

Pantelleria

Lampione

Lampedusa

Cap Bon

Kelibia

Monastir

TUNIS

Fonduk

Kasserine

Gafsa

El Hamma

Gabes

Mareth

Matmata Hills

TUNISIA

TRIPOLI

Castel
Benito

Tarhuna

Homs

Misurata

Buerat

Sirte

Nofilia

Marble
Arch

Mersa
Brega

Agheila

Agedabia

Beda
Fomm

BENGHAZI

TRIPOLITANIA

LIBYA

Scale of Miles

50   0   100   200   300

THE DESERT AIR WAR

CHAPTER 1

"Boundless and bare
the lone and level sands stretch far."
Shelley.

On 11 December, 1940, Flying Officer Charles Harold Dyson of No 33 Squadron R.A.F., returning alone from a patrol over the Libyan desert in his Hurricane, experienced a shock like that of a skin-diver blundering into a shoal of sharks. Emerging from a small patch of cloud, he saw seven Italian aircraft close in front of him. One was a Savoia-Marchetti S79 bomber. Its escort, flying in two Vs of three, were Fiat CR42 fighters. Dyson was returning to base at Mersa Matruh, in Egypt. The Italians, looking ahead as they also flew eastwards, did not see him astern.

He opened fire at once before the dorsal gunner, who was supposed to guard the bomber's tail, spotted him and gave the alarm. With two long bursts, he first set the three CR42s in the rear V alight, then those in the leading V. He lingered only for the few seconds necessary to confirm that all six were going down in flames or emitting smoke, to certain destruction or a crash landing, before he darted back into the shelter of cloud in case there were more enemy fighters in the vicinity.

During his pre-war service in Egypt and Palestine, and more recently when flying over the Western Desert, Dyson had made so many forced landings through engine failure that he had earned the nickname "Deadstick". Now he was about to repeat the experience. Coming out of cloud again he was immediately attacked by six more CR42s. Combat between fighters still followed the pattern of the First World War: biplanes at comparatively low speed were as nimble as a swallow and pilots had to be as dexterous as a one-armed juggler trying to keep three balls in the air while he scratched himself. Even the monoplane Hurricanes, Spitfires and Messerschmitt 109s fighting over France and southern England used the same tightly-turning swooping and soaring tactics,

1

as the R.A.F. strove to penetrate a mass of escorting fighters to reach the bombers. The technique would change later, as it had in 1916, when fighter pilots would try to despatch an opponent in one fast, diving attack and then either zoom up for a belly shot or depart the scene. For the time being circumstances had forced them to revert to the earliest form of air combat, particularly when one man was beset by several other fighters.

Dyson had used most of his 14.8 seconds' worth of ammunition. Conserving what little he had left, to use it most effectively, he began to twist and jink among the Fiats, which needed less space for their manoeuvres than a Hurricane, until he could get in a telling shot. If he could not bring his sights to bear on one of them, he would either have to resort to a spin, which would make him the most difficult target to follow and to aim at, or rely on speed to dive steeply. Diving out of trouble could be risky, because for a few seconds he would be extremely vulnerable as he followed a straight path instead of zig-zagging, which would have reduced his speed. He fired at the nearest CR42 and saw strikes that caused it to lurch from side to side and lose height, apparently out of control, before he ran out of bullets. The others were shooting at him and red flashes and orange sparks skittered along the Hurricane's cowling. He put its nose down, shoved the throttle forward and felt the exhilaration in his senses and the pressures on his body of a high-speed dive. With a final judder and a puff of oily black smoke the engine stopped, but the enemy were too slow to catch him. Unhurt, he put his machine down somewhere near Sollum, 120 miles from his home airfield.

When he did not return to the squadron that night he was automatically reported missing and, as he failed to turn up the next day or the day after that, he was presumed dead. When at last he reached base on 17 December and claimed to have destroyed six enemy aircraft he was gratified to learn that the true total was seven. Soldiers had watched his fight and found the wreckage. One of the burning fighters had collided with the bomber and it too had gone down. This number of enemy aircraft shot down in one action was not attained by any other Allied pilot throughout the war. He claimed also a probable victory in his brief second engagement, but this was never confirmed.

In 1938 Dyson had won the Distinguished Flying Cross for ground attack operations against rebel tribesmen in Palestine. For his latest feat he was awarded a bar to it. Had he been adrift in the desert for those six days a few months later, he would have qualified for another, but unofficial, award − the winged silver boot of The Late Arrivals Club, to pin − against regulations − beneath his wings. The Club, whose motto was "It is never too late to come back", was originated by Squadron Leader G.W. Houghton, a Public Relations Officer, in mid-1941 to encourage aircrew who found themselves in a similar predicament to Dyson's by drawing attention to the many who had already survived such an ordeal. In addition to the small insignia, each member received a certificate that stated: "This is to certify that — of — Squadron is hereby nominated a member of The Late Arrivals Club. Inasmuch as he, in — on —, when obliged to abandon his aircraft, on the ground or in the air, as a result of unfriendly action by the enemy, succeeded in returning to his squadron, on foot or by any other means, long after his Estimated Time of Arrival."

That dazzling achievement and his earlier record before the war were not Deadstick Dyson's only distinctions. He had already destroyed five enemy aircraft on the ground in one strafe and went on to shoot down two more in the air over North Africa. Between January and May, 1941, when the Squadron was in Greece and Crete to meet the Axis invasion, he claimed a further sixteen victories; but the Squadron's records did not survive the campaign, so confirmation of these was lost. Dyson was captured in Crete and spent the rest of the war in a prison camp.

The only man who is thought to have exceeded Dyson's score in a single engagement allegedly established not only this record for the Axis Powers but also a global one for the greatest number of victories in a day — one of the most famous airmen of the war, Hauptmann Hans-Joachim Marseille.

On 1 September, 1942, Marseille, then an *Oberleutnant*, was commanding a *Staffel* of Messerschmitt 109s in I/JG27. During the night of 30-31 August General Rommel had opened an attack that was intended finally to defeat the British Eighth Army. The battle for Alam Halfa, a tactically dominant ridge that became known to the Germans as "the Stalingrad of the desert", was at its height. The air fighting, strafing and bombing were as fierce as the infantry, armoured and artillery conflict. At 7.30 am the *Staffel* joined a formation of dive bombers as escort. They were at 3,500 metres and approaching their target when Marseille gave a radio warning that he had sighted the enemy. According to the German report, "Ten minute dots that swiftly grew bigger".

A few kilometres further on, as the Stukas began their dive, Marseille reefed into a climbing turn to the right and called, "I'm attacking". The account continues:

"In a twinkling, his No 2 saw him swing to the left, position himself behind the last of the suddenly scattering Curtiss P40s [Kittyhawks] and shoot at a range of 100 metres. The enemy aeroplane lurched abruptly on to its left wingtip and, burning, fell like a stone vertically to the ground. The time was 8.20." But these were not Kittyhawks, they were Hurricanes of No 1 Squadron South African Air Force. Nor were there ten of them, but twelve.

At 8.30, according to his No 2, Marseille sent down another "Kittyhawk" in flames. The Stukas had bombed and the fighters had descended to 100 metres to join them on their homeward course. One "Kittyhawk" had preceded them, evidently intending to attack the dive bombers, but Marseille pounced on it and "the flames from burning wreckage lit the desert". It was now 8.33 by his No 2's watch. A few minutes later came the alarm call "Spitfires!" The other Me109s had stayed with the Stukas. Six Spitfires of 92 Squadron swept down on Marseille and his wing man from above and astern. Marseille waited for the right moment to break. He saw one of the Spitfires open fire with cannon and machine guns. Tracer streaked past as he went into a climbing turn so that their opponents would overshoot beneath him and his No 2. Turning tightly, he came in 80 metres behind the last Spitfire and sent it crashing down, emitting smoke. His winger's watch showed 8.39.

Allied records prove that during this action, in which twelve Hurricanes of 238 Squadron also joined, Major Metelerkamp and Lieutenant Bailey of 1 S.A.A.F. were wounded and crash-landed their severely damaged aircraft. Flying Officer Matthews of 238 Squadron also had to crash-land. Pilot Officer Bradley-Smith of 92 Squadron baled out. The German account ignores the fact that some six Messerschmitts were damaged.

When Marseille landed at 9.14 he had used only eighty rounds of cannon and 240 of machine gun in making his four kills. That was good shooting, but not the best. Squadron Leader J. H. "Ginger" Lacey, the top-scoring R.A.F. pilot in the Battle of Britain, when commanding a Spitfire squadron in Burma in 1945, shot down a more difficult target, a Japanese Zero, with nine rounds of cannon at twice the range.

At 10.20 am Marseille took off at the head of a *Kette*, a section of three, to cover another Stuka raid. Although it was the Luftwaffe that had introduced the fighter tactic of flying in pairs separated laterally by 200 metres and in height by about 150 − copied after the Battle of Britain by the R.A.F. − and two pairs together were usually the smallest fighter formation, they had recently reverted to threes on some occasions in North Africa. (The German account emphasizes that there were *only* three on this mission, not the twelve sometimes attributed.) Shortly before reaching the objective he saw two British formations, each of fifteen to eighteen bombers escorted by twenty-five to thirty Kittyhawks. Twelve of the Kitties belonged to No 3 Squadron Royal Australian Air Force. "He had never been a man to be impressed by superior numbers of the enemy," the German account says. He waited a few seconds until eight Curtiss P40s peeled off and made for the Stukas, before turning his section towards them. As the Germans approached, the P40s formed a defensive circle. "This tactic was effective in normal circumstances, but not against Marseille." He put himself in the middle of the circle and shot down a Kittyhawk at 50 yards range. The time was 10.55. Half a minute later he took out a second. "Suddenly the circle fell apart. The leader had lost his nerve and they all broke away to the north-west." In two minutes Marseille overtook them and a third victim fell. The remaining five turned eastwards, Marseille in pursuit. They changed direction north-westerly again and presently were over the sea with only four left. They turned inland once more. Two minutes after this the fifth went down. The sixth followed one minute later. Three minutes more sufficed for Marseille to shoot down the last two. He had scored eight victories in ten minutes.

When he landed at 11.35 he found that Field-Marshal Kesselring, commanding Luftflotte 2, had come to visit the *Geschwader*. Marseille reported that his *Staffel* had just returned from shooting down its twelfth aircraft of the morning.

"How many did *you* get?" Kesselring asked.

"Twelve, *Herr Feldmarschall*."

Eyewitnesses relate that " The *Generalfeldmarschall* shook the officer by the hand, then sat down lost for words." His legs must have buckled as though he had been treated to that favourite Nazi mind-boggler, a couple of hundred volts through the crotch.

Marseille set off at the head of his *Staffel* on its third sortie of the day at 5 pm, this time escorting Ju88s. The German version is that fifteen fighters, which, as Marseille usually did, he reported as Curtiss P40s, but were in fact twelve Hurricanes of 213 Squadron, spotted them and attacked. It is not clear how any of the German pilots was able to keep his eye on the time and the points of the compass in the pace and turmoil of the ensuing dogfight. It is scarcely credible that anyone could, while hurling his aeroplane about in his attempts to shoot down the enemy and simultaneously trying to avoid the latter's fire. But the German narrative states confidently that "at heights between 1,500 and 100 metres, Marseille's first four victims fell at roughly one-minute intervals between 5.45 and 5.50, the fifth at 5.53. The places where they went down were 7 km south, 8 km south-east, 6 km south-east, 9 km south-south-east and 7 km south-south-west of Imayid". Marseille's claimed tally for the day was therefore seventeen. To mitigate post-war Allied scepticism about his score, the archives confirm that 213 Squadron lost five aeroplanes in this fight: Flying Officer Woolaston was killed and Sergeant Potter was missing, presumed dead. Sergeant Garrod baled out and Flying Officer Avise and Flight Sergeant Ross crash-landed, all three unhurt. But *Leutnant* Stahlschmidt, flying with Marseille, claimed two of these.

Marseille was one of the many fighter pilots who were more interested in adding to their scores than in the worth of the aircraft they destroyed. He would try to pick off escorting fighters rather than cut through to the bombers, which should generally have been every conscientious fighter pilot's priority targets, because the bomber is the prime instrument of aerial warfare and does the greatest damage. He also used often to order the other members of his *Staffel* to hold off while he went in to make the kill, as was demonstrated in his second engagement that day. In such an event there might have been time for his No 2 to note details of time and place, but on this occasion all the Messerschmitts mixed it with the Hurricanes. Such suspect details about an air battle, said to have been recorded by a participant whose attention surely cannot have been wholly concentrated on his leader throughout, is not the sole reason to doubt the veracity of Marseille's claims on that day and throughout his career. German fighter pilots' aircraft recognition was generally poor and it is now well known that his was among the worst. They could seldom distinguish between a Warhawk, a Tomahawk, a Kittyhawk and a Hurricane. Moreover, the total Allied fighter losses for the day were twenty, but the Germans claimed twenty-six. Further, Marseille's total claims during his career, added to the verified kills of other German pilots, exceeded the number of Allied fighters that were actually lost. The most that can be conceded to him for September, 1942, is that he shot down more than a dozen, of which eight might have been on one sortie, which is good enough to be a desert record at least.

On the next five successive days he was credited with five, six, four, four and two respectively. After three barren days he despatched another two; then, four days later, claimed seven more. On 28 September he claimed seven victories again, to make his total for the month fifty-four. With an official aggregate of 158 kills, 151 of them in North Africa, he was to date the Luftwaffe's top scorer. The Allied air forces allow that he must have made more than a hundred kills over the desert. On 24 September, two months before his twenty-third birthday, he had been promoted to *Hauptmann*, the youngest in his Service. On 30 September he was returning to base in a new Me109G when his cockpit filled with white smoke from a coolant leak, then black smoke from a resultant overheated engine. He half-rolled and baled out over base. But, blinded and not knowing that his aircraft was nose-up at an angle of 70 degrees, he struck the tail unit. This either killed or stunned him and he hit the ground from approximately 2,700 metres without having pulled the ripcord.

These episodes, 21 months apart, in the lives of two fighter pilots on opposing sides in the North African campaign, exemplify the essential qualities of the air forces engaged over the Western Desert. In the R.A.F. during the first months of the desert war, with its paltry numbers and aircraft on solitary patrols and reconnaissances, pilots and crews had to be self-reliant, constantly alert and bravely decisive. When Dyson chanced upon a numerically superior enemy force he joined battle without hesitation. The Regia Aeronautica, comfortably aware that it greatly outnumbered its adversary in all types of aircraft, went about its work slackly self-confident and suffered a succession of lethal surprises. The Luftwaffe, when it eventually appeared, showed its habitual thoroughness, determination and discipline.

The Late Arrivals Club was a manifestation of the British way of taking hardship lightly, cocking a snook at adversity, and the R.A.F.'s traditional style of treating misfortune as a joke. To the Italians, such an institution would have been evidence of phlegmatic Anglo-Saxon insensitivity: any heroic aviator lost in the wilderness — for whom his fellows would have indulged in transports of weeping — who survived to return deserved praise and extravagant displays of joy. The Germans it would have baffled, their essentially coprological sense of humour touched only if camel droppings had figured somewhere.

Dyson, with his two DFCs, his nine confirmed victories and probably sixteen more, was no average performer, but to his fellows the vagaries of fortune that had earned him his nickname were comical rather than dramatic, and a not uncommon experience, which made him, in their view, just another normal desert pilot. Any of them given the same lucky chance to jump seven enemy aeroplanes and be presented with the easiest of shots — dead astern with no need to estimate deflection — would probably have done as well. Marseille was a genius whose impeccably precise flying and astoundingly accurate shooting made him known even to his enemies. *Generalleutnant* Adolf Galland, the Luftwaffe's Commander-in-Chief of Fighters from November, 1941, to the war's end, who made 104 kills and was a major-general at 29, says categorically "He was the best".

The desert war began as a sideshow to the Battle of France, which was in its last throes, and the Battle of Britain, which was about to start: an apparently minor production staged by the Italians, whose fighting qualities the British, and later the Germans, held in little respect. This did not mean that North Africa was a theatre to which the second-rate could safely be despatched. Small though it was, Desert Air Force in 1940 was already a first-class force under a formidable commander who had himself shot down sixty German aircraft in the First World War, the third highest scorer of the British Empire. And when Germany entered the fray, she did so with some of her best of all arms.

From the First World War the distinction "ace" has been bestowed on fighter pilots with at least five victories. Of the many aces on both sides in the desert campaign, Britain and the Commonwealth produced the most. The achievements of the most successful German pilots mistakenly appear to suggest a far greater ability than the best among the Allies, because they had much the bigger scores. The reason is that the R.A.F. and Commonwealth air forces alternated tours of operations with periods of rest in ground or non-operational flying posts, whereas the Luftwaffe served continuously with only rare short leaves away from the Front.

Since 1916, when increasingly large formations of aeroplanes began to do battle in many cubic miles of sky, the victory claims of fighter pilots have been, inevitably and understandably, difficult to confirm. In the confusion of air combat more than one pilot would fire at the same enemy machine and honestly believe that he was the one who sent it down. Often an aircraft diving away from a fight with smoke pouring from it was thought to be on fire and doomed, but many a smoking aircraft has returned to base. Sometimes, when an aeroplane pulled away from a dogfight at full throttle, exhaust smoke billowing from its engine was mistaken for a fatal conflagration. Pilots could not verify that opponents whom they had damaged over enemy territory, but had not actually seen hit the ground, did in fact crash. This is not to insinuate that any high-scoring ace deliberately made false claims, but it has to be said that some were conspicuously more optimistic than others, not only in North Africa, but also in every aerial battle zone there has ever been, until jet engines and guided missiles put an end to combat between formations of fighters. In the desert it was harder than anywhere to make an accurate count.

An empathy that creates an esoteric bond exists between fighter pilots of all nations. It arises from the essential characteristics they have in common, of which Dyson and Marseille are exemplars. There is a unique cheerful brutality about the fighter pilot's trade: catch me if you can, and if you can't I'll kill you; no hard feelings either way. If Dyson and Marseille had met, even if one had shot the other down and made him a prisoner, they would undoubtedly have been on friendly terms and probably even liked each other. Not that the aerial campaign in

Egypt and Libya, Algeria and Tunisia, or from 1943 in Italy, was entirely a fighters' affair. As will be seen, the bombers were no less embroiled, and from the men who flew them equal skill and courage was demanded, in the most difficult environment of terrain, climate, living conditions, communications, servicing and supply by which air operations had ever been beset. But there has never been a mutual understanding between bomber crews on opposing sides like the personal bond between those who fly fighters.

It was the terrain, as much as the battles, that demanded special qualities of toughness and equable temperament from the soldiers and airmen who fought on it and above it.

The seabord from the western frontier of Egypt to the Atlantic Ocean, haunt of pirates from the fifteenth century for three hundred years, was known in ancient times as the Barbary Coast. The Romans had called the inhabitants Barbari, the barbarians, from which their name Berbers was derived. Successive invaders over the next twenty centuries knew the hinterland as the Barbary States, but to the Arabs it was Al Jezirat al Maghreb — shortened in modern days to The Maghreb — the Island of the Sunset. It is this fusion of the threatening with the romantic that characterizes the whole battleground.

Our concern here is with Egypt and only part of The Maghreb: Libya, whose eastern province, Cyrenaica, adjoins Egypt, while its western, Tripolitania, marches with Tunisia and its southern, Fezzan, with Algeria. To mark the frontier between Libya and Egypt, the Italians had built a barbed-wire fence. Twenty feet wide, with four rows of five-foot steel posts to support the strands and coils, it ran from the coast due south into the desert for 400 miles. Tanks could smash through it, but otherwise it was impenetrable without wire-cutters.

The conventional image of a desert is a monotonous flat waste of tawny sand, relieved, as in the Sahara, by dunes shaped by the prevailing wind into graceful crescents. The Western Desert, which stretches from the Nile to the Tripolitanian border and extends southward to the Sahara, is a dreary and hideous wasteland but the drab monotony is relieved at different seasons of the year and hours of the day by mutations of the prevailing buff colour into streaks and patches of beige, ochre and grey. On its northern boundary there are glimpses of beauty.

At first, going westwards from Alexandria along the coastal road, the landscape is featureless and ugly. The desert's dun surface is stony and gritty, with outcrops of rock, scattered with stunted scrub and clumps of camel thorn. In the 1940s torpid seaside villages and small ports that have grown today into bustling towns gave some variety of hue to the harsh monochrome with grass, palm trees, silvery beaches and a sight of blue water. At Mersa Matruh, with its fig trees, white domes and minarets, once stood Cleopatra's summer palace where she entertained Anthony. Between the two world wars it had become a popular watering place for rich Cairene families. At Ma'aten Bagush, Sidi Barrani, Sollum and Bardia, dominantly sited on a clifftop, fishing boats and trading dhows found harbour. Tobruk and Benghazi — Euhesperides to the ancient Greeks, Berenice to the Romans — were ports with anchorage for naval and merchant ships.

At Derna — the Roman Darnia — a town of glistening white buildings and purple bougainvillaea, the Jebel Akhdar, the Green Mountain, springs abruptly from the plain to a height of 2,000 ft. This is really a range of hills, 50 miles across at its widest, which extends for 150 miles following the curve of the coastline and separated from it by a strip that is between 10 and 30 miles broad. It was a place of scrub oak forests and extensive cultivation by poor farmers from Italy, whose Government had offered them fertile land, with irrigation and ready-built houses, on which to settle. They prospered among their pastures and cornfields, olive groves, orchards, vineyards, market gardens and flowers, which gave the area a look of southern Europe rather than of Africa. Twelve miles inland from Derna lie the ruins of the Greek and Byzantine city of Cyrene.

If the topography is boring for the most part, the legends, romance and history with which the region is saturated make it one of the most fascinating on earth. In 814 BC the Phoenicians founded Carthage, which became independent two and a half centuries later and the centre of a great empire. In 520 BC the Spartans tried to conquer the city and many Greek buildings still stand. At intervals between 262 and 146 BC the Romans fought the Carthaginians in three long conflicts, the Punic Wars, which they won after an aggregate of 42 years' campaigning. They destroyed the city but its remains were still there for the warriors of the 1940s to see. In 74 BC Cyrenaica became a Roman province. In 429 AD the Vandals landed in the Maghreb and ten years later captured Carthage. Ninety-five years passed before the Byzantines took it and held it until 698 AD, when the Arabs, advancing across the Maghreb from Egypt and creating shock waves of Islamic fervour, ousted them and built Tunis only three miles from where Carthage once stood. Between these dates of particular significance there was a plethora of lesser wars and rebellions, such as the Jewish revolt in Cyrenaica of 115 AD that spread throughout the Middle East amid huge destruction and loss of life. In 1567 the Turks occupied Tripolitania and, in 1640, Cyrenaica.

The Italians drove them out in 1911 and annexed all of Libya. The

Italian Air Corps, formed in 1910, took part with seven aircraft based on a makeshift aerodrome at Tripoli. *Capitano* Carlo Piazza flew the first operational sortie in history when he made a reconnaissance on 23 October, 1911. *Sotto Tenente* Giulio Gavotti, flying the world's first air raid, dropped a two-kilogramme bomb on Ain Zara and three on Tagiura. The whole region had never known enduring stability. It pulsated with the memories, and was strewn with the relics, of 3,000 years of intermittent warfare, a fit setting for the demolition of Mussolini's last African colony and of Hitler's ambitions in Africa.

The opposing air and land forces in this latest trial of arms soon learned that the desert is a capricious, dangerous, and, even at its best, uncomfortable dwelling place. All day the shimmering fierce light hurt the eyes, the heat threatened to curdle the brain, the ubiquitous flies tormented the skin and clustered on food. No 459 (Hudson) Squadron had a standing joke about the flies. "Every time I go to the latrine, all the flies in the desert are there." "Why don't you go at meal times?" "What difference would that make?" "That's when the flies all congregate in the mess tent."

The Western Desert is not the totally arid wilderness of popular misconception. From autumn to spring sudden heavy rain turned landing grounds into bogs, flooded tents and bedevilled the incessant maintenance work on aircraft. The desert wind, the Khamseen – Arabic for fifty, the number of days for which it notionally blew – whipped up sandstorms whose stinging fine grains formed an opacity as thick as smog. Men groped their way about with a cloth tied over mouth and nose so that they could breathe. The grit permeated their food and drink. It penetrated the entrails of the aeroplanes: a fighter that waffled soggily through the air and flew like a brick could be found to have 80 lbs of sand aboard, mostly in its wings. Boredom was the greatest threat. Shared adversity bred a special kind of comradeship and high morale in those who had the fortitude to resist it. In others, who lacked a national toughness of character, it produced a sulky reluctance to face the enemy.

The dry air and meagre rations gave everyone an appetite that could not be wholly satisfied and, aggravated by heat, a thirst that was never fully satiated. The salt in the atmosphere created a craving for sweets and chocolate, which were unobtainable. The unbalanced diet caused desert sores. The nights were chilly and, in autumn and winter, bitingly cold. But in the extremes of temperature germs could not thrive and there were no infectious diseases. All ranks may have been undernourished and grubby, but they kept their health.

Among the most decisive factors of the three-year North African

11

campaign was the different manner in which the nations involved came to terms with their alien setting. The Italians had never adapted to desert life. Instead, they strove to create a facsimile of familiar domestic conditions. Luxury, not military efficiency, was their first consideration. They settled into permanent buildings wherever possible; mobility they disregarded. If they had to make some concession to being on field service, their huts and tents were furnished with good carpets, drawing-room furniture and spring beds. The officers burdened themselves with luggage that contained such superfluities as ceremonial uniforms and bottles of toilet water. Their messes, even under canvas, were lavishly stocked with wine, spirits and epicurean delicacies.

To the Germans the desert was an enemy. They treated it as they handled people: bullied it, dominated it, hammered it into submission. A hardy and practical race, they accepted Spartan conditions and arrived with the appropriate dress and equipment to *fight* with the maximum competence.

The French, with their experience of governing Morocco, Algeria, Tunisia and Syria, were long familiar with desert conditions. The key to maintaining a Frenchman's morale is to feed him well and provide him with a copious daily ration of wine. A French cook, even in the armed forces, can do wonders with the least sybaritic material. For the rest, the French soldier, sailor or airman is natural philosopher and logical reasoner enough to make the best of unalterable privation and accept the inevitable. The French fed and fought well in their enforced circumstances; with the added incentive of battling their way back to their homeland and kicking the Boches out of it. North Africa was a step towards home.

The British, more than any people, felt at ease in the desert. As founders of the biggest empire in history, they had learned to assimilate their surroundings anywhere from pole to pole. Their desert experiences in Iraq, Syria and Palestine from the First World War until the present, had been an excellent preparation. They were already familiar with fighting in the Western Desert: in 1915 Germany had incited the Senussi, Libya's hardiest, fiercest tribe, to cross into Egypt and challenge the British, who had thrust them back. The South Africans, Australians, New Zealanders and Canadians, rugged men of pioneering stock accustomed to an outdoor life, had the same attitude.

All, whether native British or from the Commonwealth, seemed to relish desert life, to take a delight in improvisation, in fashioning some semblance of comfort out of the scantiest means, in tolerating the most monotonous diet. Keep your British serviceman supplied with several mugs of tea a day and he won't grumble about hard lying, desert sores, enforced celibacy or lack of beer. He is a natural extemporizer who makes any problem seem trivial. You want a fire for a brew-up? Easy, fill an empty petrol can with sand, pour petrol on it and apply a match. Then drop the matchstick into the billycan to prevent smoke tainting the contents. Need a glass to drink from? Find an empty bottle, pour in oil to the required size, then light it. The glass will break smoothly all round at the oil's surface, leaving the bottom half for a tumbler. The rations are the same every day, bully beef and hard biscuits with perhaps a repellent lump of soapy "processed" cheese (the process undefined but scatalogically conjectured). Put the lot into a cooking pot with a little water and stew it rather than eat them separately. For variety, grind biscuits into makeshift flour and fry bully beef fritters. Sometimes there were tinned potatoes. After a while, sausages called soya links, made of pork and soya and tasting like sawdust, were added. For pudding, biscuits and jam had to do. Tents to be camouflaged? Daub them with oil. One quart of water a day per man for ablutions? Shave, wash face, armpits, feet and crotch in that order: you won't stink and you'll feel clean. The dirty water was saved to fill motor vehicle radiators.

The Americans, when they joined the desert fighting in 1942, took the hard lying with cheerful ingenuity and tastier rations than the R.A.F. issue. The British thought highly of spam, which the Yanks were always ready to swap for corned beef. The whisky occasionally available to officers and sergeants from the NAAFI was the most valued instrument of negotiation in bartering between the two nationalities: it was not unknown for a jeep to change hands for a couple of bottles of Scotch.

That was the background against which Desert Air Force, with the Eighth Army, won a great victory after being more than once on the edge of defeat as the battle front moved back and forth across the desert. Few who survive a long war look back on any period of it with pleasure. Memories of the first campaign in France that ended with the humiliating evacuation from Dunkirk, of Burma, of the Pacific or of the rampage across France and Germany after the 1944 landings do not commonly evoke pleasure. It is a unique feature of the desert war that, tough though its every aspect was, those who fought it see it in retrospect with a certain wry affection. "Happy days," reflects Squadron Leader Maurice Smyth, DFC, who flew tours of operations over Europe as well as North Africa. Virgil understood this brand of sentiment: "*Forsan et haec olim meminisse iuvabit* . . . Maybe one day we shall be glad to remember even these things".

But how and why did the fighting in the desert, the sky above it and on the sea that bordered it, break out in the first place?

13

CHAPTER 2

The Desert Fighting Starts

In June, 1940, the Germans were winning the Battle of France, which had been smouldering since Britain and France declared war on Germany on 3 September, 1939. It burst into flame with Hitler's invasion of Belgium, Holland and France in May, 1940. By the first week in June the *Blitzkrieg*, the lightning war in which the German Army and Air Force advanced rapidly in close co-operation, had driven the bulk of the British Expeditionary force out of France. The last of the R.A.F. squadrons based there withdrew two weeks later. The French land and air forces were on the point of surrender. Mussolini, the Prime Minister and Dictator of Italy, foreseeing that the French must succumb within a few days, expected Britain's conquest and occupation by the Germans to follow swiftly. Hoping for an easily-gotten share of the spoils — in particular a large area of south-eastern France — that would go to anyone who succeeded in conquering the British, he declared war as Germany's ally on 10 June. On 22 June, France accepted Hitler's peace terms.

The only serious threat that Italy offered to Britain was in Africa and the Mediterranean. Egypt, a British Protectorate since 1880, was the most vulnerable. Strategically it was of crucial importance not only to the British Isles but also to the whole Commonwealth. The Sudan, on Egypt's southern border, was divided into two areas, French and Anglo-Egyptian. The administration in the latter was, in practice, British and the garrison consisted of 9,000 British and Sudanese troops. On Sudan's eastern frontier lay Abyssinia and Eritrea, Italian colonies where an army of 200,000 was maintained. The Italians also menaced Kenya, which adjoined Ethiopia on the latter's south and was lightly defended. Oil for Britain from Iraq and Iran, and Britain's trade with India, the Far East and Australasia, passed through the Suez Canal. Egypt's two main ports, Port Said and Alexandria, were essential for the supply and reinforcement of British land, air and sea forces and as naval bases. The Royal Navy controlled the Mediterranean from three points, at each end and in the middle: Egypt, Malta and Gibraltar.

In Egypt, on 10 June, 1940, 36,000 British, New Zealand and Indian troops opposed an Italian and colonial force of 300,000 in Libya. Egypt's security was now also threatened by the Italian Navy, which comprised two battleships — with four more nearing completion — several cruisers and destroyers and 116 submarines, the world's largest under-sea fleet.

Italy's entry into the war put Malta at risk from attacks by bombers stationed in Sicily and British shipping in danger from the Italian Air Force and Navy when passing through the narrows between Sicily and Tunisia. This meant that the protection of shipping devolved increasingly on the R.A.F. and enhanced the importance of its desert aerodromes.

Britain's planning for a probable war against Germany and Italy, with France as her ally, had assumed that the main attack against Libya would be made by the large French Army and Air Force contingents based in Tunisia and Algeria. But when France capitulated to Germany the British armed services in Egypt were left to fight alone. They lacked the resources to make an immediate large-scale attack: the Committee for Imperial Defence had stated in 1939 that "The role in general assigned to our Air Forces operating in this country is the defence of Egypt."

The R.A.F.'s function in Egypt was more precisely defined as: "To maintain close co-operation with the General Officer Commanding the Army in the Western Desert." This was General Sir Archibald Wavell, whose Headquarters was in Cairo. Air H.Q. Middle East, under the Air Officer Commanding-in-Chief, Air Marshal Sir Arthur Longmore, KCB, DSO, an Australian, was also there. His authority and responsibility covered vastly more than the area in which the desert war was to be fought. It comprised all R.A.F. units stationed or operating in Egypt, Sudan, Palestine, Trans-Jordan, East Africa, Aden, Somaliland, Iraq and adjacent territories, Cyprus, Turkey, the Balkans, Mediterranean Sea, Red Sea and the Persian Gulf: a spread of 4,500,000 square miles. Middle East Command embraced many countries that are not geographically within this area. But, for the R.A.F.'s purposes, it was a logical extension. The Italians were being fought in Ethiopia, Eritrea and Somaliland. Kenya and Sudan had to be defended, as well as the Red Sea and Persian Gulf. The Balkans were the gateway to the Levant and Near East. Reinforcements would need to be shifted from one zone to another. The most efficient way to manage these complicated operations was to vest overall authority in one commander for the entire air

15

force and one for the whole of the land force. General Wavell's area of command was the same as Air Marshal Longmore's. When considering Western Desert operations the Commanders-in-Chief had to bear in mind that every decision they took about the desert campaign affected those in the Horn of Africa and could impinge on what developed in places as far apart as Iraq and Sudan.

There were R.A.F. stations on the Suez Canal and in the Nile Delta at Helwan, Heliopolis, Abu Sueir, Aboukir and Ismailia. These included stores depots and maintenance units as well as aerodromes. In the Egyptian desert lay twelve landing grounds: Amriya, El Hamma, Dhaba, Qasaba, Khataba, Ma'aten Bagush, Ikingi Mariut, Burg El Arab, Fuka, Mersa Matruh, Bir Hooker and Sidi Barrani. Their surfaces varied from hard gravel to loose drift sand. All were reasonably flat and little work other than clearance of scrub had been needed to prepare them. If unused for a few months they became rutted, but it was easy to change sites. Between November and April heavy rain made many unserviceable, but six hours' sun sufficed to dry them. All ranks lived in tents, the airmen's cookhouse and dining room were prefabricated-section huts, the hangars were canvas Bessoneaux.

On 9 June, 1940, Longmore ordered H.Q. 202 Group, whose Air Officer Commanding was Air Commodore Raymond Collishaw, DSO, OBE, DSC, DFC, a Canadian, to move from Cairo to Ma'aten Bagush. Both officers had flown in the Royal Naval Air Service in the Great War, which gave them a mutually sympathetic understanding. (In April, 1918, the R.N.A.S. and Royal Flying Corps amalgamated to form the R.A.F.). The two men's characters together created a formidable combination. Longmore was a skilled strategist and a former Commandant of the Imperial Defence College. He was also a vastly experienced pilot: in 1910 he was one of the first four naval officers selected by the Admiralty to learn to fly and became an instructor at the Central Flying School when it opened in 1913. Collishaw, with his sixty victories as a fighter pilot between 1916 and 1918, a squadron commander by 1917, was the quintessential aggressive leader. Having served in the Middle East during the 1920s and 1930s, he had experienced operational conditions in the desert.

A separate formation, 252 Fighter Wing, comprising two Gladiator squadrons, protected the Nile Delta and the Suez Canal.

Collishaw's eighty-one aircraft in the desert were opposed by an enemy force of 282, commanded by *Generale Squadra Aerea* Felice Porro, a leader of small calibre compared with Longmore and Collishaw. In 1915, as a 24-year-old infantry officer, he had transferred to the air force as an observer. Serving first with an artillery observation

202 GROUP ORDER OF BATTLE
11 June 1940

Squadron No.	Type	Strength	Base
Fighters			
33	Gladiator	21	Mersa Matruh
Bombers			
45	Blenheim	12	Fuka
55	Blenheim	12	Fuka
113	Blenheim	12	Ma'aten Bagush
211	Blenheim	12	Daba
Army co-operation			
208	Lysander	12	Qasaba

LOCATION OF OTHER UNITS

252 (Fighter) Wing H.Q., Helwan
80 Sqdn, Gladiator and one Hurricane, Amriya. 112 Sqdn, Gladiator, Helwan.
5 Sqdn Egyptian Air Force, Gladiator, Suez.

201 Group H.Q. Alexandria
228 and 230 Sqdns, Sunderland flying boats, Alexandria.

30 Sqdn, Blenheim, in reserve, Ismailia.

216 (Bomber/Transport) Sqdn, Bombay, Heliopolis. 70 (B/T) Sqdn, Valentia, Helwan.

No 1 (Army Co-op) Sqdn R.E.A.F.: one flight at Suez and one flight at Qasaba.

---

squadron, then, as a captain, commanding a reconnaissance squadron, he won two Silver and one Bronze Medals for Military Valour, the second and third highest decorations. In 1924, when a major, he converted to pilot. In 1927, promoted to lieutenant-colonel, he was given command of the 20th *Stormo*. A year later, as a full colonel, he had a Staff appointment before being put in command of the 4th Fighter Stormo. Thereafter he held various Staff posts, then took command of the 1st *Squadra* in 1938, as a *Generale di Squadra* (equivalent to Air Marshal R.A.F.). He did not serve in the Spanish Civil War and had no great reputation as a fighting commander. Perhaps he is best known for his excellent book on the Italian Air Force in World War 1, *La Guerra Nell' Aria*, published in 1935.

The Italian Air Force was better off than the British for reinforcements and the replacement of aircraft destroyed and damaged. Initially the R.A.F. squadrons were fully serviceable, with a reserve of one hundred per cent, but the outlook for the supply of new aeroplanes was bleak: the bulk of British fighter production was needed at home. While the threat of a German invasion of England following France's defeat continued, this would not change. If the situation improved, supplies would still have to come by sea − a journey of two weeks, with the Atlantic and Mediterranean infested by enemy submarines. The passage along the North African coast was under constant air threat. The Regia Aeronautica's maintenance was far inferior to the R.A.F.'s and it was only sixty per cent serviceable, but spare parts and more aeroplanes could be flown from Italy in a few hours.

An air force cannot be fully effective without a Control and Reporting system to give information about encroaching enemy aircraft and provide a means of directing the defending fighters to intercept them. At this Britain has excelled since the First World War. The organization set up at home by 1939, incorporating radar (known until 1943 as Radio Direction Finding, referred to as R.D.F.), was the most sophisticated and efficient in existence throughout the Second World War. Other components were the Royal Observer Corps, who tracked by sight and sound; fixer stations to take bearings on voice transmissions by friendly fighters and pinpoint their positions; and the Y Service, which monitored enemy radio messages, both Morse code and voice.

The Italians were ignorant of radar. A German had invented it in 1904 and it remained unknown outside Germany for three decades, but was neglected there until the late 1930s. The British had discovered radar for themselves in 1935 and pressed far ahead of Germany with its development.

The R.A.F. had established a simplified C. & R. system in the Middle East. To give warning of the approach of hostile aircraft, chains of wireless observer posts, each manned by three or four troops with a wireless-telegraphy set, were stationed at intervals of ten or twenty miles along the coast of Egypt and Palestine, and across the deserts to the east and west of the Delta area. Like the civilian Observer Corps at home, these men relied on vision and hearing to detect aircraft. The Egyptian Police and Coastguard also kept watch on the coast near the Delta and the Suez Canal. Mobile direction-finding stations on the landing grounds, known as Homers, could take bearings on pilots' transmissions and gave them a course that would bring them back to base.

By June, 1940, three R.D.F. (radar) stations were operating at Ikingi Mariut (near Alexandria), Aboukir and El Dhaba (20 miles west of

18

Helwan). These did not perform to the same high standard, in range or height-reading, as those in the United Kingdom and were too few to allow the combining of their reports to produce accurate tracks. They were of little value for the control of fighters attempting to make an interception, but did provide some warning of enemy raids. Reports from all sources were made by telephone or wireless to the Air Report Centre at Helwan, whence they were passed to Sector Operations rooms at Alexandria, Bir Hooker, Al Maza and Port Said. The C. & R. system was improving as mobile R.D.F. equipment arrived, but at the time when war came to North Africa it was still rough and hardly ready. It was of no help to the 202 Group squadrons on forward airfields out in the blue.

In theory the Italians were at an advantage not only in numbers but also because they had recent experience of modern air warfare. Like the Luftwaffe, the Regia Aeronautica had sent units to fight on the Fascist side in the Spanish Civil War of 1936-1939, and many of the pilots who had served there were now in North Africa. The commander of the 4th *Stormo, Tenente Colonnello* Ernesto Botto, known as *"Gamba di Ferro"* or "Iron Leg", was a leader of unusual quality. He had scored five kills in Spain, shared in fifteen, lost a leg yet was still flying. *Maggiore* Carlo Romagnoli had shot down nine enemy aircraft in Spain and now commanded the 10th *Gruppo*. But the Italians' casualness, inefficient servicing organization, lack of stomach for battle, preoccupation with creature comforts instead of adaptability to desert living, and polished aerobatics in the place of marksmanship and combat technique, negated their numerical superiority and operational seasoning.

The opposing aeroplanes were fairly evenly matched. The Gladiator, the R.A.F.'s last biplane fighter, was obsolescent and being replaced by the Hurricane and Spitfire. It had a maximum speed of 253 mph and was armed with four .303 inch machine guns. The Fiat CR42 fighter, also a biplane, could attain 267 mph and had two 12.7 mm machine guns. The Blenheim MkIV's top speed was 285 mph, its range 1,125 miles and bombload 1,000 lb. The Savoia-Marchetti S79 bomber had a best speed of 270 mph, a range of 1,243 miles and could carry up to 2,200 lb of bombs.

Even with superior strength, the Italians showed no inclination to start the fighting. They had the reputation of being reluctant warriors who had evinced enthusiasm for battle only when facing poorly armed tribesmen in Eritrea and Abyssinia, whom tanks and artillery had slaughtered while bombers obliterated their villages. Despite this, the R.A.F. had expected air raids on the Egyptian airfields immediately

Mussolini declared war. This would have been in accord with the doctrine of aerial strategy originated by *Generale* Giulio Douhet (1869-1930), who had commanded Italy's first military aviation unit in 1912, rose to Commander-in-Chief of the Regia Aeronautica in the 1920s, and was known as "the father of strategic air power". He maintained that strategic bombing was essential to disorganize and annihilate an enemy's war effort, that decisions about air operations must precede those about land and sea operations; and that "the bomber will always get through" because no anti-aircraft or fighter defence could ever be totally effective. The last of these tenets was also accepted by most British, German, French and American air strategists. Air Chief Marshal Sir Hugh Dowding and the whole of Fighter Command, of which he was Commander-in-Chief, begged to differ, as they were about to demonstrate in the Battle of Britain.

Italy's delay in launching an attack on Egypt was not caused by her generals' lack of fighting spirit alone. Their preparation for a war in North Africa had, like Britain's, been based on the expectation that the major assault on Libya would be made by the French from the west. They were therefore as unready to defend one from the east as the British were to launch it. Similarly, they were poorly placed for making attacks on Egypt. But the British did not expect a long delay before the enemy showed aggression. Not only did the Italians outnumber the British both on the ground and in the air, but also, because of this, their morale was high. Not being among the world's most renowned fighters, it was only when the odds appeared invincibly in their favour that they showed some spirit and optimism. The Regia Aeronautica was an élite with a respectable record in the First World War, untainted as yet by the Italian Army's reputation for speed in retreat and the reluctance of the Italian Navy to leave port. Its pilots were among the best in the world at formation flying, aerobatics and testing. But their successes in Spain owed more to their aeroplanes' superiority to the Russian-built aircraft of the enemy than to guts.

Mussolini had promised his army and air force that they would "soon be bathing in the green waters of the Nile". With the confidence of bullies facing apparently much weaker opponents, they believed him and were eager to dive in. First, however, they had to reorganize the disposition of their squadrons. The Army also had to make a switch from an anticipated western front to an actual eastern one. But Iron Leg Botto and his fellow *Stormo* commanders thought there was no hurry. Their Intelligence experts had assured them that the R.A.F. in Egypt was "small and devitalized". They thought they could knock it out whenever they chose. British Intelligence hadn't been much brigh-

"One of the most famous airmen of the war, Hauptmann Hans-Joachim Marseille". (p.3)

2 Flying Officer Charles "Deadstick" Dyson, 33 Squadron, "was no average performer". (p.7)

"Franco Lucchini showed the courage that made him Italy's third-highest scorer . . . before being killed over Sicily in 1943". (p.30) (*Italian Air Ministry*)

4 Alas, poor Yorick . . . or Antonio? Warrant Officer Ron Lawson, DFC, (p.44) with the skull of an Italian found near Derna. (*R. Lawson*)

5 Flight-Lieutenant Fred Harrison, whose Blenheim was set on fire during a low-level attack on a 3-masted Schooner. (p.67) (*F. Harrison*)

6 "Doug Peacock sported a chef's toque" (p.53); in the port waist gunhatch of a 216 Squadron Bomb (*S.A. Hall*)

7 "The only bearded member of the RAF and the leading fighter pilot in the desert" (p.46); Pilot Officer Ernest "Imshi" Mason.

ter: it put the Regia Aeronautica's strength at 200 fighters and 200 bombers.

Generale Arnaldo Ceccato, retired from the Regia Aeronautica, commenting nearly half a century later, says: "Mussolini thought he would win the war in North Africa and East Africa in one month", a complacency that further explains the lackadaisical manner in which the Italians addressed themselves to their task.

The R.A.F. did not allow lack of preparedness to deter them. On the night of 10 June Longmore ordered 202 Group to come to immediate readiness. At midnight war between Britain and Italy was confirmed. Nine minutes later Collishaw had a signal from Longmore: "A state of war with Italy exists. Carry out reconnaissance as arranged. Bomber formations as available should accompany reconnaissance in northern area. Favourable targets observed, especially concentrations of aircraft."

He defined 202 Group's tasks as:-
1. Reconnaissance of the road to Libya.
2. Reconnaissance and attack of submarines.
3. Attacks on vessels in Tobruk and Bardia harbours.
4. Reconnaissance of enemy air activity at Amseat, El Adem and Derna.

Collishaw, a burly and rumbustious extrovert, was not without his idiosyncrasies. As a young squadron commander in Flanders during the First World War he had delighted in a ruinous game played when dining in another squadron's mess: swinging on the cross beams of the wooden hut and collapsing the roof. In 1917 he had survived a mishap that would have been fatal ninety-nine times out of a hundred. In combat at 16,000 ft with three German Albatros fighters, he had made a manoeuvre so violent that his safety strap broke and he fell out of the cockpit of his Sopwith Triplane. He grabbed the two centre struts and hung, with his legs trailing in the slipstream, as the "Tripe" dived with full power until it suddenly nosed up, stalled and began to spin. Managing to get one leg into the cockpit, he hooked the stick back with his foot and, as the aircraft began a sudden climb, he fell back into his seat. That near miss seemed to sharpen his appetite and contempt for danger. In 1919 he had been selected to command 47 Squadron, which formed part of the British Expeditionary Force sent to fight the Revolutionaries in Russia, where he added one more victory to his name and blew a gunboat to bits with his bombs.

He was itching to turn his love of action on to the Italians in this new war. They had awarded him two decorations in the first one, whose ribbons he continued wearing but concealed, eccentrically, under black silk. Everyone else who had sported medals from an ally-turned-enemy removed them. Not "Collie", as his Service knew him: blacking them out was intended to express greater disdain. More practically, he ordered 45 Squadron to attack El Adem, the airfield near Tobruk, at dawn.

At first light on 11 June the R.A.F. made the opening moves in the desert campaign when 211 Squadron flew a reconnaissance into Libya, while 33 Squadron patrolled between Daba and Mersa Matruh – the most westerly British position, 120 miles from the Libyan frontier – to intercept any Italian attackers who ventured into Egypt; none did. As an adjunct to the C. & R. system, 30 Squadron at Ismailia was standing by to shadow such raiders back to their bases and inform 202 Group of their locations, so that these could be attacked as soon as possible after the enemy had landed.

The sun had been up only a couple of hours when the first blow was struck, again by Britain. The eight Blenheims that 45 Squadron sent off went in at low level to drop high explosive and incendiary bombs and strafe with their guns. Instead of the expected defensive patrol of fighters near the aerodrome and flashes at the muzzles of anti-aircraft artillery and heavy machine guns from a score of different sites around it, the bomber crews were astonished to see that apparently the entire manpower at El Adem was assembled on parade. In front of the flag-post stood two figures, presumably the station commander and his adjutant. But not for long: they and the ranks drawn up before them ran for their lives as the raiders' bullets struck sparks off the parade ground and bombs exploded. It was learned later that the Commanding Officer had been reading out a signal from Marshal Graziani, Italian Commander-in-Chief in Libya, announcing the declaration of war: a formality that 45 Squadron's interruption rendered superfluous. By the time the anti-aircraft defence opened fire, two hangars had been hit and were burning. Several of the aeroplanes that were parked in rows, as in peacetime, instead of dispersed about the airfield perimeter, were also alight or smashed to bits.

One Blenheim was hit as it turned for home, caught fire and plunged into the sea off Tobruk, taking its crew to the bottom with it. Another was badly damaged but managed to struggle back to Sidi Barrani, where it burst into flames on touchdown and all aboard were killed. A third, which had had an engine failure over the target but was not hit, put down without mishap.

Meanwhile a 208 Squadron Lysander made a tactical reconnaissance for the 7th Armoured Division but saw no enemy movement. The Division went forward during the day and four aircraft, five pilots and thirty-two ground crew of the Squadron's B Flight moved to the advanced landing ground at Sidi Barrani, less than 50 miles from Libya. From there they operated under the Divisional Commander, Major-General Creagh, who at once began a series of raids across the frontier.

That afternoon Collishaw transferred Nos 55 and 113 Squadrons from Ismailia to Fuka, 50 miles east of Mersa Matruh. Here they each bombed up nine Blenheims, which took off again to strike El Adem once more at 2.15 pm. The Italians were so indolent that they had not dispersed their aircraft, despite that morning's raid. Several were destroyed or greatly damaged and hangars were bombed again. The clouds of dust that rose from the explosions and mingled with the smoke hindered accurate assessment. Anti-aircraft fire damaged two Blenheims, but they all returned to base. Antiquated CR32 fighters, whose top speed was only 233 mph, chased the attackers fruitlessly.

At dawn on the 12th the Navy carried out a sweep against Tobruk while the R.A.F. bombed the port to drive shipping out of harbour into the guns of the waiting fleet and to destroy at their moorings those vessels that did not flee. Twenty-nine Blenheims were briefed to be over Tobruk at sunrise, but this operation provided an early lesson in the vagaries of warfare that cannot be reproduced by exercises staged in time of peace. In fog and low cloud, the six of 45 Squadron failed to find the target. Of the nine from 211 Squadron, two crashed on take-off and one collided with a Bombay (bomber/transport aircraft). The remainder reached Tobruk, where they were engaged by CR42s, two of which they claimed to have shot down. Of 55 Squadron's five, an engine of one would not start. The observer of another was hit by a propeller, so it did not leave the ground either. A third turned back over Mersa Matruh with engine trouble. The two that reached their target met about fifty CR42s, but these did not attack them and they returned to base unharmed. Nine Blenheims of 113 Squadron hit Tobruk and an old cruiser, the *San Giorgio*, which foundered on a sandbank and remained half-submerged, to be used as an anti-aircraft gun position by the successive occupants of the town.

By immediately stealing the initiative from the enemy in the air, on the ground and at sea, the British established a mental ascendancy over them and forced them into a defensive attitude of mind, which always erodes morale.

The Army made a foray across the frontier assisted by long-distance reconnaissance by 113 Squadron and tactical reconnaissance by 208 Squadron. One of the latter's Lysanders attacked a frontier post, Fort Capuzzo, with eight 20lb bombs. Despite his effort to provoke the enemy into activity, the pilot reported no movement.

The best news of the day was delivered by 33 Squadron, one of whose defensive patrols forward of Mersah Matruh reported the arrival of three Hurricanes from England, making a total of four in Egypt, but with the promise of more to come.

On the 13th air reconnaissance provided a picture of the enemy's dispositions and particularly of the frontier posts. In preparation for an attack on Fort Capuzzo, which was reported to be weakly held, B Flight of 208 Squadron was sent to Buq Buq to be near Divisional H.Q. for two days, and a flight of six aircraft from 33 Squadron moved to Sidi Barrani to be within range for escorting bombers the next day.

Early on the 14th, eight Blenheims of 211 Squadron dropped 250lb bombs with 11-second fuses on the fort from low level. Again hazards impossible to rehearse and more demoralizing in the heat of action than any measures taken by the enemy, awaited the crews. Some fuses failed, bombs exploded prematurely and most aircraft were damaged by splinters from their own or their comrades' bombs. But the target was extensively battered and swiftly captured by a small force of eight officers and 200 troops. To protect both bombers and ground force, 33 Squadron flew offensive sweeps as far as Bardia, shot down two CR32s and a Caproni 133 over Capuzzo and strafed bombers on the airfield at Sidi Azeiz. Two aircraft of 45 Squadron, of which one was lost to ground fire, also bombed Sidi Azeiz and three others attacked Fort Maddalena.

Keeping fighters on patrol is inefficient and wasteful of fuel and engine hours, but, lacking early warning of enemy movements, 33 Squadron patrolled Mersa Matruh and over Army operations at the periods of greatest danger, dawn and dusk. Scarcity of trained R.A.F. and Army observer teams meant that all those available were positioned in defence of the Delta and the canal, and the Y Service was as yet rudimentary, so Collishaw had to rely on reports from the most advanced Army units.

That day's work stirred the enemy into slightly increased activity. Bombs fell on Sollum — which had already been evacuated — and frontier posts at Shegga and Weshka, but caused negligible casualties.

Reconnaissance found Tobruk harbour congested and revealed large naval oil reserves on the wharves. There were army and air force headquarters in the town and thirty-four aeroplanes on the airfields at El Adem and El Gubbi, on its outskirts. Longmore decided to place one Bombay of 216 Squadron under Collishaw's control for a week at each moon period, effective immediately. It was to arrive at Mersa Matruh at dusk every day and take off at dawn to return to Heliopolis, to avoid damage if the forward landing ground were bombed. The duty Bombay on the night of 14th/15th made the first moonlight raid when it dropped eight 250 lb bombs on Tobruk from 10,000 ft through slight haze. Photographs confirmed direct hits on small craft and a warship. From that altitude and in poor visibility, using the crude bombsight of the period, this was creditable. But no bombs fell on the oil storage. The Italians were somnolent and neither fighters nor the twenty searchlights ringing the town nor anti-aircraft fire disturbed the lumbering, obsolescent bomber-troop transport. The next night another Bombay attacked Tobruk and blew up part of the oil dump.

At dawn on the 16th nine Blenheims from each of 55 and 113 Squadrons took off to raid El Adem and El Gubbi, but, emphasizing the problems of operating from airstrips on the sand, engine trouble again meant that three of 55's failed to reach the target. Those that did met at least twenty-four fighters and the consequent dilemma so familiar to day bombers: take evasive action on the run up to the target and spoil your aim, or hold steady and risk the loss of precious aircraft for which no quick replacement was available. Their bombs fell among the parked aircraft but damage was estimated as slight. There was a dawn take-off also for six of 33 Squadron detailed to carry out protective patrols near Sidi Barrani. These were impeded by the one constant menace to air operations, the greatest contributing factor to the squandering of airmen's lives, the world over: the weather. Thick mist over their destination forced them to return to base. Of three pilots who lost their way, F/L Bolingbroke, DFC, crashed into the sea and was killed; the first fighter casualty. The other two forced-landed on the desert. It is not only Englishmen whose first talk when they meet is, as Dr Johnson said, of the weather: flying men of all nationalities share the habit. At that stage of the desert war there were scant facilities for meteorological forecasting in the forward area. Later, "Met" sections moved up – and back – with the rest of Western Desert Air Force (a designation that did not yet exist).

In the evening three Blenheims of 113 Squadron went singly to bomb dispersed aircraft and hangars at El Adem, surprising the enemy by making a glide – engines off – approach from out to sea. That night, using the same method, a Bombay again bombed the oil store at Tobruk. Its crew saw fighters, which did not attack.

To date the enemy's air offensive had consisted only of attacks on forward positions and on Sidi Barrani and Mersah Matruh airfields by formations of up to twelve bombers. As the Gladiators were some 10 m.p.h. slower than the Savoia-Marchetti S79s, Collishaw asked Longmore for a section of Hurricanes, but there were still only four of these 312 m.p.h. eight-gun fighters in Egypt, all with 80 Squadron. The Blenheim Mk1s of 30 Squadron had by now been converted to fighters by the installation of four .303 machine guns under the nose, to augment the one forward-firing gun in the port wing and the rear-firing weapon in the dorsal turret. Their top speed was also, at 260 m.p.h., rather less than the S79s'. A section of two Blenheims and a Hurricane — which became known as "Collie's battleship" — was formed and attached to 33 Squadron on the newly built landing ground at Ma'aten Gerawla. Collishaw tried to bluff the enemy into thinking that he had several Hurricanes, by frequently operating his solitary one from different landing grounds. To make the best use of it, he ordered that only selected pilots were to fly it and it must always be accompanied by the Blenheims. F/O P.G. Wykeham-Barnes, who flew it regularly, became one of the R.A.F.'s most gifted fighter leaders. He had joined the Service as an apprentice but won a scholarship to the R.A.F. College, Cranwell. Ultimately he rose to be Air Marshal Sir Peter and truncated his surname to Wykeham.

On receiving warning of the enemy's approach, the three fighters were to take off and climb to 15,000 ft north-north-west of Mersa Matruh and 35 miles off the coast. On this patrol line they should intercept enemy aircraft flying east. For special operations they could use the advanced landing ground at Buq Buq and escort bombers attacking enemy airfields. The Blenheims, with five front guns, were capable of destroying bombers and could also, because of their long range, shadow them. They were not designed for taking on highly manoeuvrable fighters such as the CR32 or 42. Therefore they had to maintain high altitude on patrol and be closely escorted by Gladiators. The Hurricane pilots in particular were instructed to adopt aggressive tactics and frighten the opposition. Collishaw's instruction read "Success will adversely affect Italian morale and he (sic) will be fearful that Hurricane fighters may attack at any moment". He would have relished flying the Hurricane himself and frightening the wits out of the enemy in a fight with CR42s and S79s. He had also made an accurate assessment of the intestinal fortitude of the average Italian aircrew that a team of psychologists could not have bettered.

On the 19th the fighters scored their first success when four Gladiators of 33 Squadron, flown by Squadron Leader Johnson, Flight Lieutenant Hawkins, Flying Officer Lynch and Sergeant Green, with Flying Officer Wykeham-Barnes in the Hurricane, and the two Blenheims, on patrol in the Sollum area, met five CR42s and seven other aircraft that were either CR42s or RO37s: precise identification was difficult because of similarity. For aircraft of three different types, with their disparate cruising speeds and other characteristics, to keep formation needed first-class airmanship. When they broke to make individual attacks, Wykeham-Barnes shot down two CR42s while the Gladiators accounted for two more. Sergeant Green was attacked by three of the enemy. He kept firing short bursts as a target fleetingly appeared, in the intervals of violent aerobatics to avoid the bullets that the Fiats were aiming at him from different directions, until at last they sent him down. Later that morning the Hurricane and four fighter Blenheims intercepted a formation of CR42s. The Hurricane took out one, while the Blenheims, despite their handicap of comparatively slow manoeuvrability, destroyed two. They also damaged two that probably did not get home. Longmore signalled Collishaw to congratulate him "on the splendid work of the fighters this morning. The results are most encouraging".

The same could not be said about the supply of reinforcements. The three Hurricanes recently delivered had staged through Algeria and Tunisia, but with the obviously imminent French surrender this route would be closed. In the 1920s and 1930s an alternative had been reconnoitred by Squadron Leader Coningham and Howard Williams. This began with a voyage from Britain to the West African port of Takoradi. Thence the stages were, by air, to Lagos, Kano, Maidurguri, El Geneina in the Sudan, El Fasher, Khartoum and Wadi Halfa to Abu Sueir: 3,700 miles. Although this route was safe from the enemy, it was not immune from risks to both aircraft and crews. Each stage involved a long flight, which, particularly in a tropical climate, put severe stress on the engines. The whole journey was over wild country, often in changeable weather. Anyone who was forced down by mechanical trouble, a storm or lack of petrol, might not survive an emergency landing, and, if he did, might not be found for an uncomfortably long time.

On the 16th Longmore had signalled the Deputy Chief of Air Staff: "The situation now is three have arrived here and have been fitted with their guns and are ready. We thus have four Hurricane fighters. Two more and a Hudson are waiting at Tunis. The stock of spares which had reached Gibraltar in H.M.S. *Delhi* was dumped ashore there and now appears to have gone for a ride around the Cape in a merchant ship; goodness knows when we shall get them. You have just signalled news of twelve more MkIV Blenheims and they will be very welcome. If their spares can be sent through the Mediterranean by fast destroyer it will be better still."

Because the situation at home was precarious, no definite plan for the reinforcement of the Middle East could be carried out. But while France was collapsing, Britain was doing its best to secure as much French equipment and as many overseas bases as possible. The War Cabinet appreciated that the Middle East was an important sector in the economic blockade of Europe and that Britain's ability to maintain its position there depended largely on reinforcements reaching Egypt. Air reinforcements could be made in small numbers through Malta, if it were held, and the Takoradi route was being urgently developed. The only possible policy was to conserve resources in Britain and release what could be spared for Egypt whenever available. Even so, such supplies would, for the time being, only re-equip squadrons with more modern aircraft than those they currently flew and replace wastage, not increase front-line strength.

The existing force had obviously to be used with the greatest economy. Longmore posted 45 Squadron to the Sudan and curtailed operations in the Western Desert. As he explained to Collishaw, they might soon have to face German air and land forces in Libya as well as the Italians. Loss of control of the Western Desert would certainly make it impossible to prevent this. His message to Collishaw accordingly concluded: "I therefore feel that we must consider very carefully every air operation we embark upon". Future support of Army and Navy operations would be restricted to those of strategic importance, as the loss of even a few aircraft on operations of merely tactical significance was unaffordable.

One of 113 Squadron's Blenheims was saved from destruction by an act of initiative that is recalled by ex-LAC armourer, K.E. York. "The squadron was short of an observer/bomb aimer. To make up the crew, an armourer/air gunner, LAC Ian 'Jock' Blair, volunteered: as an armourer, he knew the bomb switches etc and the Mk 9 bomb sight. His place in the turret was taken by another air gunner, LAC Hutchinson." Blair was, says his old comrade, "an outstanding young man who joined the R.A.F. in 1934 as a boy armourer". Just how outstanding was about to be demonstrated. Over the target the Blenheim was intercepted by Italian fighters and a burst of machine-gun fire killed the pilot. Blair scrambled from his position in the front to the cockpit, while Hutchinson extricated himself from the dorsal turret, squeezed through the narrow space between his position and the pilot's and joined him. With the aircraft in a shallow dive and its wings rocking, the two Leading Aircraftmen hauled the dead pilot out of his seat, slipping and sliding as the uncontrolled Blenheim swayed and bucked. Blair eased himself into the driving seat and flew the Blenheim 350 miles back to Ma'aten Bagush. When the airfield came in sight he told Hutchinson that he should bale out rather than risk being killed or injured in a landing made by someone who had never before flown an aircraft. "I'll stay and give you moral support," Hutchinson said. Blair informed ground control what had happened. York says, "We all stood and watched him make a very good landing." His rewards were the first Distinguished Flying Medal awarded to the Squadron and recommendation for a pilot's course. "I am pleased to say Jock Blair survived the war – I met him in 1947 as a Flight Lieutenant pilot."

Soon after the fighters' good hunting on the 19th, the Army withdrew from Libya to temporary positions on the Egyptian side of the frontier. Mobility was the essence of Wavell's strategy to make the most effective use of his small resources and induce the enemy to concentrate, which would provide the bombers with the most profitable targets.

Meanwhile the enemy tried to force the R.A.F. to abandon the airfields at Mersa Matruh and Sidi Barrani by frequent air raids. From high altitude they also bombed, but only straddled, petrol and ammunition dumps at Mersa Matruh, which were duly shifted. On the 28th eleven bombers attacked the airfield, copying the British glide approach but not venturing as low. They cratered it but it was serviceable by the evening. The Italian bomber crews' style of attack was reminiscent of the way in which cheeky, scared small boys stealing apples defy an angry farmer who is driving them out of his orchard with a big stick: jeering and putting out their tongues, then turning tail to bolt while he is still at a safe distance. Their caution made an unseemly contrast with the gallantry shown by their predecessors in the First World War, whose feats, often at the deliberate sacrifice of their lives, matched any performed by British, French, American or German airmen. It was ironical that *Generale* Felice Porro, in his book on the First World War, wrote "The moral strength of traditions is by now a powerful reality in the air force". This was not apparent in 1940. The lack of enthusiasm shown by the Italian Army and Air Force might be largely attributed to a general reluctance to support Mussolini. This was concealed at the time, both inside Italy and from the world. But the Deputy Secretary of the Fascist Party had estimated that 50 per cent of the nation were against Fascism, 25 per cent were indifferent and only 25 per cent were actively in favour.

On 21 June the name of *Capitano* Franco Lucchini of the 10th *Gruppo* figured for the first time in a report of a successful air combat in North Africa. Lucchini had joined the Regia Aeronautica in 1935, two months before his 21st birthday, and was posted to Spain with the 4th *Stormo* in 1937. He was shot down a year later and spent seven months as a prisoner of war. On 21 June, 1940, he was on dawn patrol near Tobruk in a formation of three CR42s when he spotted a Sunderland flying boat of 230 Squadron on reconnaissance. At the same time three CR32s appeared. The six Italian fighters attacked the Sunderland, making concerted dives at it from ahead, astern and both sides. With a top speed

29

of little over 200 m.p.h., the flying boat could not escape, but it sent one CR32 crashing into the sea before being itself forced down. The Sunderland carried four machine guns in a nose turret and four in its tail turret, and a waist gun on either side. Some had four more in the bows. It was a formidable adversary, regarded askance by the Luftwaffe, who called it "the flying porcupine". In attacking one, Lucchini showed the courage that made him Italy's third-highest scorer, with twenty-one individual victories and fifty-two shared, before being killed over Sicily on 5 July, 1943.

The last ten days of the month saw some larger-scale operations, with the further inter-Service cooperation for which Desert Air Force was already distinguished. Two hours after the loss of the Sunderland, four Royal Navy cruisers and the French battleship *Lorraine* bombarded Bardia, while a flight of 33 Squadron protected them and the Fleet Air Arm spotter aeroplanes. In preparation, 113 Squadron had photographed the harbour. Nine Blenheims of 55 Squadron set out to bomb the warships in port. Only seven reached the target, where they met a heavy anti-aircraft barrage and were chased by CR42s, but set a large ship on fire. Two Blenheims were damaged.

On the same morning, at the request of the General Officer Commanding Western Desert Force, 113 Squadron sent eleven Blenheims to attack troop concentrations at Bir el Gubbi. Sidi Azeiz was captured and dummy aircraft were found on the airfield. It was suspected that dummies were also being used at El Adem and El Gubbi. The Allies had not yet adopted this form of deception overseas, although decoy aerodromes had already been built in Britain to mislead German bomber crews and by the end of 1939 nearly 400 fake aeroplanes were in production. (The aviation industry had quoted £2,000 each, but the film studios were supplying them for £50.) That night the Italians raided Alexandria. It was an unintelligent choice of target. Alex was strongly defended by both the artillery and the fleet. The best target would have been the less well protected workshops at Aboukir, damage to which would have crippled the desert squadrons. The pilots of five 80 Squadron Gladiators, who made an unsuccessful attempt to intercept the bombers, experienced a hazard that soon became familiar to all aircrew by day and night: the "friendly" anti-aircraft gunners tried to shoot them out of the sky. If the Army wasn't blasting off at the R.A.F., the Navy would oblige whenever an aircraft strayed close enough. The R.A.F.'s desert war was daily becoming more like operating over Britain and France.

To give as many of his fighter pilots as possible a chance of combat and to allow those who had been right forward a brief rest, Collishaw began to rotate them between 33 and 112 Squadrons on short detachments. On the 24th three more Hurricanes arrived for 80 Squadron: the last to come via Malta and Tunisia. On the 25th one of these, flown by Flight Lieutenant Montague T. St. J. "Pat" Pattle, also of 80 Squadron, relieved Wykeham-Barnes and his Hurricane at 33 Squadron's landing ground. Pattle, a South African who had joined the R.A.F. in 1936, accumulated forty-one confirmed victories before being killed in action on 20 May, 1941, over Greece, the highest score credited to any Allied pilot. Despite this stupendous record, he has remained in obscurity, because he did not receive the publicity that was accorded to pilots who fought over Britain, France and Germany.

France, under her new Government in Vichy that Germany permitted in a travesty of self-rule, was now at war with Britain. But not all Frenchmen were willing to turn on their former ally. Some 100,000 French troops had crossed the Channel to England with the retreating British Expeditionary Force in June, to fight on under the command of General de Gaulle. Now others began to leave her colonies for the nearest British territory. On the 27th *Capitaine* Jacquier of the *Armée de l'Air* flew his Potez 63-11 three-crew fighter-bomber from Syria to Ismailia, to continue fighting the Axis Powers. On the same day *Lieutenant* Peronne and *Adjutants-Chefs* Ballatore and Coudray arrived in their Morane 406s, France's most modern fighters (302 m.p.h., one cannon and two or four machine guns) at El Amrya, near Alexandria, from their Syrian base. Five N.C.O. mechanics accompanied them in what the French archives call "an R.A.F. liaison aircraft". Two days later all the French escapers had been assembled at Ismailia.

Graziani had doubled his force on the frontier and thus contrived to recapture Fort Capuzzo and Sidi Azeiz on the 28th. This was the first instance of what was to become an occurrence peculiar to the desert war, the repeated loss and recovery of a military feature: town, village, fortification, landing ground, ridge, or merely a map reference.

Later that day the world lost one of its most renowned pilots, Marshal Italo Balbo, Governor-General of Libya. In 1933 he had led twenty-three aircraft from Rome to Chicago in the world's record long-distance formation flight, a phenomenal feat of immense significance in the history of aviation. The R.A.F. paid tribute to it by instituting a new noun, "balbo", to refer to any large formation. Flying near Tobruk, he was shot down by an Italian anti-aircraft gun and killed. Collishaw sent a Blenheim to drop a wreath at his funeral.

Next day three Gladiators of 33 Squadron, on patrol in the Capuzzo area, came across three CR42s, of which P/O Woodward shot down two. On a similar task two pilots of 112 Squadron destroyed a RO37 —

an Army cooperation aircraft – and two CR32s. On the last day of the month a section of 33 Squadron sent down a CR42 and a CR32 in flames. To exploit these successes Collishaw moved six more aircraft to Sidi Barrani for offensive patrols. The Italian Air Force began showing greater enterprise: standing patrols of ten fighters were encountered over El Gubbi and patrols of two in the Capuzzo area.

On 1 July two French Air Force Caudron three-place liaison types flew into Egypt from the Levant with three N.C.O. pilots, two N.C.O. mechanics and an armourer aboard. During the succeeding two days more aircraft and men came from Algeria and Syria to join the French party, followed soon after by two lorries, via Trans-Jordan and Palestine, bringing an officer and fifteen other ranks. By now ten aeroplanes of five different types, none of them with any spare parts, had shown up, *Capitaine* Jacquier, unable to make contact with London, went to see Air Marshal Longmore to regularize the position of the *Armée de l'Air* personnel. The C-in-C decreed that if enough of them assembled, with the necessary equipment, they could form a unit of their own within the R.A.F. Otherwise they would be accepted into the R.A.F. with the equivalent ranks. On 7 July they were split into three detachments. The fighters, Morane and Potez, would stay at El Amrya. The bombers – two Glenn Martins – would be posted to Djibouti, staging through Aden. The rest would go to Heliopolis. On 8 July the fighters became No 2 Free French Flight, destined to move forward to the combat zone when their machines had been fitted with sand filters.

While the French volunteers were arriving and being dealt with, there was brisk action at the sharp end, although the numbers involved were still small; perforce on the R.A.F. side, from its lack of aircraft, and on the Italians' part owing to their timidity and poor servicing.

On 4 July three of 33 Squadron intercepted two CR42s and shot them down, one in flames. Later in the day when six 33 Squadron Gladiators, four of them flown by 112 Squadron pilots on detachment, were escorting a Lysander they spotted nine CR42s taking off from Monastir. One section peeled off and took the Italians by surprise at the moment when they were at their most vulnerable: either just airborne, too low to take evasive action and without the speed to escape straight and level, or in a climb or committed to take-off and with no option but to leave the ground and fly right into the R.A.F's bullets. Flying Officer Worcester of 112 Squadron destroyed four of them. Flight Sergeant Cottingham and Pilot Officer Woods, of 33 Squadron, sent down two and one respectively. While the three British pilots were fully occupied creating mayhem, two of their adversaries were able to fly away. This calamity did not deter the Italians from pressing on with their take-offs. Whether they thought they and their aircraft would be in greater danger from a ground strafe than by taking their chance in the air, or whether they were willing to make a fight of it now that half the Gladiator flight had used most of their ammunition, is uncertain. Either way, five more CR42s took off. But the second section of 33 Squadron, all of them this time from 112, were already diving into an attack. They killed three of the Italians and wounded two, one of whom had to bale out. The other landed back at Monastir. One Gladiator was damaged and its pilot had to take to his parachute on the way home. That evening, 80 Squadron cut off ten S79s near Alexandria and shot four down. Worcester's fine marksmanship in his first successful engagement promised him a high place among the aces if he kept on as he had begun, but he was not to figure on the roll. That erratic foe, the climate, brought low cloud two weeks later and he was killed flying into a hill.

Collishaw's bombers had flown 106 effective sorties during the initial offensive between 11 and 16 June. Between 17 June and 5 July there had been increased enemy activity over both the desert and the Delta. The R.A.F. had scored thirty-four kills in the forward area but the bomber effort had produced only about a hundred sorties, on which four Blenheims and one fighter, a Gladiator, were lost.

The pattern of operations for the defensive period that was now forced on Longmore entailed long-range strategic reconnaissance by 113's Blenheims while 208's Lysanders, escorted by 33's Gladiators, carried out tactical reconnaissance and observation of artillery shoots. Forward patrols rested with the Gladiators, Hurricanes and Blenheim fighters operating by flights from Sidi Barrani. When Blenheim bombers attacked targets in Libya, fighters provided a protective screen to cover their withdrawal. To economize in the use of the Blenheims and, at moon periods, Bombays, no raids would be made for periods of up to five days but frequent reconnaissances would be flown to gather target information. Day bombers approached their objectives from 30 miles out to sea at medium to high altitude.

Avoiding casualties to aircrew and damage to aircraft was the guiding principle. A 202 Group raid at low level against a concentration of motor transport on 5 July, on which a pilot was wounded and an observer killed, evoked criticism for Collishaw from Longmore, who wrote: "Whilst fully appreciating the initiative and spirit shown by the squadrons operating under your command in the Western Desert, I must draw your immediate attention to the urgent necessity for conserving resources; instances are still occurring when Blenheims are being used for low level machine gun attacks against defended camps and aerodromes." He quoted the episode on 5 July. "I consider such operations unjustified having regard to our limited resources of which you are well aware." Collishaw excused the infringement of laid-down policy as a deviation from his instructions and assured his C-in-C that he had taken "suitable action". It was not easy for pilots who were by instinct and training bold and aggressive, or for Collishaw, with his forceful character, to accept restraint and reconcile themselves to the significance of two casualties in the present straitened circumstances.

Better times were promised. It was appreciated in London that retention of the Allied position in the Middle East formed an essential part of the Chiefs-of-Staffs' grand strategy. Success in that area depended heavily on air reinforcements reaching Egypt. The Air Ministry announced the immediate despatch of twelve Hurricanes, twelve Blenheims and twelve Lysanders, with a further monthly supply of twelve Hurricanes, twelve Blenheims, six Lysanders and spare parts. Also, 150 American Glenn Martin bombers that *L'Armée de L'Air* had ordered would be built and delivered to the R.A.F. in the Middle East over the coming six months.

All this seemed pettifogging compared with the fighting over the English Channel, the defence of Britain, the scale of aircraft production and the numbers being retained for home supply. Nonetheless, it was a crucial part and a critical period of the war. Troop reinforcements in the desert were growing. From the performance to date of the slender Allied air and land forces in Egypt it was clear that they could contain the enemy for the time being. There was no threat from Germany while Hitler concentrated his whole effort on the invasion and conquest of Britain.

CHAPTER 3

The First British Offensive

The declared enemy in the field was not Britain's only cause for concern: treachery in the Egyptian Government was a constant threat. Egypt, as merely a protectorate, was a sovereign state ruled by a constitutional monarch served by his ministers and two Houses of Parliament. As all occupying powers are resented to some degree, the political situation was unstable, and heavy with the ambiguity of mutual malevolence masquerading as amity. King Farouk, barely in his twenties, was a voluptuary who lacked any regal balance of qualities and in the place of moral fervour displayed only a sinister sullen gravity. The British Government regarded many of his advisers with contempt and suspicion. The British Ambassador had unsuccessfully demanded their dismissal. Among middle-class Egyptians there was much goodwill towards Britain, but mixed with doubt that the British and Commonwealth armed forces present were adequate to defend the country. Courage was not a predominant feature of the Egyptian nature; fear of heavy aerial bombardment was widespread. This had prompted the King to request the removal of the Army and R.A.F. H.Qs from his capital. Wavell and Longmore ignored him.

The Egyptian Armoured Brigade had consented to move to Qasaba, so Longmore tried to persuade the Director of the Royal Egyptian Air Force to send a fighter flight forward to defend it. But the Director would not commit himself, since aircraft were more likely than ground units to be called on during a static period. The Egyptian Government's policy of non-belligerency embarrassed the Commanders-in-Chief but may have restrained the Italians from making air raids on the cities, to avoid disaffecting a populace whom they hoped would revolt against the British. As a gesture, No. 5 Squadron R.E.A.F. did fly patrols in defence of Cairo and Suez.

After 33 and 112 Squadrons' successes on the 4th, July ran on at an almost placid tenor with the occasional loss of an aircraft by both sides.

The Italian Army was fully occupied with massing on the eastern border of Cyrenaica, preparatory to an assault on Egypt. The Italian Air Force was almost entirely engaged on standing patrols to cover these ground movements and the ports where *materiel* was being unloaded. The number of aircraft employed and the accumulation of engine hours meant a worsening in the already poor serviceability state and consequent reduction in available aircraft. The constraints on the R.A.F. have already been made clear. On the 23rd three of 33 Squadron engaged eighteen CR42s and shot four down. Italian news bulletins alleged that three Gladiators had been destroyed, but in fact none was. Two days later three 33 Squadron Gladiators sent down five out of seven CR42s for the loss of one.

On 28 July *Capitano* Lucchini figured again in a successful combat. He took off at 6.30 am, accompanied by two sergeant pilots, to intercept three Blenheims of 113 Squadron approaching Tobruk. The fighters together attacked the leading bomber head-on and sent it down. They then engaged another, under fire from both surviving dorsal gunners, and damaged it so badly that "they could be sure it would be lost". They also hit the third Blenheim, but "with no visible effect".

On 1 August more good news came from London. The monthly rate of deliveries to Middle East Command was being increased to thirty-six Blenheims and eighteen Hurricanes. Batches of six Wellington heavy bombers, coming via Malta, would replace the Bombays. An aircraft carrier, H.M.S. *Argus*, would ferry a further twenty-four Hurricanes as soon as possible and another twenty-four were being sent to the South African Air Force.

Now that the bulk of the Regia Aeronautica had been shifted eastwards, it was seen more often over Wavell's forward positions, particularly Sidi Barrani and Buq Buq. The landing ground at the latter was on a dry lake bed, where bomb craters had filled with water and could not be repaired, so it had to be abandoned. Italian fighters patrolled their assembling land forces in ever greater profusion, but the pilots remained reluctant to engage their opposite, and much fewer, numbers. On the ground the enemy's increase in strength, coupled with wear and tear on the British armoured fighting vehicles, imposed a lessening of patrol work.

Again the fourth day of the month yielded more than the daily average of colourful incidents. Late on the evening of 4 August a 208 Squadron Lysander set off to reconnoitre the Bir Taieb el Esem area with an escort of four 80 Squadron Gladiators positioned well above it and far out on its flank, which enabled them to keep the widest possible surveillance. Near the objective a red Verey light fired from the "Lizzie" drew their attention, so, while Wykeham-Barnes and Sergeant Rew remained circling, Pattle and Pilot Officer Lancaster split off to investigate. Seeing no cause for alarm they turned to rejoin the other two, but before they could re-formate Wykeham-Barnes spotted seven Breda Ba65 bombers making for the Lysander and instantly led Rew into an attack. His first burst had just set one alight when six CR32s appeared and opened fire on him and Rew. He shot one down but his Gladiator was taking heavy punishment and he had to bale out. Meanwhile Rew's aircraft was going down, burning. Pattle and Lancaster tackled the Bredas, which scattered, but Pattle took one out, although only two of his guns were working. Lancaster's guns were also suffering stoppages and, in trying to dogfight two of the Italian fighters, he was wounded and had to pull out and go back to base.

Pattle headed homewards too, but five CR42s intercepted him. In a confused and whirling engagement he destroyed one, which discouraged the remainder sufficiently to induce them to abandon the fight. He was still over Libya when he ran into twelve CR42s escorting three Ba65s and was once more in battle. This combat stretched out to 15 minutes, which is testimony to Pattle's exceptional skill as a fighter pilot and the incompetence of his round dozen of opponents. Finally one of the Italian pilots did manage to put a crippling burst into the Gladiator and Pattle baled out. He and Wykeham-Barnes had come down many miles apart and each had a long trudge to Egypt, but friendly armoured patrols found them both next day.

202 Group's bombers were by now widely dispersed and using satellite airfields to minimize the risk of bomb damage. The three Gladiator squadrons had been operating in three flights of four instead of the normal two with six aircraft each. Collishaw withdrew 33 Squadron to refit at Helwan and sent two of 112's flights and one of 80's to replace it. But the Naval C-in-C was carrying out a major docking programme in Alexandria, so one flight from 33 moved to Amriya to join 80 and the R.E.A.F. in maintaining patrols throughout daylight.

The Italians' strength on the frontier having caused the British to retire, Wavell chose Mersa Matruh as the place at which to make his major attempt to stop the enemy's advance. This did not please the R.A.F., since it meant losing the airfield at Sidi Barrani. The bombers used it to bring important targets in Cyrenaica within range, the fighters used it to extend their coverage on patrols and escort missions, and aircraft flying from Malta to Egypt staged through it. While awaiting Graziani's attack, the British bombers' main targets were Derna and Tobruk.

On 8 August there was an episode that cast an enlightening ray on the capacity of Italian propagandists for obfuscating failure by a fog of fiction. The Lysanders, capable of around 200 m.p.h. at low level, armed with one moveable machine gun in the rear cockpit and two fixed machine guns mounted bizarrely over the wheel spats, were the only aeroplanes the enemy fighter pilots could approach closely with impunity. 208 Squadron was meeting stiff opposition, evidently because the Italians were intercepting its Morse transmissions.

Collishaw dealt with this by laying on an exchange of spoof signals between Lysanders on the ground, simulating preparation for take-off, then sending fourteen Gladiators to take on the Italian aircraft that reacted. They intercepted a gaggle of eleven RO37s and a sixteen-strong escort of CR42s. Pattle sent down two of the Fiats and Wyke-ham-Barnes one, out of a total nine downed in five minutes. Three of the Italian pilots abandoned their aircraft and three made forced land-ings. The other three weren't so lucky. The survivors compensated for this defeat by reporting that they had been set upon by twenty-seven Gladiators, of which they took out five. Actually, one Gladiator pilot was killed and one forced down but rescued by the 11th Hussars. In the course of this mediocre performance, however, one of the Italians, Ser-geant Lido Poli, lived up to the high standard of gallantry set by his predecessors in the First World War. Staying in the fight despite grave wounds in the arm, it was he who forced the second Gladiator down before having to make a forced landing himself. His captors took him to hospital where his arm was amputated. When details of the action reached his own side he was rewarded with Italy's highest decoration, the Gold Medal for Military Valour.

On the 12th, No 2 Free French Flight began its operational life by joining a flight of 80 Squadron's Hurricanes at El Amrya. The French-men were delighted by being admitted to the battlefront. But gratitude is not one of the most obvious qualities of the French, and most nations whose pride is affronted by having to accept the charity of others even-tually resent their benefactors. As the war went on the Free French forces bit with increasing rancour the hands that fed, clothed, paid and equipped them: British at first, joined later by American. The prime exemplar of this sour ingratitude was that shining specimen of piety and object of France's veneration, General Charles de Gaulle. The pilots who had been posted to R.A.F. squadrons in Britain began to com-plain from the outset that they were not put into the front line at once, despite their self-judged greater experience than their British comra-des. It would not be long before those in North Africa alleged that they were being slighted by omission from operations, or given the most dangerous position in a formation when they did fly. Garrulous emotional exhibitionism did not dovetail easily with the R.A.F's laconic, ironical and intensely practical style.

On the 17th Italian bombers came up against a Hurricane for the first time: four S79s bombing ships off Bardia were interrupted by Flying Officer J. H. Lapsley, who quickly despatched three of them. On their modest scale, these occurrences were indicators as significant as those of much greater magnitude happening concurrently in the Battle of Britain. The French, Poles and Czechs had been given their own squadrons in the R.A.F. Spitfires and Hurricanes, flown with indomitable bravery and unequalled skill over southern England by pilots outnumbered five to one, were beating the German bombers and Messerschmitt 109s and 110s. Thanks to the BBC and British agents in occupied and neutral countries, news travelled fast. In the Western Desert, French airmen who defied the Nazis and France's subservient Government were an inspiration to their former comrades in Syria, Morocco, Algeria and Tunisia. The mayhem that one Hurricane had wrought was a daunting portent of what was to befall the Italian Air Force.

With a touch of histrionics on the part of the Regia Aeronautica, August ambled on, though dangerously enough for those who faced the daily prospect of encountering superior enemy formations. Every small enhancement the month brought to the embryonic Western Desert Air Force was magnified by urgent need. One flight was taken from 33 Squadron and one from 80 Squadron to form No 274, the first all-Hurricane squadron in the Command. Squadron Leader P. H. Dunn, 80's C.O., took over the new unit. Wykeham-Barnes, Lapsley and No 2 Free French Flight were posted to it. No 80 lost their Hurricanes, which were replaced in the coming weeks by Gladiators. The members of No 3 Royal Australian Air Force Squadron arrived and were equipped with aircraft already to hand. They were organized in three disparate flights: Gladiators, Lysanders and Gauntlets, the Gladiators' immediate predecessor, 230 m.p.h. two-gun fighters, now to be used as makeshift dive-bombers.

Graziani's simmering bellicosity – more accurately, a reluctant acceptance of the obligation to make some aggressive gesture – began to bubble. On 9 September reconnaissance showed vehicle concentrations at the Tobruk airfields and at Tmimi, Gazala, Derna and El Gubbi. On the 10th Lysanders reported 700 lorries moving towards the frontier. The Italian Army lumbered towards the battlefield as sedately as a Lord Mayor's procession. A screen of motorcycles was followed in succession by tanks, light armoured vehicles, infantry in lorries, mobile field guns, lorried machine-gun units and mobile anti-aircraft batteries. At night they leaguered, surrounded by illuminated barbed wire and guns.

A day later the Blenheim fighters again proved their effectiveness against S79s; two pilots of 30 Squadron each shot one down while Lapsley in his Hurricane was eliminating two and a fifth fell to an 80 Squadron Gladiator.   On 13 September Graziani's six divisions and an armoured group of 200 tanks (not all of which would be serviceable when the day of reckoning came) at last crossed the frontier. Still his resolution to join battle did not come to the boil. Instead, he penetrated cautiously no more than 50 miles, which took him 15 miles south of Sidi Barrani; then, on the 15th, with 70 miles to go before he reached the British front, he paused to shorten his lines of communication. Here his force went to ground behind a minefield in a chain of fortifications while he built up his supplies and a fresh *Stormo* flew in from Italy.

His hesitancy gave the defenders eight welcome weeks in which to reinforce. Three armoured regiments were rushed out from Britain to join the desert army. Longmore transferred No. 6 Squadron from Palestine to Qasaba. No. 33 Squadron began converting to Hurricanes and handing on its Gladiators to 3 R.A.A.F. Squadron. No 33 Squadron, taking their Hurricanes into combat for the first time, began to emulate the successes of Nos 80 and 274. A renowned Hurricane Squadron, 73, was on its way from Takoradi. It had fought throughout the French campaign of September, 1939, to June, 1940, and given the R.A.F. its first ace of this war, New Zealander E. J. "Cobber" Kain (seventeen victories before being killed). One flight of 208 Squadron shed its Lysanders, used for close reconnaissance and artillery spotting, and acquired Hurricanes for long-range reconnoitring. No. 45 Squadron brought its Blenheims back from Sudan. Three Wellington squadrons, 37, 38 and 70, came out via Malta.

Typical of 216 Squadron's sorties was one on the night of 24/25 October, recalled by Stephen Hall, DFM, as his crew's first. A flight rigger/air gunner, he had joined the Squadron as a 19-year-old Leading Aircraftman in March, 1939. Before the war, airmen of any ground category could volunteer to be air gunners. They were trained by the Squadron, sent on a short course to a gunnery school if they were lucky, and earned an extra ninepence a day for flying. Uniquely, in 216 Squadron all air gunners were skilled tradesmen. Thus any aircraft could be detached from base and serviced by its crew, returning only for minor or major overhauls. The other two in LAC Hall's crew were Hadley, a fitter, and McKay, a wireless operator. In addition to the nose and tail turrets, the Bombay had a waist gun, fired through a hatch, on either side. When these were to be manned, two extra crewmen were carried. On this occasion, they were not needed.

Heliopolis cannot have been the most reassuring place from which to set off to face enemy gunfire. The aerodrome abutted an Egyptian Army cemetery, which was used as the bombing-up area. To park one's aircraft among tombstones as a prelude to risking one's own life seems hardly inducive of a cheerful frame of mind. Nor is a graveyard the landmark for which most aviators would eagerly look out on returning from a long sortie. But it seems that familiarity had bred a phlegmatic indifference to such reminders of aircrews' mortality. Before taking off from Heliopolis on this occasion, the aircraft had to be fitted with internal bomb racks, and 120 anti-personnel fragmentation bombs were stowed. After an early afternoon briefing they made the two-hour flight to Ma'aten Bagush, where they topped up with fuel, fed and waited for nightfall. Having left Ma'aten Bagush they first made a rendezvous with H.M.S. *Ladybird* before flying inland to attack troops and vehicles at Sidi Barrani while *Ladybird* shelled them.

The normal drill for bombing from a Bombay was laborious enough. At the main door was a bomb rack with a carriage that held five bombs. After it had been loaded and the second pilot, who was also navigator and bomb aimer, had released them, the rack was swung back and reloaded: a procedure that appeared satisfactory on the practice range but was uncomfortably slow under fire over the target.

The method of dropping anti-personnel bombs was even more archaic. To start with, an extra man had to be carried and stationed at the flare chute. The front escape hatch was opened and the second pilot positioned himself beside it after guiding the aircraft captain over the target. The wireless operator was at his set, the fitter/A.G. was at the main door and the rigger/A.G. was in the nose turret to report hits, fires and other events of interest to the captain. When the captain switched on a green light the men at the flare chute, front hatch and main door began picking up bombs, pulling out the safety pins and throwing the bombs out of the aeroplane. "The faster the bombs were disposed of, the sooner one could say goodnight to the enemy," as Hall puts it. "The moment the red light showed 'stop releasing', this meant the skipper was having a re-run, Green light on, back to the task in hand."

The Naval Communiqué next morning stated that, in co-operation with the R.A.F., an enemy concentration had been successfully attacked and large fires started, without casualties to own forces.

After de-briefing at Ma'aten Bagush, the crew returned to Heliopolis to sleep, feed and service their aeroplane, then flew back that evening for another operation. The cook grilled sausages for them in his slit trench covered with galvanized sheeting; there was the usual tense waiting, then at last they were off. "Each now alone with his own thoughts," Stephen Hall says. "The excitement, the unknown. We gather speed and with the moon for company I watch Bagush fade. Within minutes we pass near Mersa Matruh. They open fire with a few ack-ack guns as we continue climbing steadily to 12,000 ft. Our target, Tobruk. Suddenly reality. This is it, a gigantic firework display yet something more sinister, a feeling of excitement, fear, the hypnotic effect of the flaming onions, these huge bright balls of fire chained together in sevens, slowly reaching our height. Then suddenly, darkness and knowing that every streak or spot of light is lethal. Meanwhile the brain is conscious of talk on the intercom between the skipper and second pilot. 'Bombs away!' alerts me to try to pinpoint where they explode." Back to Bagush to report to the Intelligence Officer, have a meal, refuel, then off to Heliopolis.

While the rest of the crew went to bed, Hall and Hadley, who had to service the Bombay, could snatch only catnaps. For that night's raid they loaded aboard eight canisters, each containing ninety incendiary bombs. The target was Bomba, a flying-boat base. Once more they refuelled and had a meal at Ma'aten Bagush before a night take-off. Presently they were "passing the first coastal landmark, a few welcoming bursts of shellfire from our own gunners". Past Tobruk, then "Bomba seems quiet, no reception committee". They are to strafe as well as bomb, so "We wheel and come in low, fire at will, what excitement and thrill intermingled with the noise of gunfire, our own bursts, the lines of tracer and incendiary bullets finding their target. Our sticks of incendiaries rain down, we climb steadily inland and set course for home." Meanwhile, "I am puzzled by the strange glow that appears to be radiating up from under water. No answer could be found." Many months later, after Bomba was taken, the mystery was solved: "A submarine was at the jetty and we had straddled it, causing extensive damage."

After returning to Heliopolis via Ma'aten Bagush, Stephen Hall had hardly fallen asleep when he was roused to clean the guns and prepare for yet another sortie that night. His weariness as he went about his work became so apparent that he was excused the mission and sent back to bed.

The respite was short. The following day the crew was one of three detailed to attack Tobruk once more. They took off first and "Nearing the target my mind registers the fact that we are not alone. We have the company of three night fighters. I warn the skipper. He immediately dives for cover in the clouds. We go in, drop our bombs, then homeward bound." At Ma'aten Bagush, when they reported to the Intelligence Officer, "At the mention of night fighters he seemed to become quite indignant. Night fighters? Rubbish, none reported in that area." They awaited the return of the second aircraft. "Its crew report night fighters and have a bullet hole to prove it." Both air crews stayed for No. 3 to arrive. This story was worth waiting for: "They were attacked by night fighters, the port wing was set on fire, the skipper ordered bale out. Jock, in the rear turret, couldn't believe his ears, so, to clarify things, he made his way back to midships. Here, he found the midships gunner standing beside the open door, his parachute clipped on to his chest and holding his mug and irons [knife, fork and spoon] in his left hand. Jock, seeing this, rushed back to his turret, lunged at the perspex dome, omitting to release the safety catches, and bumped his head with such force that he was slightly dazed. The fire went out, the bale out order was cancelled. The second pilot was frantically searching for his revolver. He couldn't believe what he was witnessing: there, formating under the starboard wing, was an Italian night fighter with a pilot giving a thumbs-up. He gave a final wave and peeled away." Hall concludes: "The Intelligence Officer never recovered from the shock of our visit to Tobruk." The crews who underwent the experience seem to have got over their shock quite quickly; there was worse to come.

Graziani's delay and the arrival of British reinforcements were, however, accompanied by deprivation. On 28 October, civilization's bogeyman in the Mediterranean, Mussolini, unalterably flamboyant and absorbed in self-aggrandisement, sent his troops into Greece. In 1939 Britain and France had guaranteed to go to the Greeks' help if their country were invaded. The Greek Government invoked this promise. Although France had reneged, Britain felt honour-bound not to withhold help, and Churchill, Britain's Prime Minister, confirmed that it would be given. The Chiefs of Staff, who mistakenly expected Germany's collapse within twelve months, favoured participation in a Balkan War. Longmore, on his own initiative, decided that he must support Greece and immediately ordered 30 Squadron (Blenheims) there, backed up soon by the Blenheims of 84 and 211 and the Gladiators of 80 and 112. As parsimonious replacements, Collishaw received two flights of Blenheims, one each from 11 and 39 Squadrons. No 2 Free French Flight left for Palestine to convert to Hurricanes, but this would be to the Allies' advantage later.

Despite this depletion of its strength, 202 Group never ceased to afflict the enemy. Derna, Tobruk, Bardia, Apollonia, Gazala and Sollum were so rigorously attacked that their use as ports had dwindled or ceased. Tanks could no longer be brought ashore at Tobruk. They had to be landed at Benghazi or Tripoli, which added a further 250 or 600 miles to their road journey. On their way to the Front most broke down and waited days or weeks for repair. Many never completed the odyssey. The damage by bombing and strafing inflicted on the Italians during their sluggish incursion into Egypt had forced them to strengthen their standing patrols over the miles-long column, at the expense of protecting their airfields, which promptly received the R.A.F's fierce and accurate attention.

Among Longmore's vexations was the habitual incomprehension of technicalities by laymen. His statements of requirements and requests for supplies prompted Churchill to write: "I was astonished to find that you have nearly 1,000 aircraft and 16,000 air personnel in the Middle East, excluding Kenya. Surely out of all this establishment you ought to be able, if the machines are forthcoming, to produce a substantially larger number of modern aircraft operationally fit? Pray report through the Air Ministry any steps you may be able to take to obtain more fighting value from the immense amount of material and men under your command."

Of the 1,000 aircraft distributed around the huge Middle East area, 250 were used for training, communication and other non-operational work. Also, Churchill assumed that all those sent to the Command would figure in the Order of Battle in two or three weeks, according to their route. Something he had not learned at the Royal Military College, Sandhurst or in the Hussars, before resigning from the Army forty years previously, was that aeroplanes are vulnerable to a multitude of mechanical and other unpredictable afflictions. Small wonder! The flying machine had not then been invented. He did not realize that some of the aeroplanes sent from Britain would never arrive at their intended destinations. Many had to be written off after accidents, which are more common than outsiders are aware. Aircraft are peculiarly liable not only to loss but also unserviceability in the course of a long flight. On the way from Takoradi or via Gibraltar and Malta there were always several awaiting assembly, inspection, repair or spare parts. Further, ground staff essential for putting them into the air travelled by the Cape route and usually landed weeks after the aircraft that did complete the flight.

About the impediments that confounded the Malta route, Warrant Officer Ronald Lawson, DFC, could have enlightened the Prime Minister. The Wellington in which he was rear gunner took off from Hampstead Norris — no connection with the north London suburb infested by trendy socialists, but a satellite of Harwell — and landed at Gibraltar ten hours later. "We put a wingtip over the Spanish border and were fired at." Two days later they set out for Malta, another ten-hour flight, "during a battle," which is Lawson's laconic way of describing a heavy air raid against which the defence numbered a handful of fighters. "Got out of the aircraft, which was attacked and destroyed, so had to wait for someone to bring another one out [from England]."

To ease the C-in-C's burden, a deputy, Air Vice Marshal Boyd, was appointed with the main task of looking after the Western Desert. On the way from England his aeroplane ran short of petrol and had to land in Sicily instead of Malta, where the enemy took possession of him for the next few years. One of the cleverest and most cultured men in the annals of the Service, Air Vice Marshal Arthur Tedder, Air Member for Development and Production at the Ministry of Aircraft Production, replaced him. He had the sense to go via Takoradi, thus avoiding the enemy and personally experiencing and inspecting the long air route.

Finally, Graziani was poised to assault. But the brilliant commander of the Western Desert force, Major-General Richard O'Connor, whose policy was "aggressive action whenever possible", struck first. The operation, codenamed "Compass", saw the revival of close tactical co-operation between air force and army that had been practised in 1917 and 1918 by both the British and the Germans, then neglected in Britain for the next twenty years. A sophisticated development of it, the Blitzkrieg, had demonstrated its irresistible effectiveness in Poland in 1939 and in Denmark, Norway, Holland, Belgium and France in 1940. Compass did not duplicate the pattern of the Blitzkrieg, it evolved its own, adapted to the great expanse of the desert, the ports that fed it and the narrow coastal strip along which ran the road from Alexandria to Tripoli and the single-track railway from Alex to Tobruk. Wavell and Longmore had always been advocates of combined land-air action. O'Connor and Collishaw, ardent exponents of it, had set up their Headquarters on contiguous sites. From this cordial and perceptive combined planning and effort grew the whole concept of modern tactical warfare and the tactical air forces that were instrumental in bringing the Allies victory in, successively, North Africa, Italy, France and Germany.

The basic tactical lesson of the First World War was that air power is not merely a matter of numbers of aircraft, it is the power to establish air superiority applied to conquest. The side that is unable to establish air superiority over the vital area must fail to frustrate the enemy's major plans and cannot hope to influence decisively the course of the land battles to gain and hold territory. The British had proved in 1918 that they understood this, when the Royal Air Force was created as an entity entirely independent of the Army, instead of a mere branch of it as the Royal Flying Corps had been. The Chiefs of Staff at that time had learned that while one army can overcome another by attrition, the modern way must be first to blind the enemy by eliminating his aerial reconnaissance and then to defeat his bombers and fighters. The British had forgotten these principles in the interim between the 1918 armistice and the new war of 1939. The Germans had not. Hence the rapid and overwhelming success of the Blitzkrieg whenever they had inflicted it on some country that stood in the way of their evil craving to subjugate the whole of Europe. But Wavell, Longmore and Collishaw had not forgotten what they had learned between 1914 and 1918 either. Also, unlike the Italians, they had drawn the right conclusions from the Germans' victories.

As a preliminary to Compass, a Lysander and a Blenheim had photographed the Italian positions. The nine Hurricanes and six Gladiators escorting them had shot down seven of the CR42s that unwisely intervened. The Royal Navy had shelled Sidi Barrani. On 7 December Wellingtons based in Malta bombed Castel Benito and destroyed twenty-nine aeroplanes. On the 8th Wellingtons from the Delta destroyed ten at Benina. Day and night bombing of Italian defences was unflagging.

The enemy mustered 80,000 men. O'Connor had only 30,000, but his 275 tanks were opposed by no more than 120. On the night of 7 December the British and Commonwealth force set forth on its 70-mile approach march to go around the minefield's flank and take the enemy from the rear. Soon after dawn on the 9th the attack went in with the 7th Armoured and 4th Indian Divisions in the van. No 3 R.A.A.F.'s Gauntlets did their first dive bombing, 33 Squadron strafed and 274 Squadron, intercepting five CR42s, shot down four; one more each for Wykeham-Barnes and Dunn and one, which marked his first victory, for Pilot Officer Ernest Michelson Mason. This pilot, who joined the R.A.F. in March, 1938, did his training at Abu Sueir before being posted to 80 Squadron. By then he had acquired the nickname of "Imshi", the Arabic for "go away", a word to which he resorted with vehemence when importuned by vagrants, pedlars, pimps and other undesirables. Diversely accomplished, he was a natural pilot and shot, as well as a saxophonist, and had been, at the age of 15, a dirt-track rider. He was transferred from 80 to 274 with Dunn, Wykeham-Barnes and the others who formed its nucleus. Presently he became notorious for being the only bearded member of the R.A.F. and the leading fighter pilot in the desert.

Sandstorms delayed O'Connor on the 10th, but by the next day he had overrun Sidi Barrani, taken 40,000 prisoners and 400 guns, and advanced beyond Buq Buq. Nos 3 R.A.A.F. and 33 Squadrons each lost a fighter in the course of downing six of the enemy.

On the 10th, while the Italians were scurrying back whence they had come, Wavell had withdrawn the 4th Indian Division and sent it to the Sudan, where he expected an attack. It was on the following day that Deadstick Dyson put his name in the record book with his seven kills in one fight. On the 12th No 3 R.A.A.F's Gauntlets were retired owing to their antiquity and the consequent servicing problems, and replaced by Gladiators. The 13th was unlucky for this squadron. Having attacked five CR42s near Sollum and shot one down, they were set on by eight more, which took out five of them: one pilot was killed, two baled out and two crash-landed. In 274, one pilot was lost and one forced down, while a third destroyed a CR42. No 33 scored three CR42s and two S79s. The 14th saw more R.A.F. successes. Eight of 274 shot down six S79s on one interception. Later, nine of the same squadron intercepted five CR42s and destroyed them all. Squadron Leader Dunn accounted for two but had to crash-land again. Flight Lieutenant Lapsley, who also got one, now had a total of six, the highest so far in the desert. Wykeham-Barnes and a Canadian in 33 Squadron, Flying Officer V. C. Woodward, each had five.

Sandstorms, and floods caused by exceptionally heavy rain, had impeded the enemy's air effort. Sollum was captured on 16 December; it had needed only a week to drive Graziani's army and air force out of Egypt. There was no complacency in the squadrons; the tempo of air activity did not slacken and both sides inflicted daily losses. Wykeham-Barnes added an S79 to his tally on the 16th, Dyson brought down two CR42s on the 18th and Lapsley got another. Reinforcements for the Regia Aeronautica kept coming in from Italy: on the 16th, twenty-three S79s and twenty-three CR42s; on the 18th a whole *Gruppo*, the 20th, with thirteen Fiat G50bis fighters on its strength. These monoplanes, capable of 385 m.p.h., were armed with two machine guns and a cannon.

The new year began with a display of pugnacity and courage by an Italian fighter pilot, who, flying a Singleton CR42, attacked nine Blenheims that had just taken off from Derna and damaged five of them. Wherever he hailed from, he fulfilled Shakespeare's exhortation: "What's brave, what's noble, / Let's do it after the high Roman fashion".

The 6th Australian Division had arrived from Palestine and the surge forward could continue. O'Connor resumed his thrust on 3 January, 1941, and Bardia, yielding 45,000 prisoners, fell three days later.

On the 7th Longmore received a signal from Churchill. "Greatly admire your brilliant support of Army operations. We shall soon be as usual torn between conflicting needs. Probably four or five squadrons will be required for Greece and yet you will have to carry the Army forward in Libya."

This baleful forewarning was the outcome of Churchill's enthusiasm for meeting Mussolini's challenge in the Balkans, fuelled by his admiration of the Greeks for holding the Italians at bay. He offered an armoured and artillery force to the Greek Prime Minister, General Metaxas, and ordered Wavell to make the necessary preparations. Metaxas refused the offer.

Churchill's next signal to Wavell and Longmore began: "Nothing must hinder the capture of Tobruk", but continued stubbornly, "thereafter all operations in Libya are subordinate to aiding Greece. We [the Cabinet] expect and require prompt and active compliance with our decisions, for which we bear full responsibility."

The chorus of a popular song in the mid-1930s went "With a fine old English gentleman, our Maggie caught a cold last night." It was several fine old English gentlemen, the War Cabinet, who were the authors of this warped strategy, and it was the British and Commonwealth airmen, soldiers and sailors fighting to hold North Africa, Greece and Crete who caught a cold.

On 11 January Longmore ordered 11 (Blenheim) and 112 (Gladiator) Squadrons to Greece. To bring No 11's strength up to establishment, 39 handed its Blenheims over and re-equipped with the first Martin Marylands to reach the Command. These bombers, with a top speed of 278 m.p.h. and a bomb load of 2,000 lb, were also highly regarded for photographic reconnaissance.

Imshi Mason's score by now had mounted to five CR42s, four S79s and a Ca310. On the 12th 33 Squadron was detailed for Greece, where Pattle, who had left the desert with four victories to his name, had shot down seven more and was the top-scorer in the Command.

Tobruk, which had been by-passed, was attacked on 21 January and surrendered next day with a further bag of 30,000 prisoners. After a brief pause O'Connor was allowed to push on, with Benghazi as his objective. The Italians were strongly entrenched at Derna, which he intended to attack as soon as supplies and more tanks reached him. But the Australians, who had advanced beyond it by 2 February, found that the Italians were pulling out. Air reconnaissance confirmed that Graziani was retreating all the way to El Agheila, where he could establish a narrow front between the coast and the Great Sand Sea. Boldly moving to cut the Italians off before they could do so, O'Connor sent a force of armour, artillery and lorried infantry across the desert south of the Jebel Akhdar. This reached the coast at Beda Fomm, half-way between Benghazi and Aghelia, by the afternoon of 5 February. In the battle that followed at Beda Fomm, where the Italians displayed uncommon bravery, O'Connor's force of 3,000 took 20,000 prisoners, 216 guns and 120 tanks and had thrown the enemy right out of Cyrenaica.

The Regia Aeronautica had lost fifty-eight aircraft in action, and ninety-one intact and 1,100 damaged were captured. O'Connor paid Collishaw a handsome tribute: "I wish to record my very great appreciation of the wonderful work of the R.A.F. units under your command, whose determination and fine fighting qualities have made this campaign possible. Since the war began you have consistently attacked the enemy air force, dealing him blow after blow until finally he was driven out of the sky, and out of Cyrenaica, leaving hundreds of derelict aircraft on his aerodromes. In his recent retreat from Tobruk you gave his ground troops no rest."

The way was open for O'Connor to sweep on across Tunisia and empty Libya of every last Italian soldier, sailor and airman. Black-bearded Imshi Mason was not there to share in this triumph. On 30 January he had been promoted to flight lieutenant and posted to command a flight in 261 Squadron in Malta. By then he was the top-scoring pilot in North Africa, with fifteen and a half kills, and had equalled Pattle's present tally. Had these two still been in the desert when the Italians decamped from Cyrenaica, they might disgustedly have echoed, more forcefully, Plutarch's words 2,220 years earlier, after Pyrrhus had defeated the Romans at Asculum: "One more such victory and we are lost". For on 29 January Metaxas had died suddenly and his successor, Alexander Karisis, accepted Churchill's renewed offer of military reinforcements; at the expense of immediate total victory in Libya.

With an impetuosity and lack of foresight that were to cost the unnecessary deaths in North Africa and Italy of tens of thousands of British and Commonwealth fighting men of all three Services, Britain's Prime Minister ordered Wavell on 12 February, 1941, to stop O'Connor's advance, to leave the smallest possible holding force in Cyrenaica and to make ready to send the bulk of his army to Greece. Churchill was the war's most inspiring figure on either side, but his judgment this time was as sound as that of someone who opens a vegetarian restaurant in cannibal country.

The Germans were coming.

Hitler had issued his first directive ordering German troops to Africa, to save Tripolitania, on 11 January, 1941. The unit designated was the 5th Light Division, which included a Panzer Regiment. It was to be commanded by *Generalmajor* Erwin Rommel, who had led the 7th Panzer Division with scintillating flair in the Battle of France.

The Luftwaffe's *Fliegerkorps X*, under the command of *Generalmajor* Hans Geisler, had begun establishing itself in Sicily in December, 1940. By 12 January, 1941, it mustered 245 aircraft, of which 179 were serviceable, began attacks on Malta and made one on the Suez Canal. At the end of January, 1941, part of it, under *Fliegerführer Afrika* began moving to Castel Benito, Cyrenaica.

On 6 February, 1941, Hitler decreed that the air force in North Africa must be strengthened, "if necessary, withdrawing units from warfare against the British Isles".

On 11 February Rommel called in at Sicily to confer with Geisler. On the 12th he arrived at Tripoli. On the 14th the advance guard of his force, a battalion of light infantry and an anti-tank unit, came ashore.

On 18 February, 1941, Hitler created the Afrika Korps and decided to send Rommel a full Panzer Division and other reinforcements.

The desert war that the British and Commonwealth forces had come so close to winning was about to be transformed. From a conflict in which small numbers, great bravery and clever leadership confronted huge numbers and pusillanimity poorly led, it became a struggle between soldiers and airmen of equal courage and strength and commanders of comparable ability.

The Allies had been deprived of victory by a flaw in the character of a Prime Minister of prodigious talent who was vulnerable to distraction by his obstinately long-held romantic visions. For a former officer in the Regular Army, and taking into account his unimpeachable moral and physical courage – he had changed political parties on a matter of principle (or was it cynical expediency?), he had ridden in a cavalry charge at the Battle of Omdurman (1898) – to make so crass a concession to vanity and so clumsy a strategical decision was an enormity. Those who abetted him must be suspect of an intellectual capacity more consonant with disporting themselves in the treetops among the lower primates than with high office. Thanks to them the war dragged on for another four and a half years and the life-expectancy of hundreds of thousands of Service and civilian men and women and children was drastically shortened.

The stupidity of the policy is even more obvious when one recalls that the Greek Commander-in-Chief, General Papagos, had warned that the British would be wiser to complete their conquest of Africa than to divide their forces and fight on another front simultaneously. No doubt to the British Cabinet he was "some sort of a dago chap who hasn't been to Camberley", (the Staff College), so his opinion must be worthless. But the German Supreme Command, whom they might have respected, shared the Greek C-in-C's view. One of Hitler's staff, General Warlimont, reports: "We could not understand at the time why the British did not exploit the difficulties of the Italians in Cyrenaica by pushing on to Tripoli. There was nothing to check them. The few Italian troops who remained were panic-stricken, and expected the British tanks to appear at any moment."

The armed forces of the Balkan states with which Churchill daydreamed that Britain could form a conquering alliance against the Axis powers were primitively equipped and poorly trained. It was obvious to any intelligent person, let alone to statesmen and senior military commanders, that, facing the Luftwaffe and German tanks, they would have as much chance as a tethered goat against a tiger.

In North Africa the Allies were now committed to two and a half years more of air and land battles against a military genius, which could have been avoided by the exercise of plain common sense.

CHAPTER 4

Rommel's First Attack

The fighting and the stampede across the desert had left the battlefield and landing grounds littered with the motley detritus of modern war. Italian aircraft, ruined or repairable, stood among empty oil and petrol drums. Tanks, burned out, blown up or merely with shattered tracks, wallowed in the sand, often with a row of mounds beside them where their crews were buried. Graves, unmarked or with a crude cross, perhaps with a rifle thrust bayonet-deep at the head, a steel helmet over the butt, were scattered wherever one's eyes roved over the devastation. Overturned armoured cars and soft-skinned vehicles lay with their working parts spilling through gashes torn by mines, bombs, grenades or gunfire. There were piles of ammunition, water cans, tins of rations. Clothing of all kinds was spread amid ammunition boxes, water bottles, boots and gasmasks. Letters and photographs fluttered in any vagrant breeze. Lorries, staff cars, personnel carriers and motorcycles that had not been smashed by bombs, bullets or shells stood ready for the taking.

And they were taken. Officers and other ranks drove cars or rode motorcycles between their living quarters and the dispersed aircraft, offices and workshop tents. The informality that characterized the desert army and air force was emerging. Among Army officers, fawn corduroy trousers from Cairo tailors were replacing battledress slacks. Khaki jerseys were becoming more common than battledress blouses, bazaar-cobbled suede, crepe-soled boots were preferred to regulation shoes and issue leather boots. This jaunty rig gradually permeated the R.A.F. as well. Troops who normally went about bare-headed adopted Italian military headgear. Khaki drill shirts and trousers issued to the enemy found a place in many kitbags. The almost universal item was a coloured silk scarf, a strip of parachute silk or any piece of cloth to pull up over nose and mouth in sandstorms or when riding in the back of a lorry. Fighter pilots wore them also to keep their necks warm and

8 The Ship Inn, Mersah Matruh. (*T. Davies*)

9 A Wireless Truck of Air Support Control System. (*D. Thomas*)

10 A typical squadron airmen's cookhouse. (*R.C. Duncan*)

11 Christmas Dinner in the Blue. (*R.C. Duncan*)

avoid stiffness when constantly turning the head in search of enemy air-craft. Stephen Hall wore a British sun helmet of the kind worn by the R.A.F. in Asia and Africa before the war for flying in open cockpits. His fellow gunner in the crew, Doug Peacock, sported a chef's toque. Discipline was as relaxed as the uniform regulations; for air and ground crews alike, as for combatant soldiers, clerks and technicians, unremit-ting hard work and efficiency were all that mattered. Not that indis-cipline or disobedience was tolerated.

From the outset, the usual sleeping accommodation was a small tent over a slit trench to give increased head room and some shelter in air raids. The standard tent for most purposes was known glibly to all ranks as the "E.P.I.P.", without, in most instances, any certainty of its deri-vation. "European personnel, Indian pattern" was a favoured version. The right one was equally odd: "Egypt pattern, Indian patent". Now, Italian tentage was often acquired.

With the fall of Tobruk 216 Squadron reverted for a day to the trans-port role when it fetched captured Italian Staff officers to Cairo. Among them was General Berganzoli, commanding in the field, who was known to the British, on account of his abundant and bristling facial hair, as "Electric Whiskers". The Squadron then moved to El Adem, where they were warned not to kick any of the bottles littered among the tents. It was only when the wind blew the sand aside that the mines attached to the bottles were revealed; but neither the time nor the equipment nor the trained men could be spared to clear them away. Lengthening lines of communication also brought privation and for some months yams substituted for potatoes, to be replaced in turn by rice.

These aberrations in day-to-day life on the ground were accompanied by diversity of experience in the air. The squadron had a new C.O., who, says Hall, "believed in the high level glide-in attack". Briefed to bomb and strafe Benina airfield, he promised to light the target for those who followed; with the light of the fires he would start was the implication. "Brave words," and "I remember the skipper saying on the intercom 'he's kept his word.' It was certainly ablaze. From the rear turret I could not yet see anything burning, yet the smell of burning was reaching us many miles away. Our new high level glide bombing technique had evidently brought us lower than the skipper realized, for as soon as I started strafing I heard the crunch of our bombs and felt the back pressure. The raid was a resounding success. From photos taken next morning it was estimated that 70-100 aircraft were damaged or destroyed."

The imperturbable Ronald Lawson (who, on return to England, flew as mid-upper gunner in Lancasters, with the great "Mickey" Martin, regarded by many bomber pilots as the best of them all) found his work monotonous. "The long haul to Benghazi was fairly uneventful and a bit binding, as it was unusual to meet opposition until we reached the target. On the trip back we used any excuse to land at Heliopolis, a peacetime station where the food was more appetizing than at Shallufa or Landing Ground 09, and the sanitary arrangements first class. We were not very popular with the permanent staff, they being Regulars and we RAFVR." The authorities at Helio complained about these unwelcome visitors going into the officers' and sergeants' messes in flying kit. At briefing for a trip, the squadron commander "used to 'bollock' us, then say 'See you at Helio in the morning and hope you have a good shower and breakfast'."

Lawson's bravery was rewarded in 1944, when the *London Gazette* announced that "The King has been graciously pleased to approve the following award for gallantry and devotion to duty in the execution of air operations: Distinguished Flying Cross, Warrant Officer Ronald Lawson. This officer has now completed two tours of operations. During his first tour he was seriously wounded and temporarily blinded and he made determined efforts to return to operational duties and eventually succeeded. His courage, keenness and invaluable assistance to other gunners in his squadron are most praiseworthy."

On the depletion of 202 Group's strength in Libya, Air H.Q. Cyrenaica was set up and Group Captain L. O. Brown given command of the nugatory air force that remained. The fighters of 3 RAAF and 73 Squadrons protected harbours and forward troops from bases as far west as Benina. No. 55 did bombing and reconnaissance, and No. 6 tactical recce. These and the Wellington squadrons based on Malta and in the Canal Zone persistently attacked enemy airfields and Tripoli. Collishaw's command became 204 Group.

The Luftwaffe was flying in. The first to land, in late January, 1941, were Me110s of ZG26, based at Sirte, "Marble Arch", where Mussolini had erected a vainglorious triumphal memorial on the Cyrenaican border, and Castel Benito. They were joined by the Ju87s of StG3, Ju88s of KLG1 and He111s of KG26. The first loss was a Ju87 under the guns of an Italian fighter: not surprising, most airmen would say, cynically mistrustful of other people's aircraft recognition. The first Luftwaffe victim of the Allies was a Me110 that forced-landed on the wrong side of the line. The second was a Ju87, which anti-aircraft gunners brought down. The first to be shot down in an air fight was a Ju88 credited to Flying Officer Saunders of 3 RAAF on 15 February. The Stuka crews quickly tasted Isaiah's "bread of adversity, and the water of affliction", as their predecessors had in the Battle of Britain: two days later, 3 RAAF intercepted twelve Ju87s: Flight Lieutenant Steege and Flying Officer Jackson each bagged three, Flying Officer Saunders two. On the following day the squadron suffered the Me110's first successes when two Hurricanes went down.

In pressing so far forward to attack enemy air strips and put Alexandria out of the Regia Aeronautica's reach, Collishaw's squadrons had destroyed Italian stores that could have sustained them when they occupied these vacated sites. Consequently, they depended on the Army for supplies. But the Army, now far from its depots in the Delta, was in the same predicament. And when the Luftwaffe began to bomb Benghazi, the Royal Navy declared the port untenable as a naval base, which meant another weakening of the supply line and consequent inability to mount a large-scale offensive. Collishaw lamented that his group was "prevented from further demoralizing the enemy's routed troops which (sic) were escaping westwards to El Agheila in crowded masses on the main road."

To compound its folly, the British Cabinet defied the quickly increasing number of German military and air force units in Tripolitania and persisted on its disastrous course. No. 208 Squadron was sent to Greece in late February, while British, New Zealand, Australian and Polish troops began embarking for Greece on 6 March.

The aircraft strength remained too low. In the first three months of 1941, 184 were lost and only 164 replacements received.

The 7th Armoured Division had been replaced by the inexperienced 2nd Division. The 6th Australian was in Greece and the newly arrived 9th Australian lacked equipment. Rommel had immediately deceived the Allies by deploying dummy tanks. O'Connor was recuperating in Cairo. While General Neame, who had replaced him, hesitated to attack, Rommel made his first aggressive move on 24 March by sending armoured cars against British outposts, which retreated to Mersa Brega. On 31 March he launched fifty tanks backed up by two fresh Italian divisions and drove the Allies back in confusion. Benghazi fell on 3 April and by 11 April Neame's force had retreated all the way to Egypt, leaving Tobruk isolated and under siege. The town was bombed and strafed daily and its airfields were shelled by observed artillery fire.

The silent sub-text of war is fear. The courage of those who had to fly Stukas must have been the worst fractured, and all the more fragile because of their initial easy tasks in killing and terrorizing civilians in Poland, the Low Countries and France. On the morning of 5 April three Hurricanes of 3 RAAF and four of 73 shot down five dive bombers of nine they encountered. That evening two 73 Squadron Hurricanes and seven from 3 RAAF intercepted twelve and destroyed nine. It was not only the Hurricane pilots who potted them like clay pigeons: six days later the ack-ack gunners at Tobruk brought three down.

No. 6 Squadron, which now had one flight of Hurricanes, and No. 73 continued to operate from within the defence perimeter, while the rest of Collishaw's units withdrew eastwards. On the 12th German armour tried to concentrate for an attack on Tobruk, but air reconnaissance reported them. Bombers of 45 Squadron from the Delta and 55 from Maraua — both recently transferred to 204 Group, whose H.Q. was at Ma'aten Bagush — refuelled at a landing ground within the Tobruk perimeter, then broke up the massing armour. Both Hurricane squadrons spent much of their time strafing, and the Blenheims on bombing, troops and vehicles, an occupation that proved its worth and contributed hugely to the enemy's failure to take Tobruk. This wise impromptu tactical use of aircraft in support of the ground forces did not exactly emulate the Blitzkrieg stratagem, but it did foreshadow the deliberate employment of fighters, fighter-bombers and bombers on low-level ground attack that was about to be developed.

An attack on the 14th was a sample of the pressure to which the Tobruk garrison was being subjected and the scale of the air fighting, with the odds much in the enemy's favour. At 0730 hrs seventy aircraft comprising Ju87s escorted by Me110s, CR42s and 650s appeared overhead. No. 73 Squadron scrambled to take them on. One of the flight commanders, Flight Lieutenant J. D. "Smudger" Smith, a Canadian who had scored a victory in France, two during the Battle of Britain and two over the Western Desert, engaged five 650s and shot two down before being killed. Sergeant R. W. Ellis, who had also served with the squadron in France, then made four kills in the Battle of Britain, took out two Ju87s before having to land and rearm. Quickly airborne again, he destroyed another.

This was the day when a new predator, menacing, powerful and confident, arrived in North Africa: the Messerschmitt 109E, whose speed and rate of climb exceeded the Hurricane MkI's by 38 m.p.h. and approximately 1,000ft a minute. It was armed with two machine guns and two 20mm cannon. Three *Staffeln* belonging to I/JG27, which comprised many battle-hardened pilots — among whom was Marseille with seven kills to his name — were assembling at Gazala. This *Geschwader* claimed more than sixty successes in the Battle of France and over thirty in the Battle of Britain. The *Gruppenkommandeur, Hauptmann* Eduard Neumann, who had a tally of nine victories, displayed the brand of panache and eccentricity that his opponents had already brought to desert warfare. He turned up with his living quarters in tow: a gypsy caravan.

The Me109s fired their first shots on 19 April, over Tobruk, when 274's C.O., Squadron Leader J. H. Lapsley, DFC, who had destroyed eleven Italian aeroplanes, was shot down. The Huns, who made such a parade of fighting cleanly, machine-gunned and wounded him after he hit the ground. Three other Hurricanes also went down. In the afternoon the first 109 fell victim to Pilot Officer Spence of 274.

Operating again from Heliopolis, Stephen Hall's crew was among those detailed for a raid on Benghazi. This meant carrying three 90-gallon tanks in the cabin, their contents to be pumped manually into the main tank as required. "Symonds attack system to be used: gain maximum height before reaching target, line up objective and throttle back to quarter revs for a gentle dive to 5,000-6,000 ft. Drop bombs, full throttle and climb away. The theory was quietness in approach, speed in getaway, and at final height over target we should be below the heavy ack-ack barrage and above the medium stuff."

They approached Benghazi from the sea, concentrating on the cathedral mole so that any bombs that overshot would hit the dock buildings. "The fire from the ground defences was murderous. Everything imaginable seemed to be exploding around us. The chat on the intercom between the skipper and bomb aimer was intermingled with my own thoughts." He displays the ironical, deprecating humour that is a speciality of the R.A.F. "Think, lad, of the privilege of sitting in a lovely cramped turret with the beautiful moon and stars and all hell let loose, while someone down there is intent on killing you. Suddenly the nightmare of all nightmares: the whole heaven above illuminated by some twit dropping a parachute flare whose brilliant glare silhouettes us. Seconds ago we had a 50/50 chance of survival. The engines are put into overdrive and we're climbing as we've never climbed before. Too late . . . bangs, lights, flashes, tearing of metal. We are still in the air and over Benina. It's dark, then one solitary stream of tracer, exactly our height, is following us: a hair's breadth from my turret, so we're reasonably safe. The skipper seems concerned for my welfare. I can't convince him that I'm okay. He sends the second pilot down to look at the damage. My parachute harness is ripped, there are two massive holes in the fuselage, our tail wheel is missing, my turret is hanging on well and my guardian angel working overtime."

Half a century later, Hall is laconic about the Distinguished Flying Medal he was awarded in April, 1941. He admits only that he landed inside the Tobruk perimeter with stores and personnel. The citation also leaves much to the imagination: "Throughout, his courage and efficiency have been outstanding." Later, he received a mention in despatches.

Rommel intended to carry his attack right into Egypt, but both the Italian Supreme Command and General Halder, Chief of the German General Staff, disapproved of such dynamism and unorthodoxy. Halder sent General von Paulus, his Deputy, "to head off this soldier gone stark mad", as he noted in his diary. As a more achievable and more comfortable undertaking, Paulus sanctioned a full-out attempt to capture Tobruk. On 30 April this was set in motion, but checked and counter-attacked by the British and Australians. Only half the German tanks were left in fighting trim, and, as Liddell Hart put it, "As for the Italian supporting troops, they were slow in backing up and quick in backing out". The siege wore on.

On 12 May a convoy reached Alexandria with fifty Hurricanes and 306 tanks. By now, also, the trickle from Takoradi was becoming a steady flow. Churchill informed Longmore: "Whereas you have received only 370 aircraft from November to now, 328 more are on their way and a further 880 will start before the end of May."

* * *

Hitler had invaded Greece on 6 April, an obvious move that Churchill's Cabinet had not foreseen. By the 14th the Germans had advanced so far and Rommel had shaken the Allies so gravely in North Africa that Wavell cancelled the sailing of intended reinforcements from Egypt, the 7th Australian Division and the Polish Brigade. This was in effect a decision to abandon the Greek campaign. On the 19th General Papagos recommended the Allies to leave and London gave Wavell permission to evacuate. The bulk of the Allied forces were withdrawn to Crete. On 20 May 3,000 German paratroops dropped on the island and 19,000 more were swiftly brought in by aeroplanes and gliders. On the 23rd the King of Greece and his Government moved there. Between 28 and 30 May, 14,500 men out of the remnants of the defeated British and Commonwealth land, air and sea forces were shipped back to Egypt, along with 2,000 Greek troops. Thousands of Allied troops had been killed and wounded and 13,000 Allied prisoners were taken.

The R.A.F. had lost seventy-two aircraft in the air and fifty-five to ground strafing. A further eighty-two had to be abandoned or destroyed. Of 163 of all ranks killed, missing or captured, 150 were aircrew.

* * *

Churchill's dissatisfaction with Longmore, shared by the Chief of Air Staff, Air Chief Marshal Sir Charles Portal, had been growing. On 29 March the Prime Minister had written to him: "I have been concerned to read your continued complaints of the numbers of aircraft which are sent you. We are as fully informed as you are of what you are getting. A weekly report is submitted to me of all movements via Takoradi. Therefore, when I read a telegram from General Smuts in which he refers to 'Beaverbrook [Minister for Aircraft Production] being persuaded to disgorge from his hoard', or when I read the C-in-C Mediterranean's telegram to First Sea Lord stating that 'Only one Hurricane was received during the month of March', and when I also read your A442 which seeks to justify this absurd statement, I fear there must be some talk emanating from your Headquarters which is neither accurate nor helpful."

Despite his abundant talents, Churchill remained ignorant about the intricacies of moving aircraft to a destination thousands of miles distant. To him the number despatched still automatically equalled the number received. His rebuke to Longmore was quickly followed by punishment. On 1 June, 1941, Tedder became A.O.C.-in-C. Middle East.

Wavell was planning a new offensive codenamed Battleaxe, whose main purpose was to relieve Tobruk, but reluctant to begin it until 4th Indian and 7th Armoured Divisions had been brought up to strength. Behemoths of every kind, despite their minatory aspect of indestructibility, are abnormally sensitive to their own peculiar tormentors. Kipling revealed the elephant's nervousness of rodents and small dogs. A hippopotamus, though uninjured, died of shock when its transport had a mild accident that dumped it on an English main road. And the tanks that had recently arrived in Alexandria had – like the aeroplanes that preceded them – suffered many mechanical faults between British factories and Egyptian docks, which needed repairs that could not all be completed before the battle.

Churchill was impatient and defined Battleaxe's objective as "to win a decisive victory in North Africa and destroy Rommel's forces". Wavell modified this to "drive the enemy back west of Tobruk". Three separate columns were to make the attack; one aiming for Halfaya Pass, another for Capuzzo and a third for Hafid Ridge. The Army asked for air cover over the battle area, to protect its advancing troops from the Luftwaffe, rather than for repeated raids on the enemy's airfields to destroy his aircraft before they took off. Nobody except Collishaw seemed to recall what Marshal of the R.A.F. Lord Trenchard had said and proved in 1917: that the most effective and economical way to deal with an enemy air force was to smash its machines on the ground.

No 204 Group's Order of Battle at that date was: 6 Squadron (Lysander and Hurricane), 14 (Blenheim IV), 45 (Blenheim IV), 30 (Blenheim I), 39 (Maryland), 24 SAAF (Maryland), 73 (Hurricane), 274 (Hurricane), 250 (Kittyhawk), 1 SAAF (Hurricane), 2 SAAF (Tomahawk).

The air umbrella was to be preceded by attacks on Rommel's lines of communication. At dawn on 14 June Collishaw also sent six 73 Squadron aircraft to shoot up Gazala South airfield. Flying Officer George Goodman, DFC, led them. He had fought in France with No 1 Squadron and shot down two He111s. In the Battle of Britain he destroyed a Me109, two Me110s, a Do17 and an He111, as well as sharing in the destruction of two enemy machines over France and three over England. In North Africa he had added a CR42, an Me110, a Ju87 and a G50 and shared others, to bring his total to 14½. Over the target the formation flew into a barrage of 88mm flak, which brought down three of them. One was Goodman, who crashed somewhere deep in the desert and neither his body nor his aeroplane was ever found.

Forty-five minutes later five aircraft of 1 SAAF set out to escort a 24 SAAF Maryland, flown by Lieutenant Newborn, on reconnaissance to the same place. Bad visibility obliged four fighters to turn back. From the enemy aerodrome the readiness pilots of I/JG27 saw the Maryland and its sole remaining escort, flown by Captain K. Driver, DFC, who had shot down ten Italian aircraft in East Africa and one in the desert, pass by. Driver spotted the objective, but couldn't inform the Maryland pilot as they had no common radio frequency. After flying for a further 20 miles the Maryland turned back and this time found its target. First the 88s fired at the intruders, then *Oberleutnant* Franzisket scrambled in his Me109. Driver attacked him head-on, but missed. The German's return fire caused the Hurricane's fuel tank to explode. As the two fighters flashed past one another on reciprocal courses the propeller of each sliced a wingtip off the other. Driver baled out of his burning aircraft. Franzisket, flying one wing low, shot down the Maryland, from which one man baled out. The rest of the crew also survived.

The noise of the 88s and the aircraft's guns woke the *Gruppenkommandeur, Hauptmann* Springorum, who was thoroughly put out at being roused a couple of hours prematurely. Having lived in America, he was able to express his feelings forcefully to the four prisoners. "What the hell do you British want in Africa, anyway?"

When Newborn reasonably replied "The same as the Germans, sir," Springorum roared with laughter.

At breakfast, Franzisket learned that Driver's wife was in Cairo, waiting to see her husband, so he dropped a message for her on the

Allied side of the line, a chivalrous act that partly compensated for the behaviour of some others who strafed shot-down aircrew when they were defenceless.

The Allied ground force started forward that afternoon and opened the battle by moonlight in the early hours of 15 June. The German listening service was as good as the British, and infantry and armour exchanged as many radio messages as did aircraft. Emplaced 88mm guns were waiting for Wavell's men at Halfya Pass and Hafid Ridge. Only at Capuzzo were there no 88s and only there was the enemy overcome. The next day Rommel counterattacked and 7th Armoured had heavy losses. On the 17th the Allies pulled back behind the Egyptian frontier and Battleaxe had failed.

The air umbrella had not produced the results expected by the Army, largely because the R.A.F. and Army H.Qs, which a year before had been on adjoining sites, were by now 80 miles apart. Communication and co-ordination were therefore difficult, and exacerbated by Army wireless failures.

In the air some twenty-five Hurricanes, Marylands and Blenheims were lost, against about twenty Me109s, Me110s, Ju87s, CR42s and 650s. Many aeroplanes on both sides were damaged. It was the Me109s that had the most successes. Among the British casualties was Flight Lieutenant J. E. McFall of 6 Squadron. Three Me109s shot him down; then, as he was clambering out of the wreckage, his gallant vanquishers butchered him.

Even when successful, joint-Service operations are notoriously followed by displays of spectacular effrontery as the Commanders involved instantly set about blaming each other for any flaws that are revealed. In this instance, when failure might have been expected to provoke virtuoso performances of mutual denigration, it was characteristic of Wavell and Tedder that they were both so restrained.

Wavell complained that Western Desert Air Force had failed in its primary rôle; to master the sky over the battlefield and keep the enemy from operating there. He admitted, however, that this was owing to lack of training in the Army as well as the Royal Air Force.

Tedder pointed out that the air umbrella for which the Army had asked had proved effective. With only two exceptions in the extreme forward area, attempts to attack British troops had been intercepted and enemy bombs were dropped unaimed. Also, despite numerical weaknesses, attacks on Axis lines of communication and airfields had led the enemy to retain a large proportion of fighters in the rear of the battle area for protection. The enemy attempted no sweeps, because the rest of his fighters were used as bomber escort. Tedder also explained that an air umbrella entailed maintaining many, and therefore weak, fighter patrols which, being outnumbered when they met the enemy, suffered heavily and could sometimes be penetrated.

This subject was one that Churchill at once completely comprehended, as his edict makes clear: "Nevermore must the ground troops expect, as a matter of course, to be protected against the air by aircraft. If this can be done it must be only as a happy make-weight and a piece of good luck. Above all, the idea of keeping standing patrols of aircraft over our moving columns should be abandoned. It is unsound to 'distribute' aircraft in this way and no air superiority will stand any large application of such a mischievous practice." In a display of his multifaceted genius, he defined the roles that land and air forces must properly play, with a concision and lucidity that could not have been bettered by a Staff College instructor. "Upon the military Commander-in-Chief in the Middle East announcing that a battle is in prospect, the Air Officer Commanding-in-Chief will give him all possible aid and irrespective of other targets, however attractive. The Army C-in-C will specify to the AOC-in-C the tasks he requires to be performed. It will be for the AOC-in-C to use his maximum force against these objectives in the manner most effective."

The Prime Minister's ready grasp of the matter was not tinctured by any apparent sympathy for the military C-in-C in Operation Battleaxe. On 21 June, 1941, General Sir Archibald Wavell was replaced by General Sir Claude Auchinleck.

On the same date the last of the Italian forces in Ethiopia, Somaliland and Eritrea, where Britain had been waging another campaign, surrendered, thus relieving Tedder and Auchinleck of a considerable distraction from future operations in the desert.

Tedder immediately tackled four main weaknesses that the past twelve months' fighting had created in his Command. The organizational structure had, with expansion, become too loose; the operational training of newly arrived aircrew was inadequate; following defeats in Cyrenaica, Greece and Crete, the maintenance organization could no longer cope with its workload; the system of tactical air support was no longer satisfactory. Attending to these occupied nearly four months.

The first was remedied by raising the status of 202 and 204 Groups. No 202 became Air H.Q. Egypt, responsible for local air defence, while No 204, in the forward area, became Air H.Q. Western Desert Air Force and its squadrons were formed into newly created wings. The second was put right by the formation of new operational training units. A Maintenance Group, No 206, was formed to cure the third by reconstructing the whole repair, maintenance and salvage functions.

Operationally, the fourth defect was the most important. This was resolved when the R.A.F. convinced the Army that the ground forces would find their best protection from air attack in offensive sweeps, air raids on enemy airfields, and anti-aircraft artillery. To provide air support immediately it was needed, excellent communications and mobility were essential: mobility for the squadrons by the provision of more lorries to move ground crews and equipment from one airstrip to another, for early warning by the provision of mobile radar units. Communication had to be swift and clear between each element of the air support network.

Mobile units called Air Support Controls, manned by the R.A.F. with a small Army staff attached, were formed. One was set up at each Corps H.Q. to consider, sift and relay requests for air support. Its principal communications were with the forward infantry brigades, aircraft in the air, airstrips and H.Q. Western Desert Air Force. Requests from advanced troops could thus be considered at once and, if granted, met promptly. Also, reports from reconnaissance aircraft could be relayed in time for both air and ground forces to act on them. Another innovation was to set a bomb line. Aircraft were allowed to bomb only on the enemy side of this, which, in theory, should prevent friendly aircraft from attacking their own ground troops. But the bomb line was determined by the local commander and varied with his appreciation of bombing accuracy. Sometimes the line was dangerously close to the Allies' forward troops, sometimes the safety margin was so wide that it was behind the enemy's forward positions.

Hitherto the air force in the desert had had to rely on improvisation and subterfuge, and to grope its way from one demand on its small resources to another. It had had to make the best use of its few aircraft while deceiving the enemy into thinking these were many. Its operations had been largely impromptu, based often on scanty and inaccurate intelligence and executed with obsolescent aeroplanes. It had done well because, though small, it was a body of highly trained professionals who possessed not only the world's greatest expertise but also inexhaustible courage, led by a man of legendary bravery, adventurousness and determination. Having survived some of the heaviest air fighting of the First World War and falling out of his cockpit without a parachute at 16,000 ft, there must have been nothing the Germans, Bolsheviks or Italians could threaten that seemed more than a passing nuisance. It was providential that Collishaw was stationed in Egypt when Mussolini let slip his dogs of war in Libya.

His overseas tour had expired in July. In his parting message he wrote: "I wish to express my grateful thanks to all who served me so well and so loyally during the past two and a half years in which I have held command. You have defeated an air force numerically superior by four to one, and have never been defeated in an important engagement in the campaign."

His successor, Air Vice Marshal Arthur Coningham, however brave, could claim no feat to emulate any of Collishaw's more startling exploits; but it was only by his courage and determination that he was in the R.A.F. at all. A New Zealander, he had joined the Army in 1914 at the outbreak of war and served in Somalia and Egypt. In 1916 he was repatriated and discharged as medically unfit. So he paid his passage to England, joined the R.F.C. and shot down nineteen enemy aircraft over the Western Front. Now twenty-three years later, his experience enriched by much pioneering airmanship, a tour as an instructor at Cranwell, graduation at Staff College, and command of No 4 Bomber Group in the first two years of the war, he had matured into a shrewd tactician. Tall, deep-chested, with huge capable hands and a genial air of relaxed self-assurance, he inspired confidence. His absurdly paradoxical nickname "Mary" was a corruption of "Maori", by which he had originally been known in the R.F.C.

Eighteen hundred years before, Marcus Aurelius had commented, "As soon as anything hath appeared and is passed away, another succeeds; and that also will presently pass out of sight". So it has been with Collishaw. The name most readily associated with Desert Air Force and its dazzling successes is not his, but Coningham's; and, after that, Broadhurst's. He is in honourable company: the first Commander-in-Chief of the Royal Flying Corps and true progenitor of the Royal Air Force was Lieutenant-General Sir David Henderson, not Trenchard, to whom the distinction is habitually attributed.

Like his predecessor, Coningham was a practitioner of the closest possible air/land co-operation. He had arrived opportunely to take advantage of the new Air Support Control organization, and his first act was to move Air H.Q. Western Desert Air Force once more to stand beside Army H.Q. at Ma'aten Bagush. His first innovation was to institute aircrew messes for all fighter squadrons. Experienced sergeant pilots often led formations in which officers followed them. Irrespective of rank, apart from the C.O., pilots were commonly on first name terms without any deterioration in respect or discipline. It was fair and logical that they should all share the same off-duty amenities, which would make the team spirit even stronger. It was not a universally applicable system. On bomber squadrons, if navigators and air gunners were included, sheer numbers would make it unworkable.

Attention now was focused mainly on Operation Crusader, the first great attack under the command of Auchinleck and Tedder, which was being planned. Churchill urged haste, but Auchinleck proved adamant that he would not make a move until his force was strong enough and prepared enough to ensure a sane prospect of success. Nor would Tedder lend himself to any impetuous commitment. This was a time for readjustment and reinforcement, which made the British Prime Minister barking furious. Air Ministry calculated that although the enemy had a total of 1,190 aircraft in the Mediterranean area, only 128 German and 237 Italian would be serviceable and available for the early phase of an offensive in Cyrenaica. The very precision of this, with its suggestion that spies on the enemy airfields were able to send an exact count, put its credibility in doubt and made it ludicrous. Why not round figures, 130 and 240, which were realistically as close as Intelligence could be? Tedder more sensibly suggested 650 enemy aircraft and 500 Allied. Churchill and Portal, misreading this to mean that the enemy would have air superiority, were incensed. Tedder had implied nothing of the kind. He had conceded only numerical superiority and knew that each of his aeroplanes was worth two of the Italians', even if the Germans had to be reckoned one-to-one.

Anyone whom Churchill suspected of defiance, let alone mere contradiction, was venturing on to a quicksand that threatened to swallow him in an instant. Longmore had been gulped down: and − if a pun may be allowed about such a dangerous aberration and so serious a matter − one swallow does not, as the proverb says, make a summer. Churchill sent Air Marshal Sir Wilfred Freeman, Vice Chief of Air Staff, to Cairo to investigate, and a letter to Auchinleck saying that if he preferred Freeman to Tedder he could keep him as the new Air Commander. Immediate dismissal seemed to be the Prime Minister's panacea as much as any dictator's. Portal announced that he would resign if Tedder were ousted and signalled Freeman to ask whether he would accept the appointment if offered it. The reply was "Certainly not; repeat not" and that he would join Portal in resigning. "The role of Judas is one I cannot fill", which was honourable; and "Am convinced it would be a fatal mistake to change now", which was sapient. Tedder, anyway, revised his calculation of available own aircraft to 660 by denuding other parts of his Command. Most pertinently and with a pawky tilt at the Air Ministry's affectation of finicky exactitude, he gave the probable serviceability as 528 for the Allies and 385 for the Axis.

Untouched by the discord, misgivings and apostasy at the heights of political and military power, the squadrons never desisted from their harassment of the Luftwaffe and Regia Aeronautica. Nor did the Germans or Italians show any inclination to snatch a rest before the next big offensive. Much of WDAF's effort was devoted to protecting the convoys that bore supplies to Tobruk, while a great part of the Axis air forces' flying hours was spent on attacking them.

On 26 June an Australian, Pilot Officer Clive Caldwell, of 250 (Tomahawk) Squadron, who before long was to earn the nickname "Killer", got his first scalp when escorting Blenheims to Gazala: and Me109. Four days later he brought down two Ju87s and shared an Me110. Not the least remarkable fact about this fiery young man was that he had made his first solo flight after only 3½ hours' dual. On 21 August Marylands of 24 SAAF, Hurricanes of 1 SAAF and 229, and Tomahawks of 2 SAAF saw action in a series of engagements with Me109s and 110s. The day's losses were two Marylands, three Hurricanes, three Tomahawks and one Me110. 14 September was another exceptionally active day, on which two Tomahawks of 3 RAAF, two Hurricanes of 451 and three of 33, and a 24 SAAF Maryland were shot down. The enemy lost an Me109, a G50 and a Ju87 in combat. They were also deprived of eight Ju87s flown by Italians, which lost their way, ran out of fuel and fell into British hands.

The Italians were having a hard time wherever they showed themselves. But, stricken and hounded though they were, shifty Latin morality and extravagant distortion of unpalatable truth gave no indication of this in the combat reports that were the basis for great blasts of propaganda. On 3 September, second anniversary of Britain's declaration of war on Germany, eleven Tomahawks of 2 SAAF interrupted approximately twenty G50s that were strafing two of the Sidi Barrani landing grounds. During 25 minutes of dogfighting, the South Africans shot down five enemy machines and claimed one probable. Their only damage was, predictably, inflicted by British anti-aircraft gunners: one Tommy hit in the hydraulic system and another's tyre punctured. The baroque Italian version was, in contrast with actuality, as spurious as elevating the status of a squalid stand-up transaction in a backstreet doorway with a five-shilling tart to a glamorous five-guinea assignation in the boudoir of a high-class courtesan. "Lieutenant Colonel Bonzano, Officer Commanding No 20 Fighter *Gruppo*, has been awarded the Silver Medal for Valour. On 3 September he led a formation of twenty-seven of his fighters on an offensive sweep in the skies of Sidi Barrani. Trusting to their numerical superiority, some fifty Hurricanes and Tomahawks, which appeared on the scene, dived to the attack. The Italian pilots, with superb dash and skill, accepted battle and shot down thirteen Hurricanes and Tomahawks, while another five were seen to abandon the fight in search of a forced landing. From this engagement the vaunted prowess of Hurricanes and Tomahawks has emerged entirely discredited." The Italian archives admit only to the loss of three G50s, but allege the destruction of twelve unspecified aircraft and the "efficacious machine-gunning" of twelve Hurricanes on the ground at Sidi Barrani, as well as stupendous damage to eight buildings and some 300 assorted vehicles.

Encounters over the sea and on a less spectacular scale were no less fraught with unpleasant surprises. Flight Lieutenant Fred Harrison was a navigator/bomb aimer in 55 Squadron, whose Blenheims were operating from Fuka Main during the run-up to Crusader. "Sand, flies, kitehawks, four to a tent, a day temperature of 100 degrees and freezing at night," he remembers. On 24 October he took off in a Blenheim with Flying Officer Murison at the controls for a sea sweep south of Crete, to attack shipping in their allotted area. Any of the four 250lb bombs and eight 25-pounders remaining at the end of the trip were to be dropped on the Derna-Bomba road. "After being airborne for about an hour and a half we came upon a three-masted schooner sailing SSW under full sail. We decided to let this go and carry on the square search for bigger game. After another 45 minutes we spotted a large motor vessel on about the same course and decided to attack." The ship was some 11 miles away, so they quickly descended to sea level and headed for the attack. "When in position and about to drop the load, the ship opened up with more guns than enough. Bits and pieces flew off the aircraft and two cannon shells came through the front panel." Disconcerting for Harrison, whose bomb sight was in the nose. Worse: "One exploded in the main fuse box, so no bombs could be released." Worst: "The other exploded in the Verey cartridge rack." The cartridges ignited. Red, green and white flares hurtled and coruscated about "all over the place. The aircraft was filled with smoke and fire". The pilot pulled the stick back and scraped over the ship. The aerial strung between the fore and aft masts went with him, wrapped around the external bomb racks. "After ten minutes or so we had the fire out and then found that the air gunner (who was in a dorsal turret half way down the fuselage) had tried to bale out through the camera hatch. His chute had opened inside the aircraft: luckily, as we were still at sea level." If he had managed to escape from the Blenheim he would have hit the sea at a couple of hundred miles an hour before the parachute could unfold. They made for Sidi Barrani, where they landed with their full load. The crew heard later that the Navy had sunk the M.V., and the schooner was loaded to the gunwales with ammunition. If they had hit her, they and their aeroplane would have been blown to bits. In fact, she arrived unscathed at Derna.

The flyers were not the only ones who came under fire. Thousands of others of all ranks who were not paid to risk their lives, and could not have the satisfaction of shooting back at the enemy, were killed, wounded or felt the hot wind of near misses from bullets and bomb fragments. AC1 Lawrence Wheatley, an armourer in No 11 (Blenheim) Squadron, recalls a landing ground near Fuka where he watched "a solitary aircraft bombing the supply dump, and tracer from nose and tail hosing down on the unfortunates beneath". The Squadron moved on to another airstrip, south of the coast road between Ma'aten Bagush and Mersah Matruh, in preparation for Crusader. "One night I stayed late chatting over the evening meal and it was almost full dark as I set out for my tent. Over to my right, where the aircraft and landing area were, I suddenly perceived a shower of sparks in a semicircle, reminiscent of bonfire night", where a bomb had exploded. As a second firework display erupted, he heard the detonation from the first one and began to run for the slit trench outside his tent, 100 yards away. "Realizing the futility of this I flung myself flat, with my hands, grasping my metal plate, mug and irons, protecting my head. At the third explosion there was a loud ping and my plate was torn from my grasp to land on the desert several feet away. When quiet was restored I groped around and found my plate. It was gashed and deeply dented, right in the middle."

Far from the mechanical amenities of a permanent airfield, bombing-up a Blenheim with 250 lb bombs called for ingenuity and immense physical effort. The bomb doors were taken off, the four bombs were laid on the sand and the fitters guided the pilot to taxi over them. "Then a crew of three armourers would raise the crutches on the bomb carriers. One man at the nose and another at the tail would lift the bomb while the third knelt and got his back under it. He stood up and the man at the nose guided the lug into the hook on the carrier, the crutches were screwed down and the fusing hooks inserted into the fuse boxes. This procedure was repeated with the remaining three bombs. A good crew could bomb up a kite in seven to ten minutes. Immediately a Blenheim landed from a raid it was bombed up again, ready for the next one." On one occasion the four bombs had been stowed by the time the navigator, last of the air crew to emerge, had gathered his equipment, stretched and left the aeroplane. "The crew kidded him that he had had four hang-ups and brought his original load back! I once humped twelve bombs on to three aircraft. My back was sore for days."

12 A Bombay of 216 Squadron over the desert. (see pp. 40-41)

13 A Hudson of 459 Squadron, a variant of the Lockheed Super Electra airliner. (*R. Roberts*)

14 "The Beaufighter made a devastating entry". (p.72) (*R. Roberts*)

15 Maurice Smyth in the cockpit of a 73 Squadron Hurricane 11C. (p.95) (*M. Smyth*)

16 "The Western Desert's first dog show". (p.126) (*R. Roberts*)

17 A Baltimore of 454 RAAF Squadron. (see p.126) (*T. Davies*)

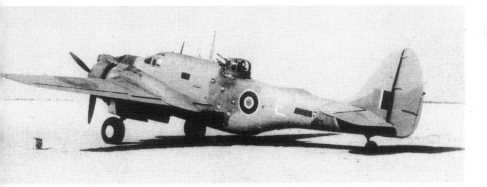

18 Kittyhawks of 112 Squadron lined up for take-off. (*V. Kaye*)

19 Ground gunner of 113 Squadron with twin Lewis guns. (see p.114) (*R. Cable*)

CHAPTER 5

The Second Major British Offensive – Operation Crusader

The primary aim of Crusader was to drive the enemy out of Cyrenaica. Success would bring four main benefits: 1. Removal of the threat from the west to Allied bases in Egypt. 2. Facilitation of the passage of shipping through the Mediterranean, by the capture of ports and air bases on the Libyan coast. 3. The relief of Tobruk. 4. The establishment of forward air bases.

Bestowal of the title Western Desert Air Force was the penultimate step towards conferment of the name by which the deeds performed by Collishaw's small 202 Group and its successors would go down in history, Desert Air Force. This was still eighteen months in the future, but another famous title had already been given to the greatly enlarged desert land force: Eighth Army. Its first commander, Lieutenant-General Sir Alan Cunningham, had led the defeat of the Italians in Somaliland and Eritrea. He wasn't about to last long, either.

D-Day for the big attack was 18 November. The air plan defined four phases, beginning on 14 October: 1. D minus 35 to D − 6, softening up; 2. D − 5 to D-Day, Army to concentrate and move forward; 3. D + 1 to D + 5, battle between opposing armoured forces and relief of Tobruk; 4. unpredetermined period, covering enemy's retreat.

On the eve of D-Day WDAF's Order of Battle comprised fourteen Hurricane and Tomahawk squadrons with 367 aircraft, of which 315 were serviceable; three Army co-operation squadrons, forty-six aircraft, forty-one serviceable, four Blenheim and three Maryland/Boston squadrons, 145 aircraft, 120 serviceable. In addition, ninety-nine Wellingtons of 205 Group (seventy-eight serviceable), could be put under AHQWDAF's operational control. Total 657, with 554 serviceable.

The Luftwaffe had ninety single-engine fighters (eighteen serviceable), fourteen twin-engine fighters (nine serviceable), forty-three bombers (nineteen serviceable), eighty dive bombers (sixty-six serviceable), reconnaissance seventeen (nine serviceable). Total 244, of which 121 serviceable.

The Regia Aeronautica's strength was 154 fighters, sixty bombers, fifteen dive bombers, sixty-seven reconnaissance. Total 296. No records exist of serviceability, but the estimate is 192.

For the beleaguered garrison in Tobruk, of whom about 100 were R.A.F. after all aircraft had left, optimism about relief was darkly qualified by resignation to daily bombardment. Getting there in the first place had been beset, for lorry drivers such as Joe Willis of No 6 Squadron, by the hazards peculiar to their job. He remembers arriving at the top of the Sollum Pass "and being told to engage first gear and stay in it. No wonder. When one looked down the side of the pass it was frightening and one held on to the steering wheel and brakes. Only one mistake, and goodbye. Another pass, Derna, was just as frightening and glad to see the end. Remember seeing Italian ships lying upside down in harbour. On along coast road to Sirte. We stayed there and loved it, in for a swim. Times changed very fast. We were on the retreat. Top of Derna Pass Germans bombed us. That was my first taste of bombs. Was not keen on them. Lucky no-one was hurt, a couple of lorries destroyed.

"Was in the siege of Tobruk. Very dangerous. Germans shelled us a good deal and their aircraft were over us nearly all day. We got rum rations and plenty of bully, etc, but only one pint of water a day. But I was healthy. Used to go for a swim, very tricky, German bombers often called at docks and other areas. One day I was only about 200 yards away when the Germans bombed HMS *Ladybird* 20 minutes after she arrived. What a sight to watch, gave you the creeps, within a few minutes ship was at bottom. All our mail etc was gone. Next day my friend and I were together when we saw a string of bombers one behind the other. Next minute they dived in turn straight down to where we were. I ran into a tunnel 10 feet away and was blown down by the blast. It was like a roller going over the top of me. Was unhurt. When I came out my friend was dead and burned black, and another man badly wounded.

"At night the place was lit up with bombs and gunfire and the noise was awful. Through it all we had our games of swimming and trying to keep out of danger. After about eight or ten weeks we were taken out by an Australian destroyer, HMAS *Vampire*, in the early hours of the morning."

His molestation by the enemy was not over yet. Anyone less stoical would have been deeply affronted by what happened soon after his return to the open desert. Couldn't Jerry leave him alone for a bit? "One evening I was walking along the edge of the landing ground when I saw what seemed like raindrops on the sand." The pockmarks were not being made by heavy rain. "It was an Me109 heading straight for me. He could not have seen me, for he stopped firing. He passed within 10 or 12 feet of me, turned his head and looked straight at me. He gave me a wave with his right hand. I hadn't seen him at first, as he was only about 50 feet high. Am sure he would have given me a different wave had he seen me earlier."

It wasn't only the Germans who might have driven a more timid character to paranoia. A few days later, "I was standing on the edge of the landing ground at Fuka when one of our squadron's Hurricanes landed and was taxiing fast when all of a sudden it turned right towards me. I got off-side as its nose dug into the ground and its tail went up in the air."

The pets that most squadrons acquired led a less than tranquil existence, too. "I drove some officers to watch a practice shoot at an old tank to test the 40mm cannon just fitted to our squadron's Hurricanes. One came in low and nearly demolished the tank. After a few moments out jumped a cat." He concluded, logically enough, that "It must have had a proper fright."

Attacks on enemy landing grounds were the preeminent component of the softening-up process. The method is described by one of the luckiest men ever to have served in the R.A.F., Air Chief Marshal Sir Kenneth "Bing" Cross, KBE, CBE, DSO, DFC, and R.A.F. rugger' "Blue". In 1940 he had commanded 46 (Hurricane) Squadron in the Norwegian campaign. The aircraft carrier *Glorious*, in which this squadron and No 223 (Gladiators) were returning to England, was sunk. Squadron Leader Cross and Flying Officer Jameson were the only pilots to survive. They and twenty-six others who were not drowned scrambled aboard a life raft. Five days later, when rescued, only nine men, including the pilots, were still alive. Within eighteen months Cross was Group Captain commanding 258 Wing in the desert. "It was fully realized," he wrote, "that the majority of enemy Landing Grounds (L.Gs) were protected by considerable and very efficient flak, and difficult to locate from low level. To overcome these difficulties a specialized form of aerodrome attack was developed. The forces taking part were one box of six or twelve Blenheims, one squadron of fighters for close support, one for top cover and one for aerodrome attack."

The Blenheims, with close and top escort, approached the target at 8,000-10,000 feet by the route likely to be least observed. The strafing squadron accompanied them slightly below and behind the bombers.

Twenty miles from the target the bomber leader signalled by rocking his wings, whereupon the strafing squadron did a 360-degree Rate Two turn while descending to ground level. This put it six to eight miles astern of the bombers. If the Blenheim leader sighted enemy aircraft on the landing ground, he bombed them. Locating the target by the bomb bursts, the strafing squadron attacked as the dust was clearing. If no enemy aircraft were seen, the bomber leader fired a red Verey light and swung away from the airstrip. Other targets for the Blenheims and Wellingtons were supply dumps, and shipping at sea and in harbour. The Bostons flew tactical reconnaissance.

For maximum mobility Coningham divided each squadron into three. One party, numbering about 150, would stay behind. Advance and rear parties, each of some eighty men able to service and maintain all the aircraft for seven days, would move forward and were allowed to take only one change of clothes. The squadrons were thus able to leapfrog across the desert from one landing ground to another that the advance parties had prepared for them. The rear parties then changed their rôle and moved beyond the new site to prepare the next.

On 17 November there were severe dust storms followed at night by thunderstorms and heavy rain. The airfields at Gazala and Gambut, where most of the enemy fighters were stationed, suddenly lay deep in mud. On the 18th the new push began, with an exhortatory signal sent by the Prime Minister at King George VI's command. "For the first time, British and Empire troops will meet the Germans with ample equipment in modern weapons of all kinds. The battle itself will affect the whole course of the war." Some hope. *Not* for the first time, a senior commander displayed an ineptitude that spoiled his initial advantage, invited calamity and brought him down swiftly. In this instance, it was the unfortunate Lieutenant-General Cunningham. He had no experience of handling tanks or operating against armour. It also transpired that he was unwell at the time.

Dust storms and rain were still alternating, but Coningham took advantage of the majority of Me109s' and 110s' and G50s' inability to take off, and sent his squadrons bombing and strafing all over the battle area and beyond.

The first Beaufighters in the desert, a flight of 272 Squadron, made a devastating entry. A two-seater and the most heavily armed fighter of the whole war, with its six machine guns, four 20mm cannon and, presently, eight 60lb rockets, the Beau was an aeroplane that exuded both aggression and the ability to absorb a tremendous amount of battering. A modification fitted by the squadron, a seventh machine gun, was soon added for the navigator. The Beau was the most versatile of aircraft. Equipped with radar, it was a wonderful night-fighter; carrying two 250lb bombs, it was a terrifying ground-attack weapon; with a torpedo slung under its belly, a formidable destroyer of ships. Here was an aeroplane with the visual menace of a fighting bull: the same humped shape for'ard, the massive strength coupled with deceptive speed and changes of direction. The pilot sat right in the bows, with a sturdy 1,670 h.p. engine and 12ft airscrew on either side, projecting beyond its blunt nose. Armed up and at the end of the runway with engines bellowing, it looked a downright bruiser with nothing but bloody violence in its character. A hefty rough handful, it demanded a lot from its pilot. A vicious swing to port on take-off or sudden stall on the landing approach had killed many a crew. Yet Beaufighters were often delivered from factories to R.A.F. stations in Britain by young women pilots of the Air Transport Auxiliary. As a flight mechanic muttered one day, seeing a pretty girl comb her hair, use her lipstick and powder her nose before emerging from the cockpit of a Beau she had just brought into an operational airfield: "Makes yer think, dunnit?" What was more, the airfield was closed on account of bad weather. And she had no navigator or navigation equipment, so had found her way with a map on her lap.

Ranging further than the Hurricanes, the Beaufighters brought perdition to airfields and transport columns before shifting their aim to the sky. Two Ju52s were the first to go down, under the guns of three of the Beaus. A couple of hours later six Beaus fell upon five more Ju52s and shot them all down before going on to bag an Hs126 and a Storch, then sending up in flames four SM79s on the ground.

On the 19th the weather cleared and the Allies maintained dominance in the air, although the enemy flew more sorties than on the previous two days as the sun dried his landing grounds. Coningham reported to Tedder: "Thirtieth Corps are very pleased with us, and so is the Army in general". On the 20th, 80 Squadron's new Hurricane fighter-bombers, each carrying two 250lb bombs, were turned loose for the first time while the pure fighter Hurricanes accounted for eight Ju87s and constantly broke up enemy formations that were trying to support Rommel's ground forces.

Amidst the powerful dramatic drive of air combat and bombing raids, infantry attacks, artillery bombardments and tank battles, and all the other violent operations of war in which men were engaged with about as much subtlety as sharks, a stealthy but no less dangerous enterprise which made an unobtrusive but equally valuable contribution to Crusader had been going forward. It had begun in the summer, following evidence that the Germans were installing radar near several crucial targets. A detachment of six Wellingtons from 109 Squadron, commanded by Flight Lieutenant C.O.V. "Scruffy" Willis, a New Zealander, was sent from England to work with 257 Wing and investigate the type of radar and its coverage. The Navy, which needed this information as much as the other Services, seconded a signals expert to fly with the detachment. He was Sub-Lieutenant P.T.W. "The Jeep" Baker, who had the salty habit of slinging a hammock in the Wellington, in which to rest on his way to and from the operational area. By the end of October he was convinced that the guns, and possibly the searchlights, at Benghazi and Derna were radar-controlled. The crews flew repeatedly across these and other ports so that Baker might judge the distance at which the aircraft could be detected by the accuracy of the anti-aircraft fire it drew. For Crusader the Army requested disruption of radio traffic between enemy tanks with airborne jamming equipment. This necessitated constant unescorted daylight patrols over the battle zone during which not a few Wellingtons were shot down by Me109s that homed on to their jammers. "A very thankless and hazardous task," Coningham called it.

On the 20th 272's Beaufighters again displayed their withering firepower when three of them shot down four Ju87s and a Storch, and five others wiped out a Me109 and fourteen Ju87s on the airfield at Tmimi.

Eighth Army was not expertly enough led to profit from the air superiority of Coningham's squadrons, flown by Britons, South Africans, Australians, New Zealanders, Poles and the Frenchmen of *Groupe Lorraine*. Although Cunningham went to battle with 710 tanks and 500 in reserve, against the Germans' 174 and Italians' 146, with none in reserve except a few under repair, Rommel out-manoeuvred him. What Rommel did have were new 50mm anti-tank guns, to replace two-thirds of the 37mm, which could penetrate any Allied armour. The Afrika Korps Commander's caustic retrospective comment cut to the heart of the matter: "What difference does it make if you have two tanks to my one, when you spread them out and let me smash them in detail? You presented me with three brigades in succession."

On the 21st Lieutenant-General C. W. M. Norrie, commanding 30th (Armoured) Corps, ordered his force to make for Tobruk and the garrison there to break out. Two German armoured columns intervened, two British tank brigades were diverted to meet them and the enemy's 50mm guns dealt with the third brigade. The next four days saw a succession of advances and withdrawals, of Allied errors and Rommel's brilliant opportunism in exploiting them, and of failure to achieve objectives. On the 24th a German tank column suddenly appeared in sight of 30th Corps' Advanced H.Q. on Gabr Saleh landing ground while

General Cunningham was there in conference with Norrie. No 108 Squadron's records note that the ground party "left hurriedly, and the Army Commander's Blenheim took off through a stampede of vehicles across the aerodrome". Wing Commander Gordon Finlayson, Senior Operations Officer at Air H.Q. Western Desert, describes the confusion as "a most interesting period, which as a study of panics, chaotics and gyrotics, is probably unsurpassed in military history".

The enemy column swept on to put the wind up the garrisons of the fighter air strips. According to 1 SAAF, "The news of the threatened German tank attack was received at L.G.123 and L.G.124 an hour before sunset. All aircraft were ordered to fly to L.G.128. Other squadrons received similar instructions, and the sky was packed with Hurricanes, Tomahawks and two or three 'Lizzies' all making for L.G.128. As most of the pilots did not know its whereabouts, the majority landed at L.G.122. So many aircraft were at this air strip that they were standing wingtip to wingtip. The pilots, because of the danger of parachute troops, were ordered to sleep under the wings of the aircraft." No. 112 Squadron diary reads: "We had 175 aircraft on the 'drome, and as the Hun column passed only 10 miles north of us, they missed a glorious opportunity of wrecking most of our fighters." No. 80 Squadron's account reveals the difficulty of identification in desert warfare. "Nearly all the columns in the so-called 'Matruh Stakes' were moving as fast as the ground and their horsepower allowed in an easterly direction, and it was singularly difficult for anyone either on the ground or in the air to pick out whether any particular cloud of dust was friend or foe."

Fred Pond was a ground gunner, and ground gunners were perhaps the most ill-rewarded and least praised members of the R.A.F's rank and file. To begin with, they were not tradesmen: their category was Aircrafthand, General Duties (ACH/GD). This, the lowest classification, was also common to embryo aircrew on enlistment. But if you had joined as a volunteer for pilot, observer or air gunner, you began your career with an added "P/U/T, O/U/T or AG/U/T" to indicate "pilot under training" etc., so your exit was guaranteed if you passed your course. For the rest, who were to pursue their lawful occasions in the Service entirely on the ground, life offered only a variety of odd jobs: scrubbing and polishing floors and windows, cleaning lavatories and drains, cookhouse chores, washing motor vehicles, guard on crashed aircraft to prevent looting, laying the flarepath, or as a "runner", sauntering about the camp bearing messages. Promotion was slow and your pay derisory. You might become a drill instructor and eventually wear two or three "tapes" on your arms, or rise to be Sanitary Corporal for the whole station. (As someone once said, fancy having to depend on your distinction for the fact that you know more about crap than anyone else on camp.)

You could also volunteer to be a ground gunner and thereby add sixpence to your daily three shillings (basic pay for an Aircraftman, Second Class or AC2). If you did, you were duly taught all about the Lewis and Vickers .303 machine guns, then took your place in the ground defence of the station. Manning, usually, a twin Lewis or single Vickers, perhaps a 40mm Bofors, you would spend your duty hours in one of the small sandbagged gun positions around the airfield perimeter or on top of various buildings. Under enemy air attack, your prospects of longevity were drastically curtailed. You were among the first objectives for enemy aircraft, whose pilots, if they were fighters, or air gunners if bombers, set about annihilating you in order to silence your guns. And all for three and six a day. Air gunners earned eight shillings and sixpence, but they, of course, defied the law of gravity as well as enemy shot and shell. (When the R.A.F. Regiment was formed on 12 February, 1942, all ground gunners became, as Fred Pond put it, "founder members".)

Pond was on 238 (Hurricane) Squadron, arrived in Egypt in July, 1941, and moved "up the blue" (out in the desert) two weeks later to Sidi Haneish. "Ground gunners lived in small groups dispersed with the kites. We were often called on to clear the landing area of stones to avoid propeller damage or re-establishing the landing strip after a sand/dust storm." When Crusader opened on 18 November, the Squadron's forward element "passed through a gap in the wired frontier fence and on to L.G.123." Caught up in the confusion and disarray of the 21st, he dismisses it prosaically now with "Twenty-fifth November found us retreating back through the 'wire' because of an armed enemy column getting too near us. Next day back to LG123". He goes on: "During Crusader, I, with 238, stayed in the 'Field', forward area. Tobruk, Gazala, Benghazi, Antelat." He says nothing of fending off strafing Me109s and dive bombers, the smoke and reek of cordite from his Lewis guns and enemy aircraft's cannon shells thudding into the sandbags of his gunpit, the flash and roar of bomb bursts, the shards of bomb-casing whining inches overhead. All this he summarizes as "We had our little fights and claims". At Tobruk: "Jerry was over. The guns were like a firework display. Trying to get all my body under the rim of a tin hat because of the falling shrapnel from gun shells when on guard duty."

But nobody, in the air or on the ground, was in action every day. The greatest hardship was not the sudden griping in the guts and the constriction of the throat as the dive bombers came screaming down or the strafing fighters roared overhead with flames stabbing at their gun ports. It was prosaic: "Life for an airman on a forward squadron or unit in the Western Desert Air Force was very hard, especially during the Crusader campaign. Sleeping in sandholes or a circle of rocks for protection. Existing on bully beef and hard tack biscuits, meat and veg. stew and tinned bacon eaten with a spoon (the heat melted it). No fresh food for weeks at a time, and of course no bread. We did, however, receive an issue of vitamin tablets. Water was tightly rationed, sometimes only a half mug of tea morning, same in the evening – that was it, none for washing etc. Often the water we did get was purified sea water with a strong salt taste, adulterated with petrol from being in transit in petrol drums. Also, when on the move in an open lorry, a mixture of dust and sweat heated by the sun formed on the face, which was painful to remove, especially without water.

"There was no off duty, we were on the whole time. No pubs or pictures, just the unit, the job and the bods. We made our own entertainment. One of our gunners was a very good violinist, so some of us found the money and a driver going back to the Delta for stores, who bought a violin. The desert was a healthy and clean place, very few flies, and most of the time no mosquitoes. The worst I suffered was sand sores and an occasional upset tummy, 'Gyppo Gut', in three years of continuous desert life." Flies abounded near the coast.

On 24 November, 1941, Auchinleck flew to the Front, found that Cunningham was on the point of retreating across the frontier and insisted that the advance must continue. Cunningham had lost confidence in his force's ability to go forward. The Commander-in-Chief had lost confidence in Cunningham and on the 26th appointed Lieutenant-General Neil Ritchie to command Eighth Army.

The following day saw an air battle of epic dimensions in comparison with what had gone before in this theatre. Twelve Tomahawks of 112 and seven from 3RAAF on a sweep over Sidi Rezegh first spotted a swarm of dots ahead at 15,000 feet, then, at 10,000 feet, another cluster. Those with the sharpest eyes could make out that the top cover consisted of Me109s and G50s, the layer below of Ju88s, CR42s and Me110s. Drawing closer and preparing to engage, they recognized, as the outlines became clearer, Stukas at 6,000 feet and, down at about 1,000 feet, more 110s. A couple of Fieseler Storch were also flitting about but were too small to discern until close to. Slicing into the beehive, which comprised some sixty aircraft, the Tommies were at once in a seething whirligig of climbing, diving, turning, aerobatting aeroplanes in a maelstrom of tracer bullets and cannon shells, reminiscent of scenes over the Thames Estuary fifteen months earlier. Down went a 110 trailing flames. Here a G50 was falling with smoke belching from it. There a Storch had disintegrated, and a crew was baling out of a Ju88. The enemy scattered, having lost nine of their number and probably three more, with eight damaged. Two Tomahawks went down: a success ratio even greater than in the Battle of Britain.

On the 30th the same two Tomahawk squadrons intercepted about fifty Me109s, G50s, Macchi 200s and Ju87s that were about to attack the New Zealand Division at Sidi Rezegh. The Ju87 was most vulnerable when it pulled out of its dive. This time they didn't even start diving. A sheet of flame, a cloud of smoke, a thunderclap and a violent buffet from the blast of air disturbed by an explosion warned the Stukas that one of their number had been blown to smithereens before it could shed its load. The Tomahawks' immediate "Tallyho!", the speed and fury of their attack and accuracy of their shooting frightened the rest of the Stuka pilots into jettisoning their bombs. The Italian fighter pilots were bewildered by the ferocity and agility of their attackers. The Germans in the 109s were blacking out and disoriented as they turned tightly to try to cut off the storming Tomahawks. The British and Australians destroyed a total mixed bag of fifteen and damaged fifteen more. It was a triumph of superb training and inter-squadron cohesion over two enemy air forces that were never in harmony in the air or on the ground, or had ever rehearsed a combined operation.

Tobruk still lay under siege but this was raised on 10 December. Success, to the relieving force, meant more than triumph. There was an Army bakery there. Fred Pond's diary entry for the 12th reads: "Had bread for the first time since leaving Sidi Haneish on 13th November".

Rommel had established a new line that ran south from Gazala with an open flank in the desert. The 13th Corps Commander signalled to the Commander of 7th Armoured Division: "The enemy is completely surrounded provided you block his retreat". But the intrepid and scorchingly successful 7th Armoured were hampered by soft sand that delayed its supply vehicles. Without petrol it was immobilized. Rommel escaped the trap. Coningham informed Tedder: "The Battle of Gazala has been a great disappointment, in that there was a promise of a complete encirclement and defeat of the enemy that has not been fulfilled. The operational aspect regarding bombing could not have been worse . . . the whole of the enemy land fighting force had been in a comparatively small area south-west of Gazala for nearly three days and had not one bomb dropped on them, although we had absolute superiority without any hostile interference in the air for two days. During that time squadrons of bombers have been 'at call' here, but always their operations have had to be called off because of the lack of identification and the close contact of the enemy forces with our own."

The battle wore on until 17 January, 1942, with Ritchie's capture of Bardia and Rommel's enforced retreat to Agedabia, where he stood firm and repulsed the Allies until he moved 75 miles south-west to Agheila on the coast. From there a broad belt of salt pans, sand dunes and innumerable small cliffs stretched southwards for 50 miles, its southern flank resting on the Great Sand Sea, a vast expanse of shifting sand. Apart from the main Benghazi-Tripoli road, only a few tracks crossed this inhospitable country, so that 35,000 enemy left out of the original 100,000 sufficed to hold it. Five hundred miles to the west of Rommel's line lay Tripoli. A thousand miles to the east of Ritchie's positions lay Cairo. The Allied air and land forces were at the extremity of a long supply line and short of fuel for aircraft and vehicles.

Crusader had not driven the enemy out of Cyrenaica. The Allies regarded this as only a brief setback in their drive across Libya. In the unlikely event that Auchinleck or Coningham was familiar with the Koran, he could have found consolation and hope in its 11th Sura: "And if we defer their chastisement to some definite time . . . will it not come upon them on a day when there shall be none to avert it from them? And that at which they scoffed shall enclose them on every side." Rommel had scoffed at Cunningham, but he would find nothing to scoff at in Montgomery's generalship when the time came.

A large part of the recently arrived land reinforcements were inexperienced as well as being led in accordance with antiquated principles of war, primarily that Staff College chestnut, fostered by infantry-minded commanders: "The destruction of the enemy's main armed forces on the battlefield is the prime objective". This was interpreted to mean: "Kill off the enemy's tanks, and then we can get on with the battle". So the order to Eighth Army was: "Your immediate objective is the destruction of the enemy's armoured forces". But, as Liddell Hart explained, "An armoured force is not in itself suited to be an immediate objective, for it is a fluid force, not easily fixed as infantry formations can be".

WDAF's air and ground crews had worked prodigiously and done all that the Army had asked of it. "Killer" Caldwell, now a flight lieutenant, shot down five Ju87s in one sortie on 5 December and by 20 December had a total of eighteen victories. A few days later he was awarded both the DFC and a bar to it. The following month he was promoted and posted to command 112 (Kittyhawk) Squadron.

Another 112 pilot, who had destroyed two Me109s before leaving England, and was destined to end the war with twenty-eight victories and go on to become a famous test pilot, scored his first individual success in the desert on 22 November by shooting down a Me109. This was Neville Duke, who wrote: "The pilot baled out and while he floated gently down . . . I circled round him and waved, a rather silly thing to do for I would have been easy meat for any of his friends. He waved back to me but once he touched the ground he bolted off for a bush and flung himself down flat. He was quite safe as far as I was concerned and he was later taken prisoner". Duke fought like a gentleman. In contrast, the previous day he had shared in sending down a CR42 with two other 112 pilots who proved to be as dirty fighters as the most shameful of the Nazis. The Italian landed and the aircraft somersaulted on to its back. "The pilot was out in a flash, bolting away from the Fiat like a scared rabbit. The two other Tomahawks began chasing him and shooting him up, but I had no stomach for this sort of thing and concentrated on setting fire to his machine." After Duke had hit the CR42 he turned and looked for the pilot. "He was dead, spreadeagled on the ground." This "rather shocked" him, because, as fighter pilots have been saying in every war since air fighting began in the First World War, although he knew that in a fight it was either his life or his opponent's, "it always seemed to me that I was fighting a machine and not another pilot". He might have felt differently had he fought in the Battle of Britain, for it was not machines that were automatically dropping bombs on civilians in London: men were operating the bomb-release.

He got a G50 on 30 November, a Macchi 200 and a Ju87 on 4 December, and was twice shot down near Tobruk. The second time, after he had taken out a CR42, three or four Me109Fs and some G50s set about him. After several exchanges of fire he turned for home "right down on the deck and flat out", knowing that the 109F was faster than his Tomahawk. Bullets smacked into the Tommy's wings and rear fuselage. "I heard the tremendous bang of an explosive shell." His aircraft turned upside down. He righted it and hit the ground, burning, bounced high and crashed down again. He got out and dragged the cockpit hood shut, hoping "the Jerry would think I was still in it, and not look for me behind a bush". He did run for a bush and heard the 109 open fire, but it was shooting at the crashed fighter. Then it departed, leaving Duke unharmed.

Radar had been of little help in Crusader. Attempts to use the two mobile units failed because of the rapidity of the advance and their short range of 15 to 20 miles. When the line was established, a more powerful type of equipment was set up 12 miles behind the Front, which normally detected enemy aircraft assembling at Martuba. This information was passed to 262 Wing at El Adem, which scrambled its readiness fighters. These headed for Gazala, where the Advanced Operations Room of 258 Wing took over their control.

Between 18 November, 1941, and 20 January, 1942, Coningham's fighter pilots destroyed 259 German and 204 Italian aircraft in the air and on the ground. The Allies lost approximately 300 in the same period.

On 7 December, 1941, the Japanese, with typical dishonesty and cunning, had bombed Pearl Harbor without having first declared war on the United States of America. After the event Japan announced its alliance with Germany and Italy, which presumably satisfied its Bushido code. America at the same time joined the Allies. British colonies and protectorates in Hong Kong, Malaya, Burma and India were now under threat. British and Commonwealth reinforcements were accordingly sent to the Far East. Some of these were air squadrons and Army formations serving in the Middle East, or on the way there and diverted. Auchinleck's and Tedder's forces in North Africa were thereby unexpectedly weakened.

In December and January two enemy convoys had slipped into Tripoli with men and supplies for Rommel, including 2,000 tons of aviation fuel. Characteristically, he decided to catch his opponents off balance and opened an attack on 21 January, 1942. Rainstorms on 19 and 20 January had flooded WDAF's forward landing grounds at Antelat, which hampered reconnaissance and occasioned half the fighter force to fall back on Msus. Throughout these two days Ju87s and Me109s, facing little opposition from Beaufighters, Hurricanes, Tomahawks or Kittyhawks, attacked Ritchie's forward troops. By 22 January the German column was fast advancing and the few Allied fighters still at Antelat quit in a hurry under shellfire. Twelve men had to push each aeroplane through the deep mire to the 500-yard-long, 30-foot-wide runway, a slow process. Many of the fighters that were flown off were technically unserviceable and some were dangerous to fly. Four Kittyhawks and two Hurricanes awaiting repair had to be burned because there were no pilots for them.

Rommel continued to send Eighth Army stumbling backwards and the wry jest about "the Matruh Stakes" turned into another, "the Sollum Derby". On 23 January 13 Corps' Commander prepared to retreat as far as Mechili and on 25th, by which time 3RAAF, 112, 229, 250 and 274 Squadrons were operating from there, Auchinleck and Tedder flew to the Front. Tedder signalled to Portal: "I hope some offensive action on land may now be taken. Only way of stopping this nonsense is to hit back. Our fighters under Cross are in angry mood. They appear to be at present the vital stabilizing force. Coningham's team working well, angry but keeping their heads." The R.A.F., versatile and multi-talented as always, did more than provide air support. Two of its own armoured car companies – soon to be incorporated in the R.A.F. Regiment – covered the withdrawal from Msus landing ground, fought off attacks by German armour and rescued several British tanks that had been abandoned because driverless.

Violent sandstorms were blowing. On 26 January 30 Squadron recorded: "The rising wind soon developed into gale force". It blew tents down and files from the Orderly Room tent were scattered over hundreds of square yards. Under cover of this Rommel thrust on. Two days later Tedder was complaining to Auchinleck: "Very concerned to hear 13 Corps have ordered Fighter Wing to withdraw from Mechili. Hope you fully appreciate how such a backward movement will hamstring our effort in the forward area." To which the Auk responded: "Infuriated to hear of this avoidable mistake. Blame rests entirely with 13 Corps Staff. Mary (Coningham) is getting them back to Mechili as quick as he can, but much valuable time has been lost." It is lamentable that a man of his consequence lacked the grammar to distinguish between "quick" and "quickly". No Frenchman, German or Italian of equivalent rank would have committed such a solecism.

On 29 January Rommel retook Benghazi and on 3 February entered Derna. On the 4th Eighth Army retreated behind the Gazala defences, where it made ready to stop Rommel at a line running south from there to Bir Hakim, protected extensively by minefields. Rommel had pressed on at such a pace that he had to leave his aircraft and most of his tanks behind. Again short of supplies, he allotted most of his petrol to the lorries that carried his troops and their fighting equipment. The only support available to him was from long-range bombers operating from Greece and the rear airfields in Libya. For five days no Ju87s or Me109s were seen in the battle area, and WDAF played merry hell with the enemy's transport. On 5 February WDAF's fighters, flying out of Gambut and El Adem, destroyed more than 100 Axis vehicles.

On 14 February Coningham's fighter pilots delivered a distinctly unloving Valentine's Day greeting to the Luftwaffe and Regia Aeronautica. At 1145 ten Kittyhawks from 112 with eight from 3RAAF were airborne from El Adem and presently saw twelve Macchi 200s below, which at once began climbing for cloud cover. Then a formation of Ju87s and Me109s hove in sight. Six high-cover 109s pounced on 3RAAF, but immediately lost four of their number under the guns of Sergeant Mailey, who took two out and Sergeant White and Flying Officer Spence, who each bagged one. Both Kitty squadrons then turned their attention to the Stukas and Macchis, with the result that between them they shot down another sixteen. This day also saw the return to the desert of Imshi Mason, now commanding 94 Squadron, equipped with new Kittyhawks, at Gambut.

Next day he was leading a flight of five aircraft when *Oberfeldwebel* (equivalent to flight sergeant) Schultz of IIJG27 shot him down and, within a few minutes, three others of his section. The death of such an accomplished pilot and respected leader was specially poignant at this juncture, when WDAF's strength had been depleted and the Luftwaffe's was increasing. But, just as the Welsh produce a seemingly endless succession of scintillating rugger half-backs, so the Royal Air Force has always bred a continuity of inspiring squadron commanders to replace those who have gone. This was particularly true in wartime of day fighter squadrons, when every leader, whether of a pair, a section of three or a flight, had to lead his wing men unwaveringly into the cannon's mouth and everyone was constantly under the plain scrutiny of his comrades. Dud ones were rare. I. N. McDougall was Mason's worthy successor.

The situation had become static. Both sides were wearied by the intensity and pace of the past twelve weeks' fighting and changes of ground. Casualties among fighter pilots had been severe. The majority of those who had survived were tired, in the corrosive mentally and physically debilitating way that is peculiar to battle fatigue. The mind becomes clouded, the limbs heavy, the will refuses to acknowledge exhaustion. Pride drives the wilting body on. The soggy brain makes errors of judgment in flying, shooting and decision. The bomber crews were no less weary. The aircraft, both fighters and bombers, were also showing every symptom of wear and tear.

Continued rain and dust storms throughout February restricted air activity. Western Desert Air Force underwent some reorganization. From 1 March No. 258 Wing was renumbered 243, comprising 112, 250, 450 and 3RAAF Squadrons. No. 262 Wing became No. 239, consisting of 33, 73, 80 and 274 Squadrons. No. 233 Wing was being formed, with 94, 260, 2SAAF and 4SAAF

This was an opportune time at which to join in the desert war and it is where a wireless operator-air gunner on 223 (Blenheim) Squadron, Sergeant (later Warrant Officer) Eric Moss enters the scene. He had volunteered on the outbreak of war, but his training, illness and bad weather had delayed his departure from England. A bout of jaundice separated him from his original crew. His new pilot was "a tall young wing commander looking for a WOP/AG. Wing Commander Johnny Monroe had seen some action and had been wounded. He had also been in plenty of trouble of the boozy punch-up type and never seemed to hold any rank for long. His overcoat said wing commander, his tunic sleeve said squadron leader, and so it was to be for the rest of his days. He looked me over and asked me some questions with a stutter. Then said 'You'll do. Go to the mess and find Flight Sergeant Harbord; he's my observer'."

After several nine-hour training sorties they left from Portreath for Gibraltar. Over the Bay of Biscay they had to return: "Oil was streaming across the windscreen and with the reduction in power we lost so much height that the pilot ordered me to send an SOS, thinking he was going to ditch." They managed to scrape over the Cornish cliffs and put down on the airfield. A few days later they took off again. Moss swung his turret constantly from side to side, looking for the heavily-armed long-range Focke Wulf Condors that preyed on the air traffic around the British Isles and out in the Atlantic. They were cruising at 12,000 feet when the Blenheim's nose suddenly dropped almost vertically. "I flailed about trying to get out of the turret. How many seconds was it going to take before we hit the sea? I couldn't get my intercom jack out of its socket, so I took off my helmet. Then I heard a bellow from the observer: 'Skipper, wake up! Wake up!' "

Slowly the aircraft levelled out. The Wing Commander's voice spluttered in Moss's earphones: "S-s-sorry, Mossy, I m-m-must have dropped off." A reasonable supposition. "He weighed fourteen stone. Drink never touched his lips — it went straight down, pints of it. He had become sleepy and fallen forward, pushing the control column. Jack, the observer, had kicked his ankle and it woke him. That ankle had been shattered by shrapnel and was tender. Even so, he deserved that kick. Bloody officers!"

A few days later they set off for Malta in company with five other Blenheims, but had to turn back alone with overheating engines. That evening "Our pilot, as befits a gentleman, was getting tanked up in the Hotel Britannia and making disparaging remarks about the black-clothed middle-aged women sitting there minding their own business. Unfortunately for him and us, one of them was the wife of the Spanish Ambassador and understood English. The next morning the balloon went up. We all got a dressing-down and were confined to our side of the Rock. This day was spent by all ranks, including the Wing Commander, in cleaning up the airfield and its environs of all paper, orange peel and the like." The notion that Spain posted an ambassador to Gibraltar is a figment, but presumably the official in question was a Spaniard of some prominence.

The next morning they were off again. Radio silence was imposed

10 Left: A tall crew: *rear left:* Ernest Coughlin (RCAF); *right:* Charles Hutchin (RAF); *squatting:* Jimmy Cline (RCAF). (p.111) (*C. Hutchin*)

11 Right: Desert Air Force Christmas Card (*F. Harrison*)

12 Marshal of The Royal Air Force Viscount Trenchard greeting Wing-Commander Howsen, CO of 459 Squadron (*R. Roberts*)

23 112 Squadron
ground crew
repairing an
Italian S.M. 81 at
Castel Benito
(*V. Kaye*).

24 145 Squadron pilots with Savoia, the Squadron mascot. *left to right:* G.
Milborrow, J.S. Ekbery, Neville Duke, J.G.M. Anderson, F/L Wooller, Colin
Sterling, (pp.112-113) (*J.S. Ekbery*)

until a given map reference was reached, when Moss sent a brief signal. They were within enemy range. On Malta's acknowledgement, the pilot descended to sea level, their propeller wash ruffling twin furrows on the water. Had they stayed at height, German radar on the North African coast would have seen them and fighters would have scrambled from Pantelleria to shoot them down. "My eyes had to be everywhere without moving the turret unnecessarily, as this could unbalance the aeroplane and tip us into the sea." Predictably, Malta was under air attack when they arrived at Halfar and they had to nip in between the falling bombs, the anti-aircraft barrage and the bomb bursts. In the Operations Room the Intelligence Officer looked at the sack Moss was carrying. "What have you got there, Sergeant?" " 'Mail, Sir.' I was immediately bowled over by the mob clawing for that precious sack."

"There was no food that first day. The breakfast we had had at Gibraltar had to last us 24 hours, as the island was on one-third rations. We had tea in the flasks we had filled at Gib. This, and the knowledge that we were better off than the long-term defenders of the island, forbade any request on our part for any form of meal. Next day, after spending the night on the floor of a ruined house, we were given one-third of a slice of toast and a cup of tea with powdered milk. As a rickety old bus was taking us out to our aircraft it suddenly stopped and the driver dived underneath. We followed as the bombs rained down, grit and dust blowing all over us. With bombs falling, we hurried to our aircraft. If we did not get away soon it was likely we never would, for the bombs would get it sooner or later. As we rolled along the runway bombs were bursting in front and behind." And so they landed in Egypt "in sight of the pyramids".

Theirs was one of several Blenheims destined for Burma. But as the crew prepared for an air test, Eric Moss collapsed, was carried out of the aeroplane and rushed to hospital. His pilot and observer went to the Far East with another WOP/AG. After twelve days he was told that the hospital was being cleared for battlefield casualties. "I was dumped on the side of the one and only road and told to make my own way to RAF HQ in Cairo." After a couple of weeks in Almaza transit camp he was sent to an operational training unit in a dry salt lake, El Ballah, and crewed up again for conversion to Baltimores: "An aircraft I had never heard of, and I doubt if anyone in England had either. My new pilot was Brian 'Jumbo' Ekbery, an easy-going, amiable sort of mutt, Civil Service trained, and of course Tory in attitudes and politics. Sergeant Roger Bates was the observer, a sincere, intense workaholic, probably a Liberal, always taking Ekbery to task. The fourth member to join us was 'Jock' Johnson, a 19-year-old Scots lad."

From there the crew was posted to 223 Squadron at a desert landing ground.

They were bombed occasionally by sneak raiders who left anti-personnel butterfly bombs, which had to be exploded by rifle fire. Another German pleasantry familiar on all L.Gs was a pyramid-shaped object about two inches from base to apex, with sharp corners. Whichever way it landed, a point was uppermost. These punctured the tyres of aircraft and motor vehicles, and hours were spent scouring the landing area for them after every air raid.

"When O.Rs were killed they were sewn into a blanket and buried in shallow graves alongside that solitary coastal road for reburial at a later date. It was said that the Wogs — wily oriental gentlemen — used to dig them up for their boots. Officers, of course, were taken into town and buried with ceremony in a churchyard of their denomination."

He took a dim view of the food. "Butter or marge was served as an oil in a saucer which was covered with flies. Corned beef was poured from its tins in a soup due to the heat, and bread was often substituted by hard tack biscuits. Most foods were tinned or dehydrated." He reserved his most virulent vituperation for his pilot, all officers and anyone whom he suspected of being politically Conservative. When he, the observer and the other air gunner dug a trench as an air-raid shelter, their pilot "flatly refused to help, as manual work was beneath his Tory dignity". A series of vicissitudes, including a heavy landing that was followed by a period of dual practice for the pilot, further delayed Moss in getting to grips with the enemy.

During the lull that began when the Allies dug in on the Gazala Line, both sides concentrated on preparing for the next round of the contest. A new R.A.F. group, No. 211, was formed to take on operational control of all offensive fighter wings in the desert. There were two Operations Rooms, a rear one underground and a mobile one in the forward area. Radar was provided at Tobruk, Gambut and Gazala and supplemented by wireless observer posts in the El Adem area. Henceforth, the Group Operations Room could order wings to scramble aircraft, to intercept raids under the direction of a forward Operations Controller. For close support work, particularly by fighter bombers, landmarks for the aircraft's use were devised. By day the ground troops would lay white strips of cloth to form letters 20 yards long. By night, they would arrange lighted petrol tins 25 yards apart in the shape of a V whose arms were 100 yards long. This was no innovation. The French had introduced cloth markers for the same purpose in 1915 and the British adopted it on the Somme in 1916.

In preparation for the coming battle the Royal Engineers provided nine landing grounds with perimeter tracks and dispersal lanes. The scale of the task was impressive and typified by Gambut satellite No. 1, which had 12 miles of perimeter track and 50 miles of dispersal lanes. Temporary blast pens for aircraft were built with 50-gallon drums filled with earth and arranged two-high in horseshoes. Similar protection was given to pilots' rest tents and operations lorries and trailers. In addition to the three landing grounds at Gambut, a decoy was laid out, with unserviceable aircraft and dummy tents and guns.

The Germans, having lost Gazala, were using Martuba, where they had built an underground Operations Room as the centre of their control and reporting system. In detail, their method was teutonically ponderous, in contrast with the flexibility of the Allies, and entailed keeping an entire *Gruppe* of JG27 at stand-by all day, with the pilots in their cockpits and ready to take off within 30 seconds.

The Air Ministry had sent the world-famous, and epicene, photographer, Cecil Beaton, to the Middle East for three months "to collect material for certain reports and to take photographs". Beaton was manifestly thrilled by the assignment, not least, one supposes, by the prospect of some rugged sunbronzed company. Certainly the change from civilian clothes into those of a war correspondent held a special appeal: "As I looked in the glass, trying on a cap and jacket (no apparel is more becoming than uniform) I felt it was a pity I was not fifteen years younger." Tedder invited him to breakfast and led him to table with a whimsical − and, one hopes, unambiguous − turn of phrase, "Shall we nibble?" Beaton described him with an artist's talent for sketching salient features: "Thick hair, twinkling eyes, bat's ears, and wiry body, with legs that stretch back at the calf like a bow." And, wittily: "He looks like a bilious schoolboy." And shrewdly: "He does not wish to impress − rather to put everyone at ease, so that they will talk most naturally and be their most interesting. He is, you feel, storing up impressions all day long, and the opinions of anyone with whom he comes in contact are grist to his mill." Tedder showed him his crayon sketches in the small notebook he always carried in his pocket and Beaton was enchanted when he learned of the AOC-in-C's enthusiasm for drawing wild flowers. Doubtless it was the pansy in the photographer that responded.

"The poverty of the desert has its paradoxes," Beaton noted. "Whisky is perhaps less rare than ginger beer or soda water: petrol is less scarce than water. Our soldiers have surprised German prisoners by the extravagance of washing out their shirts in petrol. Here, men who have given up their worldly possessions live with little more than a razor, sleeping bag, roll of lavatory paper and a packet of cigarettes.

It is reassuring to learn that it is possible, when life has been reduced to its essentials, to find that there is, after all, more in it." There were precious few sleeping bags. Neither the Air Force nor the Army was issued with them, only with blankets.

He took a shine to Coningham, rhapsodized about his gigantic physique – "Huge, good-looking, strong, sun-burnt like a peach in perfection" – and found him "delightful; no one is better at putting you at your ease". If the intensely masculine New Zealander read Beaton's book on his Middle East journey, one wonders what he thought about being likened to a fruit that is more usually a simile for a pretty girl.

Beaton's visit was timely and his genius created a subtle pictorial record of facets of the campaign untouched by press photographers. He was still there when the next big attack rent asunder the comparative calm that had endured for more than three months.

CHAPTER 6

"To the man who knows it, the desert is a fortress. To him that does not, it is a grave."

Arab Saying.

Rommel it was who again beat his adversary to the punch. Although better equipped than ever before, thanks to the convoys that had been able to reach Tripoli while the Luftwaffe relentlessly hammered Malta, he was able to put only 280 gun-armed German tanks into the field, fifty light tanks and 230 obsolete Italian tanks. Ritchie could call on 850 tanks, with 420 more in reserve. Of the total, 400 were American Grants, whose 75mm guns were more effective than the 50mm guns of the best German tanks, of which there were only nineteen anyway. Additionally, the British 57mm anti-tank guns were 30 per cent superior to the latter.

In the air, WDAF put up a mere 290 serviceable aeroplanes out of 320, while the enemy mustered 497 out of 704. Elsewhere in the Middle East, Tedder had 739 aircraft serviceable. The Germans had 215 in Greece, Crete and Sicily, and the Italians a further 775 in Italy, Sicily, Pantelleria and other places. Not only did the Axis air strength outnumber the Allied, but also the Me109F out-performed every other fighter in the desert, and there were 120 of them. It is quality rather than quantity that is generally decisive.

By moonlight on the night of 26 May the Afrika Korps, intending to attack Gazala from the rear, advanced to the south of Bir Hakim, which was held by General Koenig's 1st Free French Brigade. More than 10,000 lorries carried the mechanized infantry and supplies. When daylight came, the Italians launched a frontal attack on this fortress. Rommel had reckoned on annihilating the whole British force in two days and capturing Tobruk within a further two. Although his initiative had anticipated the intended Allied offensive, it did not take the defenders by surprise. Reconnaissance had reported Stukas and fighters arriving from Sicily and Italian units moving forward.

By nightfall on the 27th the Eighth Army had stopped the enemy's infantry at El Adem and his armour at Knightsbridge (a name given by the British Army), where two desert tracks crossed: one from Acroma to Bir Hakim, the other the Trigh Capuzzo that ran from east to west across most of Egypt and Cyrenaica. The Italians had made no significant progress through the minefields guarding Bir Hakim. Rommel wrote in his diary: "The advent of the new American tank had torn great holes in our ranks . . . far more than a third of the German tanks had been lost in this one day."

WDAF's fighters began the day with a dawn scramble by twelve Kittyhawks of 2 SAAF to intercept Macchi 202s and Me109s. The rest of the day was spent on the familiar gallimaufry of activities, with great effect. Six of the enemy were shot down − Me109s, Ju87s, a Me110 − but the greatest emphasis was on fighter-bomber operations and bombing by Baltimores and Wellingtons.

On the 28th Rommel's striking force took up a precarious defensive position east of the Gazala Line, cut off from the rest of his force. This became the target for a steady rain of bombs, repeated attacks by the Guards Brigade and other formations of Eighth Army, and passionate defence by the Germans. It was soon known as the Cauldron and the battle here seethed for two weeks. It was a tumult of confusion and satanic strife, stinking of high explosive, of charred and putrefying corpses, amid the burned-out remains of motor vehicles, to the din of shelling, bombing, exploding mines, and aerial machine-gun and cannon fire. The ferocity of the fighting grew day by day. On the 30th six 250 Squadron Kittyhawks and four of 3 RAAF dived from 6,000 feet to 1,000 feet to drop their bombs and made blazing wreckage of some fifty German lorries, staff cars and the jeep-like *Kubelwagen*. Above and around this carnage, thirteen Hurricanes, Tomahawks and Kittyhawks were shot down for two Me109s and one Macchi 202, plus several enemy fighters damaged or probably destroyed. On 31 May violent sandstorms struck the battlefield. They persisted through 1 June, but the sorties by Coningham's aircraft did not noticeably diminish and sixteen fighters were lost. Four Me109s, a Me110 and a Ju87 fell to the Allied fighters and two Me110s to the ack-ack gunners. The Me109 had been used as a fighter-bomber in the closing stage of the Battle of Britain, and some were now introduced in this role at the Cauldron. Luftwaffe bombers based on Crete kept raiding Gambut and forward airfields. Throughout, the Regia Aeronautica had barely figured. Its daily sorties dwindled from forty to eight, from lack of serviceability.

Through the real darkness of this day, created by wind-driven sand mingling with the smoke of battle, gleamed a metaphorical ray of light. One flight of 145 Squadron had been equipped with Spitfires and appeared on desert operations for the first time, as top cover for fighter-bombers.

The Ju87s had been plastering Bir Hakim, which, because it was isolated, could not be supported by Eighth Army either with direct action or supplies. The Italian Army was making a massive assault on it. On 3 June Coningham committed a large part of his effort to protecting it. He also sent it supplies, as Stephen Hall, the young armourer/air gunner in 216 Squadron recalls: "At Bagush, our skipper, a Captain Bolt, SAAF, called the crew together and told us of a possible supply drop, but we had to convince some Army types that we could do it. We got the job. This was to be a night drop, the place where we were to make it marked by a double X. Loaded and ready to take off, Capt Bolt promised me a bottle of whisky if we got through and delivered the goods. Everything went according to plan and true to his word he presented me with the whisky, which was greatly appreciated and enjoyed."

If Hall had been promoted to sergeant, the rank to which he was entitled, he would have been able to enjoy a glass of whisky in the Sergeants' Mess. That he wasn't was an injustice typical of the Treasury, which resorts to any shabby trick to deprive serving officers and men of whatever few pence it can. On 12 December, 1939, an Air Ministry Order laid down that all air gunners were to be at least of sergeant's rank. This was not strictly observed in all Commands. The compromise was grotesque: wireless operator/AGs were promoted, but those in a different basic trade were issued with sergeant's tapes, affixed with an elastic band, to wear in the air. Thus they would, in theory, be better treated if taken prisoner of war than as mere LACs.

It was not only for operational sorties that aircrew deserved to be paid as much as could be screwed out of a miserly Government department, for many died in accidents. One-third of air gunners were commissioned. Hall tells us, "Twenty-two pilot officer air gunners joined us. On their first air-to-ground firing practice, twenty crashed and were killed."

The battle for Bir Hakim had a special significance: this was the first time the French had fought the Germans since the Blitzkrieg on their own soil had shattered their armies. The national honour was at stake and they displayed exemplary gallantry. Towards the end General Koenig signalled Coningham: *"Bravo! Merci pour la RAF"*, and received the reply: *"Bravo à vous! Merci pour le sport"*. On the night of 10 June, what was left of the garrison retired. Its nine-day defence had upset Rommel's timetable and cost him dearly in men, tanks, wheeled vehicles and fuel. But it had not averted, merely delayed, the consequence of inept British generalship in the field.

Meanwhile Coningham unleashed another fresh threat to the enemy. No. 6 Squadron had received tank-busting Hurricane 110s with two 40mm cannon, which went into action on 6 June. Nothing that the air force could do, however, could compensate for Ritchie's ill-conceived tactics. Rommel noted at the time that he looked forward with hope to what the battle might bring, because "Ritchie had thrown his armour into the battle piecemeal and had thus given us the chance of engaging them on each separate occasion with just enough of our own tanks". Squandering his tanks in this way, Ritchie was forced to start retreating. Pell-mell, the Allied forces shambled eastwards. Vehicles blocked the coast road and desert tracks, easy targets for air attacks. But luckily these never materialized.

On the 18th Ritchie told Coningham that no security of forward airfields could be guaranteed. Coningham therefore sent his fighter wings back to landing grounds awaiting them beyond the Egyptian frontier. On the 21st Rommel took Tobruk, with 30,000 prisoners, three million packs of rations, 500,000 gallons of petrol and a mountain of other stores. On 25 June Auchinleck relieved Ritchie of his command and took over Eighth Army himself. On the 27th Coningham shifted Advanced HQ WDAF from the site it had shared with HQ Eighth Army to one in the vicinity of his fighters, and Eighth Army abandoned Mersa Matruh. The Afrika Korps entered it next day. Auchinleck set his new defence line between El Alamein, on the coast, and the northern edge of the impassable 7,000 square-mile, 400ft-deep, Qattara Depression, 38 miles to the south.

Although the Eighth Army had retreated 400 miles in two weeks, it had remained a cohesive entity and its losses, though heavy enough, were not as grave as they might have been. It had not been bombed and strafed into disintegration for two reasons: constant protection by WDAF, and the Luftwaffe's inability to keep up with the speed of the Afrika Korp's advance. The only apparent weakness in Rommel's mastery of tactics was a failure to grasp that if his air force were to give his troops the cover he expected, it must have enough transport to move servicing facilities and petrol forward in pace with his progress on the ground. It was not until 26 June, when his armour had entered Egypt, that he thought of this, and robbed the Italian infantry — who had to footslog — of their lorries for the Luftwaffe. Nor did General Hoffman von Waldau, *Fliegeführer* Afrika, share Coningham's imaginative organizing skill. WDAF was lean, flexible, highly mobile, a rapier force, The finely tuned mechanism in the New Zealander's dolichocephalic head turned fast and smoothly, improvising to meet every fresh situation. Waldau's command was, on the contrary, hidebound and plodding, a bludgeon. In the German's square skull the wheels churned slowly through a sludge of conformity.

Out of the calamity of Eighth Army's defeat Western Desert Air Force emerged with credit and not the smallest stain on the competence of its leadership. It was ironical that the R.A.F. had beaten the Luftwaffe at its own game, that of tactical support for the Army, the purpose for which it had been begotten and nurtured.

On 29 June Mussolini, whose Army and Air Force from general to private had, with few exceptions, played a less than admirable part in beating back the Allies, arrived at Derna. With the ineffable insolence, falsity and bombast that marked all his actions, he intended to ride at the head of the victory parade through Cairo that he was confident Rommel would ensure.

Rommel waited for the footsore Italian 10th, 20th and 21st Corps to catch up with his three German divisions before making his bid, the First Battle of Alamein, on Wednesday, 1 July. The panic that ensued in Cairo provoked wholesale incineration of secret documents in the various Headquarters. Smoke and charred paper rose thickly above the housetops and people spoke tartly of Ash Wednesday. The defenders beat off the attacks of Stukas, tanks and infantry. Kittyhawks and Hurricanes escorted Bostons on bombing missions against landing grounds. Other Hurricanes and Beaufighters strafed. The Germans and Italians were learning to dread the Beaus as acutely as the Japanese were destined to in Burma and on the Pacific islands. "Whispering Death", the Japs called them. Their hefty engines roared like the Bull of Bashan on take-off, but settled to a throaty throb in the air, which gave short warning of their approach.

That night the Wellingtons kept up the bombing and a new method of target marking was introduced. Fleet Air Arm Albacores took off in time to be over the target area fifteen minutes before the bombers. Having found the targets, they dropped flares at the Wellingtons' estimated time of arrival. This was yet another instance of WDAF's ingenuity.

By the light of the flares the captain of a 37 Squadron Wellington, Pilot Officer S. J. Thorne, picked out eight hummocks of sand that looked like dunes. But the wind did not form dunes in such uniform shapes or spaced so militarily at exact intervals. His suspicion aroused, he bombed, and hit two of them. The ammunition stored beneath the sand exploded in billows of smoke that towered 5,000 feet high, and burned with a glow that cast a red haze for many square miles around. The blast distorted the "Wimpey's" fuselage, wings and tail unit, stripped the fabric, wrecked instruments and controls. The crew baled out. Thorne, helping his front gunner through the lower hatch, fell out. The Squadron diary records that his parachute "was found unopened on the ground, unattached to the body. The harness was also found near the body, broken".

The battle raged for four days: an affair of quick switches of thrust from one part of the defence line to another, sudden brisk confrontations between small groups of opposing armour, moonlit movements by the enemy that were seen and attacked by the Wellingtons, which operated throughout every night, and enterprising counterattacks that surprised the Germans and scared the Italians.

On 3 July 1 SAAF made hay with the Ju87s in spectacular fashion. It was shortly after 6.30 pm when, with twelve Hurricanes of 274 as top cover, they bore down on a big formation of the Stukas and their escort of seven Me109s. While the Hurricanes engaged the Messerschmitts, the Kittyhawks opened fire on the Stukas. Major Le Mesurier made the first kill when one of the dive bombers exploded. In quick succession other pilots sent down a total of twelve more and a Me109. This earned the C.O. a signal from Coningham: "Personal AOC to Major Le Mesurier. Magnificent. Congratulations to you, the squadron and the wing on the great Stuka party. Your success has greatly heartened the army. We are all delighted at your warrior squadron restarting so well."

Those ninety-six hours of hectic conflict under the broiling sun and through the shivering desert nights are summarized by Rommel in a letter on 4 July: "Things are, unfortunately, not going as we should like. The resistance is too great, and our strength is exhausted." On the same day an Italian officer wrote in his diary: "From five-o'clock (a.m.) there has been no action on either side, but we still stay underground so as not to be seen by the enemy air force. We come out of our holes at night to take the air."

Churchill sent a signal to Tedder: "Here at home we are all watching with enthusiasm the brilliant, supreme exertions of the Royal Air Force in the battle now proceeding in Egypt. From every quarter the reports come in of the effect of the vital part which your officers and men are playing in this Homeric struggle for the Nile Valley. The days of the Battle of Britain are being repeated far from home. We are sure you will be to our glorious Army the friend that endureth to the end."

Auchinleck reported to London: "Our only effective defence is our air striking force."

Although the fighting continued, Rommel had already lost the battle. He had intended to take Alexandria in order to supply his army for the final advance on Cairo. He had failed and there was to be no second attempt. Without Alexandria he would have to fetch supplies all the way from Tobruk. But the R.A.F. would soon bomb him out of there, so his supply port would recede to Derna. Bombing would make that untenable, and his supply line would be stretched as far as Benghazi; for Tedder now had two squadrons of Halifaxes, four-engined, with a range of 1,860 miles carrying a 5,800-lb bombload.

To join a squadron at a time of high activity and be pitched precipitately into the fighting is probably less nerve-racking than having to kill time until a chance comes to kill the enemy. When Squadron Leader Maurice Smyth, DFC, joined 73 Squadron (Hurricane IIC) on 7 July, 1942, as a young sergeant, he had already spent eight months on operations with another distinguished squadron, No 111 (Spitfire), in England, mostly doing sweeps over northern France. On his way to North Africa he caught malaria in Takoradi, was flown to Cairo and put into hospital. So, when he reported to 73 Squadron at LG89 − near the Alexandria-Cairo road − on 8 July he had not handled a fighter for three months. On that day he flew two practice sweeps, was then considered operational and did a sweep over the desert.

The other pilots were the usual heterogeneous wartime assemblage. John Selby, one of the flight commanders, "had something to do with the BBC. Monty Ellis, DFM, had run a taxicab business. Warrant Officer Plenderleith had flown in the Battle of France and been shot down and badly burnt. He couldn't close his eyes and to go into a tent at night and see this bloke with his white eyeballs staring up at you was enough to put you off booze for evermore. Sergeant Macpherson was a most unusual character, Plymouth Brethren, very religious, didn't smoke or drink. He destroyed an ammo train in Alamein railway station on his second operational trip. The Germans erected a plaque, in English, which read 'To the memory of a brave British pilot who against intense opposition destroyed an ammunition train and in so doing lost his life.' The grave was about two feet square, outlined in white stones. Sergeant Beard, a tubby little man, was reputed to be the best shot in the squadron. When we got to Tunis he was ordered to go out and shoot a bull by hitting it in the neck. Throwing a Hurricane against a bull seemed a bit unfair to me, but we got fresh meat for a few days when we really needed it." One flight commander was Flight Lieutenant Ambrose, "quiet and efficient, had fought in Norway. The other flight commander was Flight Lieutenant Pissy Thompson, who had an operational twitch."

Among the many squadron pets were "two dogs of note. One was called Rommel, the other was Willie. Rommel was the result of an illicit liaison between one of the airmen's alsatian bitch and a pai dog that drifted into camp one night and had his evil way with her. Rommel looked like an alsatian and had a beautiful creamy coat, but was a very sneaky animal: no harm in him, he used to lie in wait and when anyone passed, jump on his back and send him sprawling. This could be quite alarming at night. Willie, a dalmatian, belonged to 'Bert' Ambrose and was a drunk, very fond of his booze, his favourite being egg nog. When he got slightly sloshed his back legs went faster than his front ones and he used to go round in circles, which rather puzzled him. Willie also travelled by air. When we moved he was put in the panel under the tailplane of his owner's Hurricane, with a blanket."

The food was conspicuously better than when out in the blue, although: "The meat was poor quality, plenty of lamb, and supposedly beef, which everybody suspected was camel. Lots of tinned bully beef and tinned fruit." Cairo and Alexandria were both in easy reach. There were WRNS in Alex. One of the pilots was married to a Wren and his comrades used to join them and her friends for parties at the Cecil Hotel and meals in the numerous good restaurants. They made the most of being close to civilized amenities while they had the chance. The airstrip was being heavily raided every night and by day the odd Stuka or 109 would bomb or strafe. One night someone took a photograph and counted 120 flares overhead.

"The place was alive with scorpions, green ones and the prize ones were the big black ones. Syndicates of airmen had fighting scorpions that they used to pit against one another. Flying Officer Hall found a Shetta spider, about four inches long, which he fed on bully beef and put in combat with a scorpion. The spider demolished it and ate it. Eventually it demolished seven in one go. Unfortunately somebody trod on it."

One night there was an air raid on Alexandria and the other ranks' brothel was hit. An airman was killed. The story went that he was gallantly covering the lady of his choice with his body when the bomb fell. It was a matter for debate whether he had been killed in action or on active service.

"They were all very good pilots on 73 and we had a superb fighting formation. The whole squadron could turn as one aircraft". On 21 July fifteen Me109Gs intercepted them at 12,000 feet. "We had a lovely dogfight that went on for 20 minutes. I was rather over-confident. When I saw one of them curving in towards me and little smoke rings blowing out over his spinner as he fired at me, and saw the tracer come out, I calculated he'd miss, so I didn't tighten up my turn. He didn't miss, he hit me right through the tail plane and along the fuselage."

By this time the Squadron had had a lot of casualties and the aircraft were well worn. It moved to Ballah to train new pilots and prepare for its future role of night intruder.

By the end of July both sides had to pause and re-supply. Churchill arrived in Egypt on 4 August. Finding that Auchinleck would not budge from his decision to postpone renewing the offensive until September, whereas he wanted it resumed almost at once, Churchill, predictably, decided to bring in a new C-in-C, General Sir Harold Alexander, and a new Commander for the Eighth Army, Lieutenant-General "Strafer" Gott, who had commanded 13th Corps at Gazala. Churchill returned Auchinleck to India, where he later became C-in-C.

Mention of Gott again recalls Stephen Hall, who recounts: "Fate or a good Guardian Angel. I had a young aircrew training with me and we were due on a normal desert trip carrying a General Gott. This lad pestered me to allow him to do the trip on his own. The officer i/c granted his request, so off he went and a break for me. The aircraft was shot down with the loss of all on board. Witnesses said an aircraft with British markings shot the Bombay down and was then escorted away by two aircraft with German markings."

Gott had been on his way to take over his new command. Churchill sent for Lieutenant-General Sir Bernard Montgomery to replace him. Montgomery assumed command of Eighth Army on 13 August, 1942, and one of his first acts was to move his Headquarters back to where Coningham's was situated. The Advanced HQs of both RAF and Army were also together. Alexander succeeded to the C-in-C-ship two days later. The impatient Churchill was in for another disappointment. Montgomery was no more willing to commit his men to a major offensive than Auchinleck had been. He insisted on ensuring that all the training and preparations he considered necessary were completed. This gave Rommel, who was another character not noted for patience, time to make the first move once again. But, at the same time, as Liddell Hart put it, this also gave him enough rope to hang himself.

One aspect of air operations that is seldom given due credit is the part played by the squadrons that flew supplies to the fighting R.A.F. and Army units and incurred their own brand of danger in the process. When a transport Group, No 216, was established in 1942, it was given three squadrons: No 216, of which and its aged but still doughty Bombays, commanded by Wing Commander Rustom, much has already been said; 117 (Boston), under Wing Commander Yaxley; and Wing Commander Wynne-Eyton's No 267, also flying Bostons.

Stephen Hall tells about a minor but daring venture in which 216 Squadron played a risky part. The Fleet Air Arm wanted to bomb a certain convoy, but their aircraft lacked the range to do so from any of the Allied airfields. A stratagem was devised to take the enemy by surprise. This was "so cheeky it's hardly believable: a satellite air strip 250 miles inside enemy territory was to be used. Gambling that the main landing area was not being bombed there would be no need to use the satellite strip." Late one afternoon three Bombays took off with a squadron of Albacores. A squad of Highlanders travelled with Hall's crew. The other two Bombays carried petrol in four-gallon cans. As soon as they landed, the troops took up defensive positions. The refuelled Albacores went off to attack the convoy. At daylight all the aircraft departed for their home bases.

On 18 August, with 1300 flying hours in his logbook, Hall was posted home, but the hazards of war pursued him. On 12 September the troopship *Laconia*, in which he was travelling, was torpedoed. He spent five days in a lifeboat, intermittently attended by three U-boats and an Italian submarine. A Vichy French naval cruiser rescued him. After a short internment in Morocco he escaped and made contact with the recently arrived American forces. He arrived in Britain on 1 January, 1943.

Having been suitably reinforced, Rommel began another major attack, which became the Battle of Alam Halfa, on the night of 30 August. Two days before, Montgomery had instructed his officers: "There will be no withdrawal . . . absolutely none . . . none whatever". Now, he at once counterattacked. On 31 August Coningham's message to WDAF was: "The battle is on. Good luck in your usual brilliant work. This defensive land fight for Egypt will be followed by an offensive some time later, and then away we go. Meanwhile go for him in the air wherever you can."

The air fighting that ensued encapsulated all that had gone before. The versatile Beaufighters of 252 and 272 Squadrons shouldered their way into every sort of action that was on offer. Strafing enemy vehicles or troops, they would break off to shoot down a passing Ju87 or Macchi 200. Running into a bunch of Ju52s whose pilots thought they were out of fighter range, they would quickly disillusion them by shooting down a few before resuming their patrol. Diving on enemy airfields they would blast everything in sight − dispersed aircraft, tents, anti-aircraft posts, men running for shelter, before sweeping away with their bellies almost scraping the sand. On 3 September the Afrika Korps began to withdraw. WDAF's contribution to the aborting of Rommel's plan was acknowledged by the German C-in-C himself: "The continuous and very heavy attacks of the RAF absolutely pinned my troops to the ground and made impossible any safe deployment or any advance according to schedule."

While these events were unfolding, squadrons of the United States Army Air Force were arriving in Egypt. Major-General L. H. Brereton led the way, with nine B17 Flying Fortresses, followed by the 57th Fighter Group (P.40 Warhawks), the 98th Heavy Bombardment Group (B24 Liberators) and the 12th Medium Bombardment Group (B25 Mitchells). By now, British aircrew training, although it maintained a high standard, had become somewhat hasty under the pressure of replacing casualties. The American crews had undergone long peacetime training and were highly efficient technically. They were introduced to operations by flying with R.A.F. squadrons.

For seven weeks the noise of battle, to borrow from Tennyson, roll'd less loudly. But the background rumble of artillery fire, bombs and aircraft engines gave notice of an impending battle of cataclysmic violence. Rommel had withdrawn only as far as the positions he had held prior to First Alamein. The atmosphere was heavy with expectation while both sides were building up their strength.

The ninth of October was a day when the cadence of those weeks of steady hard flying punctuated by combat rose to urgency. It had rained heavily and WDAF's reconnaissance showed that the Daba airfields were waterlogged and Fuka was not in much better state. Coningham set about trying to wipe out as many enemy aircraft as possible while they were bogged down. Bombers, fighter-bombers and fighters, strafing or escorting, stormed in throughout the daylight hours, in the teeth of the accustomed flak and, often, enemy fighters. They flew some 500 sorties, compared with the Luftwaffe fighters' 102. The number of aircraft destroyed or damaged on the ground and in combat by WDAF remains uncertain: the claim was for at least fifty, with another ten taken out in air fighting. The Axis admitted that ten were demolished on the ground and twenty damaged.

It was on this day that Eric Moss, the Baltimore wireless operator/air gunner, comes into the picture again. His crew, returned from leave that morning, was on the Battle Order for an attack on Daba. "We had taken off and were climbing when I heard Ekbery shout about a 'bloody oil leak' and we had to go back. This was the second time this had happened to me, and I take my hat off to the pilots for getting us down safely with black oil covering the windscreens."

He was lying on his bed reading, awaiting an air test as soon as the aircraft was serviceable, when the Squadron was called to briefing again. "We were told that a P.R.U. [Photographic Reconnaissance

Unit] aircraft had taken photographs of the results of the first raid, and the C.O. was not happy about them at all. We had bombed the bundoo everywhere except the Axis aeroplanes, and we had to go again. There were twenty-eight USAAF Mitchells with us, who had orders to open their bomb bays when we did and bomb when we did. As the bombs were painted yellow, they were easily discernible leaving the aircraft, and one of my jobs was to count them as they left us, to make sure there were no hang-ups.

"The usual approach to the target was from out at sea: we passed the target, turned inland and bombed on our way home. This time, for some unknown reason, the leading navigator, probably still suffering the effects of his hangover from last night's end-of-leave binge, led us directly to the target.

"On the morning raid Jerry had taken it without doing much in reply. Due to the heavy rain he probably thought that we too were earth-bound, and was slow to respond. This time, however, he was waiting for us, the muck from his 88mm coming up thick, fast and accurate as soon as we came into range. We were also much lower than we should have been, which helped us not at all. After the first few black puffs exploded outside our aircraft the next gigantic cracks of the explosions seemed inside the fuselage, so close were they."

There was a loud clang, the aircraft lurched and fell out of for-mation, hit in the port engine, the propeller windmilling. The bombs were released and the Baltimore rose "like a bubble in water".

The aircraft that Moss could see on the ground, diminished from the attackers' height to the size of toys, abruptly disappeared. "The ground suddenly took on the look of the head of a freshly drawn pint of bitter or a bowl of soapsuds, as about 500 bombs hit the ground in the space of less than a minute. For a few seconds the A.A. fire faltered, then started again as we passed out of range. However, we were now going the wrong way and had to turn round. This our friends did, climbing and going out to sea. We had to turn on a dead engine and go back over the target still losing height. The Ack Ack started again as we came into range. I looked down and could see the flashes of flame from the ends of the gun barrels as they fired at us. I pointed my two guns down at them and fired four 100-round belts at those flashes, watching my tracers bouncing amongst them. I threw the empty belt crates down at them.

"Their fire stopped and so did our other engine. Those stinking black gobs of smoke floated away, leaving the air clear for me to watch the multiple streamers of tracer coming up towards us. Invisible drills per-forated the fuselage about me."

With no engines, the pilot held his aircraft as flat as he dared, hoping to get as far as the Allied lines. "But no luck. Jock above me suddenly called 'There's a fighter on our tail,' and Ekbery had to put her nose down to get extra speed. The small-arms ground fire intensified. Why our floating sieve wasn't blown out of the sky I don't know. My fingers closed on the triggers of the four machine guns fixed two each side of me to fire backwards and downwards and I held them down. I hoped they were putting the enemy off aim. Four guns at 1,400 rounds per minute each is a lot of flying lead, and I didn't have to bother about saving my gun barrels. So long as Jerry was firing I kept the triggers down, until I could see stones and foxholes and sand within feet of my face.

"I had been lying belly-down on a piece of armour plate, with my escape hatch thrown to one side. This was my position to see and count our bombs away and to attend to the six machine guns in my care. At that moment I remembered the I.F.F. set [secret radio, Identification Friend or Foe] and hurled myself at it, turning the switch and punching the detonation button. Nothing happened, the electrical circuit had failed, I pulled out my revolver and fired four shots into it, hoping the bullets would rip apart the wiring inside the tiny box. The last two bullets I kept for the purpose for which revolvers were issued to us, and as I did so I wondered how many men trapped in burning aircraft had so used them."

The aircraft hit the ground and skidded along on its belly, the interior filling with sand and dust. "We had come down right amongst the enemy. With the desperation of the damned I clawed at the pile of sand blown into my face via the open escape hatch, now only inches off the ground. I hit the release button of my parachute harness and forced my body out from under the aircraft.

"Jock was out and looking at a fighter diving at us. I recognized a Spitfire as it circled us to see who and how many got out, then disappeared. So that was Jock's fighter.

"I ran across a wing to what should have been the nose of the aircraft. This portion was lying ten or fifteen feet ahead of the rest of the aeroplane. There sat Roger, our observer, calmly tearing up his logs and maps."

The pilot was looking at the wrecked engines. "He had his revolver in his hand and so had I. The lanyard which hung from my shoulder had kept it with me in my struggle to get out of the aircraft.

"Bullets suddenly pinged on the ground around us. As we turned and faced them, a line of troops about 80 yards away advanced towards us. Heads were popping up out of the ground everywhere. We were surrounded. I looked at Ekbery, his gun extended in front at waist height. I shouted, 'No, Ekbery, no,' and threw my gun as far as I could. He hesitated. For one horrible moment I thought the 'Jumbo' in him would make a futile stand with that pathetic revolver. Then he shrugged and tossed it away.

"Odd bullets hit the ground by my feet and I put up my hands, watching the enemy advance. They were Italians armed with light rifles, the fold-under bayonets now rigidly locked in the attack position. I kept my eyes on one small one who evidently was going to collect me. There was something wrong with his bayonet hinge. Every time he pulled his hand away from it, it flopped down. In exasperation he stopped ten feet from me and took a lace from one of his boots, with which he tried to tie the bayonet in the fixed position. He then approached me. I looked down at him, wondering what to do next. I asked him for a cigarette. His face lit up as he said '*Sigaretta? Si,*' and gave me one, lighting it for me.

"Striking the match made me remember the petrol in the aircraft, now swarming with Eyetie soldiers. It was also my job to destroy the aircraft if it was forced down, and a gallon tank fed from the main tanks was situated at the side of my escape hatch for this purpose. There was a cock on the tank. I should have turned it on to let the petrol flow to the ground, where I was supposed to ignite it. But, thank Heaven, the destruction of aircraft was forbidden on the raid, as it was supposed that the rapid advance of our army would allow us to reclaim them. How we were to ignite that petrol without igniting ourselves, I don't know, as there was no receptacle with which to make a trail away from the aeroplane.

"Within minutes German troops arrived in a jeep and took us away. They made some sort of tour with us, and every now and then stopped and talked to men in foxholes. We were very thirsty, so I nudged the young NCO in charge of us. 'Water?' I asked. He stopped at the next batch of foxholes and said something. A water bottle flew through the air. The young NCO caught it and removed the stopper, handing it round to us. The liquid tasted like no other water I had drunk: it was at least fifty per cent cognac. I thanked him and he threw the bottle back. A hand waved and we were off again.

"The jeep pulled up alongside a battery of 88mm A.A. guns with their snouts pointing at the sky. As the guard talked to the gunners I felt like some sort of exhibit or trophy being shown off by the proud collector.

"I then saw something which brought me to earth with a jolt. There were four shallow open graves about twenty yards away from the guns.

Three bodies sewn in blankets lay alongside while medical orderlies were sewing up the fourth. There were bullet strikes on the paintwork of the guns. My blood froze. Were they mine? They had to be: no other gunner would have opened up with all those Kittyhawk fighters of ours milling about us. We had been above as I fired, our mates were thousands of feet above us, heading for home.

"I looked at the faces of the enemy. But there was no hatred, no nothing; it was all part of the job; it was war."

In conditions of revolting squalor and starvation, Eric Moss endured prisoner of war camps in North Africa, guarded by Italians, a crossing of the Mediterranean in the crowded and stinking hold of a ship, and imprisonment in Italy. Eleven months later he escaped and was hidden by Italian peasants for many months more, until he and other escaped POWs were plucked at dead of night from an Adriatic beach by the Royal Navy.

Not many hours after Moss had fallen into enemy hands, Maurice Smyth was disabused of a dashing misconception he had long cherished. As a boy he had been given a book in which there was a picture of a Great War fighter pilot diving down a searchlight, firing his machine gun and shattering the huge lamp. On an intruder sortie over Daba, where just such an illumination was sweeping the sky, he decided to emulate the feat. He dived along the beam, but the intensity of the flak that coruscated around him was discouraging enough to merit entering a resolution in his log book: "Leave searchlights well alone".

The period of waiting, with increasing tension, was almost over. The supporting units that moved back and forth as the squadrons advanced and retreated had been static for an unwontedly long time. Don Nelson was a flight sergeant in No 32 Air Stores Park, which he describes as "a very mobile unit, more like a travelling circus, supplying squadrons (and tanks) with everything they required, clothing, propellers, fuel, [and a wide range of other items], with 31 Maintenance Unit always close by for repairs and transport". Being still for several weeks was a luxury but seemed unnatural.

Another who led a gipsy-like existence − from June, 1942, until the end of the Italian campaign − was David Thomas. He belonged to a crew of three who worked and travelled in a wireless truck. "Our unit consisted of a number of wireless vans that formed Army Air Support links from the forward landing grounds to the Eighth Army/D.A.F. HQs. Mostly we 'lived off' the wing or squadron to which we had been sent, R.A.F., South African or American. We were an unusual band, living in a style more or less as we pleased − provided we got the messages through."

Formal discipline and strictly uniform garments were irrelevant. All that mattered was efficiency in one's job, whether flying an aeroplane, being on the spot with the right spare parts, driving a lorry or bashing a Morse key. Coningham was always awake to the fact that everyone in the desert must be prevented from becoming static-minded. As soon as he noticed signs of this, and the lethargy that accompanied it, he would have a camp moved, if only a mile. "I always send batches of thirty people at a time to the beach," he used to say, "to keep them efficient and give them a thirty-six-hour break. It's essential to keep them busy all the time, and send them off for a swim as often as possible."

The least often mentioned, yet one of the most respected and appreciated, amenities for those who led this nomadic life in its various forms was the Salvation Army canteen that was always in the van of every advance.

The multifarious components of Western Desert Air Force were ready at a moment's notice to emulate the Arabs in Longfellow's poem and fold their tents; but not, as he described, "And as silently steal away". The overture to their, and Eighth Army's, even rowdier departure westwards was the din of increased activity in the air.

It began on 20 October when 450 Squadron Kittyhawks escorted 3RAAF Baltimores and 66USAAF B25s on a raid against the Daba airfields. The battering continued day-long with bombing attacks, offensive sweeps and tactical reconnaissance. WDAF's munificently increased numbers enabled operations to be mounted with a prodigality that would have made Collishaw's head reel. A typical mission took off at 11.30 am: twelve Kittyhawks of 112 Squadron as top cover, ten Kittyhawks of 3RAAF as medium cover, ten of 250 as close cover and twenty-four B25s and Baltimores. The target was Fuka. The enemy's response was also typical of the norm: eight Me109s and eight Macchi 202s intercepted them. At the end of that day WDAF and the enemy had each lost eleven fighters in the air. Two enemy fighters were destroyed on the ground and 15 damaged.

There followed three days of further aerial rough and tumble. From the final night of these preliminaries, 73 Squadron, operating from LGs 85 and 89, were ordered to concentrate on "transport busting". Smyth's logbook shows a sortie of two hours and five minutes over the Qattara Escarpment. "Strafed wadis and tracks containing M.T. at zero feet. Hits on M.T. in wadi. Many hits seen on 4 M.T. by track. Strafed tent."

At 10 pm on 23 October 1942, after 15 minutes' barrage by 1,000 guns, the infantry assault that announced Second Alamein, the largest-scale attack in the story of desert warfare, went in.

CHAPTER 7

The Decisive Battle – Second Alamein and the invasion of Algeria – Operation Torch

The Allies went into battle with an air force that handsomely outnumbered the enemy's. Western Desert Air Force comprised:- *3 SAAF Wing*: Nos 12 SAAF and 24 SAAF Squadrons, Boston, 21 SAAF, Baltimore. *232 Wing*: 55 and 223 Squadrons, both Baltimore. USAAF 12th Bombardment Group: 81st, 82nd, 83rd Squadrons, all B25. *285 Wing*: 40 SAAF, 208, Hurricane, 60 SAAF, Baltimore. 1437 Strategic Reconnaissance Flight, Baltimore. No 2 Photographic Reconnaissance Unit, Various. *211 Group: 233 Wing*: 2 SAAF, 4 SAAF, 260, all Kittyhawk. 5 SAAF, Tomahawk. *239 Wing*: 3 RAAF, 450 RAAF, 112, 250, all Kittyhawk. *244 Wing*: 92, 145, 601, all Spitfire. 73, Hurricane. USAAF 57th Fighter Group: 64th, 65th, 66th Squadrons, all Warhawk. *212 Group: 7 SAAF Wing:* 80, 127, 274, 335 R.A.F. Squadrons, all Hurricanes. *343 Wing*: 1 SAAF, 33, 213, 238, all Hurricane.

Under Air HQ Egypt:- *234 Wing*: 889 Squadron Fleet Air Arm, Fulmar and Hurricane. *250 Wing*: 89, Beaufighter, 94, Hurricane and Spitfire. *252 Wing:* 46, Beaufighter, 417 RCAF, Hurricane, Spitfire.

Under A.H.Q. Middle East and engaged in operations over North Africa and the adjacent sea were aircraft of 201, 203, 205, 207 and 216 Groups.

Among these were Beaufighters, Blenheims, Beauforts, Baltimores, Hudsons, Lysanders, Marauders, Marylands and Wellingtons.

There were also, under 216 Group, the U.S. 1st Bombardment Group: 9th Squadron, B17s, Halverson Squadron, B25s. And the U.S. 98th Bombardment Group: 343rd, 344th, 345th, 415th, B25s.

The Luftwaffe Order of Battle showed a Staff Section and four *Gruppen* of Me109Fs & Gs, one *Gruppe* of Me109E fighter-bombers, one tactical reconnaissance *Gruppe* of Me109Es & Fs, one *Gruppe* of

Me110s, two *Gruppen* of Ju88s and a third being transferred to Africa from Crete, the Staff Section and two *Gruppen* of Ju87s.

The Regia Aeronautica had two *Gruppi* of Macchi 200s and five of Macchi 202s, five *Gruppi* of Cr42s, one *Gruppo* of Ju87s, two *Gruppi* of Cant Z1007 bombers and two *Gruppi* of torpedo SM79s.

Throughout the first night of Second Alamein, sixty-six Wellingtons of 37,40,70,104 and 108 Squadrons, all in 205 Group, maintained continuous bombing of Rommel's artillery positions and troop concentrations, while 73 Squadron was strafing vehicles and troops behind enemy lines. When morning came, the fierce contest between opposing infantry and armour began, accompanied by fighter-to-fighter combat over the killing zone; and deep behind the enemy front, while Kittyhawks escorting Bostons and Baltimores fought off intercepting Me109s. Spitfires made sweeps over the enemy-held Daba landing grounds. Montgomery's tanks surged through two paths that the infantry had cleared of mines and drove a wedge into Rommel's defences, helped by No 6 and No 7 SAAF Squadrons' tank-busting Hurricanes. The night of the 24th brought eighty-five more sorties by Wellingtons with illumination over the target provided by Fleet Air Arm Albacores. The 25th saw another demonstration of versatility by the Beaufighters of 252 Squadron. Seven of them attacked a convoy approaching Tobruk, shot down both escorting Ju88s and one Do24 flying boat, then strafed the ships. On a second outing to the convoy, three Beaus escorting Beauforts and Bisleys shot down two CR42s and a Bisley sank a cargo vessel. Eight 272 Beaufighters ranging beyond Tobruk met thirty-five Ju52s and six Me110s. They shot down four Ju52s and a 110. One Beaufighter collided with a Ju52, fatally for both.

That night Maurice Smyth, on intruder patrol, found thirty to forty motor vehicles in a wadi, which he strafed from 300 ft with many hits. The next night, on patrol over the line, he "squirted at an enemy aircraft", as his logbook has it, but was uncertain of the result until a Do215E was reported to have crashed in the area.

On the 27th Rommel made a major armoured counterattack at Kidney Ridge and was beaten back.

The tanks of both sides were suffering grievous losses. The Axis managed to hold the Allies and Montgomery changed his plan, but Rommel also regrouped to meet the new, shifted, thrust. Both generals made their moves with Machiavellian deftness. The difference between their approaches to the task was that Monty refused to send his men into action until they were in sufficient numbers to ensure that casualties would be minimal and, of course, that he would enhance his reputation by winning. Rommel was no less hungry for victory, but more profligate with lives. On the 29th he wrote to his wife: "I have not much hope left . . . What will happen if things go wrong here? . . . That is the thought that torments me day and night. I can see no way out if that happens."

Four days later the desperate struggle had not lessened. The air battle was still highly charged with the Allied airmen's conviction that they and the ground forces were on the threshold of routing the enemy and that only their audacity and steadfastness could enable the Army finally to break the deadlock. Alamein was plainly to be as historically significant as Waterloo. Wellington's words then were apposite and applied again here: "Hard pounding this, gentlemen; let's see who will pound longest." It was Montgomery who pounded the *longer*: on the night of 2 November Rommel began his 60-mile retreat to Fuka. Smyth was airborne for 2hrs 45mins on line patrol. His logbook reads: "Terrific tank and artillery battle. 'Itis' getting knocked about". On 5 November, after a dusk sortie, he recorded: "Road strafed at Casaba. Road jammed with transport. Many hits seen. Explosion among 3 M/T. Bags of flak. Port long-range tank shot off."

The following noon brought Rommel an order from Hitler that Alamein must be held at all costs. He accordingly halted the retreat and brought back the columns that were on their way to Fuka. He had yet to learn that instant obedience to the crazy strategical edicts of the Dictator, whose First World War service as a corporal hardly qualified him to act the field-marshal, usually brought calamity. WDAF's reconnaissance had reported the withdrawal and incited Montgomery and Coningham to press on with undiminished resolution. Consequently, by sunrise on the 4th Allied infantry and armour had hacked their way between the Germans and the Italians and intended to prevent them from retiring further westwards along the coast road. But lack of fuel and oil, and a minefield, held up the advance. On the 6th, however, 7th Armoured Division found enough petrol to overtake the survivors of 21st Panzer Division, which had run dry, and liquidate them. Heavy rain that day held up the Allies, but confined the Axis to the coast road. The next day 7th Armoured was able to resume its chase after the German tanks. Advanced units of Eighth Army re-entered Libya on the 11th and took Bardia without opposition.

The Luftwaffe's final effort to check the Allies' tanks included a mission by fifteen Stukas escorted by six Me109s. No 2 SAAF intercepted them and their leader, Captain Wildsmith, made a feint about-turn, which drew off the fighters. Two Kittyhawks were sent down in the brief ruck that followed, but the rest went on to shoot down eight and probably four more. German rearguard actions continued, both on the ground and in the air, all the way to Tobruk, which fell on 13 November.

A Canadian, James Edwards, known as Stocky or Eddie, a rising star performer who had just been commissioned, was in the heart of the action. Soon after arriving in Egypt at the beginning of the year he joined 94 (Kittyhawk) Squadron and, after that, 260, also Kittyhawks. About this fighter he says that a strong right arm was needed to control it in most manoeuvres. When dive-bombing it would accelerate very fast and tended to roll to the right. This could be trimmed out with the left hand — which really should not be taken off the throttle — but when pulling out of the dive the Kitty rolled violently to the left. This had to be corrected by trimming out half way during the dive and holding the stick central by bracing the right arm against the right leg and the cockpit side. This improved control and less trim needed to be taken off when pulling out. If not flown smoothly, the Kittyhawk could also fishtail and skid, thus spoiling the pilot's aim. He had mastered his mount well enough to have destroyed four Me109s and a Macchi 202 by the time he was promoted to pilot officer.

The WDAF squadrons had been bounding forward like randy grasshoppers looking for a mate. On 2 November 73 Squadron moved to LG89; 4th to LG108; 7th El Daba, LG21; 8th Sidi Haneish, LG13; 11th LG75 and LG155; 13th Gambut West. Smyth's logbook entry for the 12th is "Strafed road west of Tobruk. Started one small fire. Small amount of flak. Tobruk in flames. Dropped bomb." On 17 November the Squadron moved to El Adem, the Tobruk airfield.

The confusion and bewilderment of the Germans and Italians during this period was aggravated by a small venture codenamed Operation Chocolate. Emulating the occasion in October when Bombays and Albacores had landed temporarily 250 miles behind the enemy lines, Wing Commander Darwen, 243 Wing Leader, took all thirty-six Hurricanes of two squadrons, Nos. 213 (Squadron Leader Olver, DFC) and 238 (Squadron Leader Marples, DFC) to LG125, 180 miles east of Jedabaya. Hudsons conveyed the ground crews. Enemy transport columns on their way to Agheila, thinking themselves far beyond WDAF's range, were astonished to find themselves being attacked by fighters. The Hurricanes destroyed some 130 vehicles and damaged at least as many more during their 24-hour excursion.

The Axis forces were pulling back faster than the British could follow them. By 26 November Rommel had settled into a defence line bounded by Mersa Brega, on the coast, 24 miles north-west of Agheila, and the Great Sand Sea to the south. Here he awaited Montgomery's arrival and next offensive.

One of the participants in this fervid race across Cyrenaica, representative of the myriad who, without reward, experienced the "blood, toil, tears and sweat" of which Churchill spoke in his famed speech in May, 1940, was Richard Stanfield, a motor transport fitter who had served in the Auxiliary Air Force before the war. Tears do not feature in his story, and although the bullets were often humming close by, he shed no blood, but he knew toil and sweat in plenty. He had arrived in the Middle East on 1 November and was posted to a mobile field hospital, 21 MRS (Mobile Receiving Station). "I was now on my own," he writes, "just off the boat and as green as a cabbage, given a bag of rations and told to make my own way. 'Don't bother with your kitbag,' the sergeant said, 'you'll be back.' I never saw it again." He hitched a ride on a water bowser and "spent my first night sleeping 'up the blue' ". He caught up with his unit just as they were about to move again.

"I never had any really happy days in the desert. It was all hard work keeping our vehicles serviceable, and living conditions were pretty grim under canvas all the time. The flies and scorpions were my biggest dread and the water was pretty awful, hence the tea was foul. Still, there was a war on. Every time the squadrons moved up we had to follow them. We had two large marquees, one medical and the other surgical. When we got orders to move, everybody, doctors as well, had to give a hand with all our equipment, and immediately on arrival at our new site, put up all tents again. As I was the only F.M.T. [Fitter, Motor Transport] on the unit, my job was to follow the convoy to pick up any breakdowns, which wasn't very often. In fact we reached Tunisia with more vehicles than we started with. The only trouble we had with the enemy was strafing on the sites and when travelling up, but we never suffered many casualties."

All the way from Alamein to Tobruk and beyond, the transport squadrons had played an indispensable part in making the advance as swift as possible. Pilot Officer John Newland was a Load Control Officer at Advanced HQ 216 Group/249 Wing. "No 316 Troop Carrier Wing USAAF arrived at El Adem in style," he recalls. "About a dozen C47s in close formation appeared out of the blue and landed still in close formation without bothering about wind direction, it seemed, which caused some alarm and annoyance to a Hudson pilot who was on final approach. We were told they had been training to do just that, so that the troops they carried were landed together. It was explained to the Americans that some people found it wise to fly Hudsons very carefully, especially when landing.

"It was some recompense to see that 316 had not come prepared for the desert, being equipped only with pup tents, without even a mess tent for officers and other ranks. Their rations were far better than ours — it was reported that fresh food, including steak, was flown up to them daily — and they had proper equipment for cooking. But all that must pall when one has to line up in driving rain to be served, by which time their mess tins were awash. Also their high quality uniforms were not suitable for the desert in winter. After watching 316, including their C.O., Colonel Macauley, putting up with that sort of existence, most of our men thought that bully beef and biscuits in comparative shelter wasn't so bad after all. In no time at all a thriving barter system was in operation; their Camels and Luckies and other goodies for old khaki battledress and greatcoats. At a higher level, spare tents were found." But it did not take the Americans long to learn and they soon "sorted themselves out".

C. W. Hutchin was a Hudson pilot on 217 Squadron who dismisses his service with droll brevity, "When my granddaughter asked in 1956 'What were you in the war, Gramps?' I told her, 'Frightened, girl, very, very frightened' ". The obvious comment by anyone, from ground gunners, fitters, M/T drivers and cooks on desert airstrips to highly decorated Wing Leaders, is "Which of us wasn't?" But Hutchin differed from most in age, which puts his courage, self-respect and sense of duty high: "I joined up at the age of 28. I was married with two children, and never served under any C.O. on active service who was older than I." There were not a few in similar circumstances who preferred to opt for a reserved civilian occupation or wait to be called up and make sure of a non-combatant job in uniform.

He was flying Ansons from Asmara when Wing Commander Yaxley, 117's C.O., happened to pass through. "I made a special request to him to have me join his unit, as I was fed up doing nothing useful. I shall never forget his reply. He told me to grow up, for as a pilot I was a baby. No captain under his command had less than 400 hours in his log book [on operational type, obviously not in total]. I had 190. My reply put me on a charge of insolence". Some time later a 117 Hudson crew had to take urgent supplies to the Long Range Desert Group at Kufra. The navigator went sick, so Hutchin offered to stand in. From then on the pilot, Pilot Officer May, refused to do any trips without him. "Thus I joined 117 Squadron. I shall pass over my reporting to my new C.O., Wing Commander Yaxley. I did 400 hours as second dickey [second pilot]/navigator, obtained my captaincy and took whatever was wanted to where it was wanted in the Western Desert, Sicily, Italy and Burma, resisting all invitations to join the enemy." At their Delta base, Bilbeis, Air Commodore Whitney Straight told his crews that he expected to replace many of them every four to six months. They lost five aircraft in three years. "I can only recall the funny and enjoyable times. It takes a conscious effort to remember the holes in the fuselage from flak, the sudden departure of a complete radio installation due to flak and so on." C. W. Hutchin flew over 120 hours in the Western Desert and his pilot rating was "Excellent".

Because of its great — and mostly level — expanse of manoeuvring space, and distance between supply bases and the battle front, the desert has been described as a tactician's dream and a quartermaster's nightmare. Squadron Leader Peter Hepple was, when more junior in rank, Equipment Officer in a Spitfire squadron, 601 (County of London). He found spares "very hard to come by early in the campaign, as all spares had to come from England, and progress was very slow at first. Whenever I heard that a Spit had been forced down, I used to borrow a fitter and a rigger from the Engineer Officer and take them in my Fordson 15cwt to the scene of the 'prang' and we at once cannibalized the Spit and returned with as many spares as possible.

"One of the more humorous of happenings between the pilots and myself was when there was a scarcity of pressure regulator valves. This particular precious item was not unduly large, so when I was going to be in charge of the rear party of the squadron, I asked a pilot to take the PRV in his Spit. However, the pilots had a gramophone record which had priority over everything else (I think it was a Rachmaninoff concerto)." So the record was taken by air and the pressure regulator valve followed by land. "It remained intact throughout the desert campaign. Water was another problem. At times I even had to put a guard on the water bowser. The M/T section was also my responsibility and I had to make sure that our vehicles were serviceable at all times.

"Shortly after Alamein when our squadron was on a strafing expedition, Pilot Officer Llewellyn had his Spit forced down in enemy territory. Pilot Officer Terry, his section leader, landed alongside and brought him back, I believe this was the first time two pilots flew in one Spitfire."

While the symphonic complexity of Montgomery's and Coningham's intelligently orchestrated score was booming out its diapasons of approaching doom for the enemy, a momentous descant was sounding in Algeria, with an accompaniment in Morocco. On 8 November Operation Torch was carried out, with the intention of trapping the Axis forces between simultaneous advances from east and west. Landings were made in Algeria, at Oran and Algiers, and in Morocco on the coast north and south of Casablanca. The capture of Oran was in the hands of Major-General Friedenthal, with 18,500 American troops. Algiers was taken by Major-General Ryder, another American, with

18,000 troops, half British, half American. Major-General Patton led the Moroccan force of 24,500 U.S. troops. Both Algerian landings were escorted by the Royal Navy, the Moroccan by the American.

The British and American air forces involved operated separately in different geographical areas. Their tasks were the same: to support the Army in its advance on Tunisia and to protect land and sea communications. The RAF covered Algeria east of Cape Tenez, with the title Eastern Air Command, under Air Marshal Sir William Welsh. The USAAF covered western Algeria and Morocco as Western Air Command, under Major-General James H. Doolittle. Their planning was not integrated and each reported directly to the Allied C-in-C, Lieutenant-General Dwight D. Eisenhower. Thus the table was laid for what is nowadays known as a dog's breakfast. And an indigestible and vomit-provoking meal it turned out to be.

Events in the assault from the west are not directly concerned with the story of Desert Air Force. They are mentioned because the R.A.F. units were ultimately merged with WDAF

Air cover for the eastern Algerian landings was mounted from Gibraltar. The first wing to arrive at Maison Blanche aerodrome on the outskirts of Algiers was No. 332, led by Wing Commander Petrus Hendrik "Piet" Hugo, DSO, DFC, a South African who had joined the RAF in April, 1939. In December of that year he joined 615 Squadron in France, where he shot down a He111, and a further five in the Battle of Britain before being wounded. Since then he had scored three more victories and shared in others.

Piet Hugo was but one of many distinguished pilots who took part in Torch or joined the R.A.F. wings in Eastern Air Command later. Squadron Leader (later Wing Commander) Jack Sing, DFC, another pre-war officer, scored nine kills in the Battle of Britain and was commanding 152 Squadron in the Algerian invasion. Squadron Leader Ronald "Razz" Berry, DFC, commanding 81 Squadron in the invasion, was a pre-war member of the RAFVR. He also had nine victories during the Battle of Britain and destroyed a CR42 soon after it when the Italians took part in an air raid on England. A later arrival was Wing Commander H. S. L. Dundas, DSO, DFC (soon to be, at 23, the youngest group captain in the R.A.F.), who had fought in the Battle of Britain and had a total score of at least six victories by the time he arrived in Algeria. All these pilots flew in Desert Air Force when it was formed by the fusion of WDAF and the squadrons fighting their way to Tunisia from Algeria.

Among the junior pilots of 145 Squadron who arrived at Maison Blanche in November, 1942, was Sergeant J. S. Ekbery, cousin of Brian

Ekbery, Eric Moss's pilot, who had been taken prisoner the previous month. Assessed Above Average when he completed his training, Joe Ekbery was posted to 222 Squadron in May, 1942, and flew in the air cover for the Commando raid on Dieppe in August. He then served with 243 and 232 Squadrons, before going to 145. More will be heard of him when D.A.F. moved on to Sicily and Italy, where he gained most of his successes.

After seven months as an instructor at the Middle East Fighter School, Flying Officer Neville Duke was back in action with 92 Squadron, with which he had served at Biggin Hill, and was delighted to be in a Spitfire cockpit once more. It was winter and "in the keen air of the desert we developed enormous appetites". Food supplies were often scanty, so every pilot's tent contained a "yaffle" box, in which was stored "any food we could lay our hands on: gazelle meat, which tasted like venison, collected during shoots in the desert and butchered expertly by the Aussies". They also stored cocoa, tinned food, flour, raisins, sugar and biltong — dried venison, a staple South African diet in the bush — from East Africa. The Australians and Canadians received the most generous contributions in their food parcels from home. From severely rationed Britain little could be spared. On cold nights when the wind was keen, "it was one of the more pleasant things in life to gather four or five in a tent" and cook a hot meal over the usual desert fire; a cut-down petrol tin filled with petrol-soaked sand.

Duke flew his first operation of the new tour on a defensive patrol of Tobruk, led by the C.O. Squadron Leader J. H. Heywood, DFC, who had made three kills in the Battle of Britain and a fourth by the time he was posted to the Western Desert. There, Heywood became the most successful Spitfire pilot, with nine more victories and a bar to his decoration.

Someone else, at the opposite end of the R.A.F. spectrum of rank and trade, Corporal Richard Roberts, a Fitter IIE, was also appreciating the material benefits that came from the Dominions. He was one of many Britons in 459 RAAF Squadron. The rations were "Good tucker, bacon and eggs for breakfast, bread, oleo marge (rock hard on cold mornings, pour it out by midday when it was hot, just nice at teatime, but we didn't have afternoon tea), tea or coffee (ersatz) sugar and Carnation brand tinned milk. Noon meal, tiffin, was raw cabbage, hard tack, tinned fruit, tea. Supper corned beef, various e.g. uncooked, boiled, braised, stewed: you name it, we had it. Spuds and dry pulses now and again. Substitute egg (known as prostitute egg), some meals powdered egg boiled in water. Slab cake at times. Sergeant Roy Tier was a good Aussie cook and bookmaker" and kept a pet duck, "Oscar".

Bob Cable, a 19-year-old LAC on 113 (Blenheim) Squadron, which had been posted from North Africa to Burma, was by now in the jungle and looking back on his desert days. He recalled the daily strafe by a lone Me109 that "every morning before dawn would just make a nuisance pass overhead", which sent everyone diving into slit trenches. "It was decided to fix him. Two aircraft took off to stooge around, hoping to see the exhaust. They did, and we saw the result – a flaming Jerry shot down. Squadron Leader Ford had the pleasure. Peace for a while. I can remember our aircraft going on early morning raids to Jerry's lines to wake them up with a siren mounted on nose of Blenheim to operate on approach to camps, was told it played havoc with troops. Our aircraft came back with telephone wires wrapped around wings and fuselage." Settling into a new landing ground early one morning, "No sooner had we had breakfast and our ration of one mug of water which had so much treatment it was like pure ammonia, tinned milk would curdle, shaving and washing was out, Jerry paid us a visit." High-level bombers approached from the west and Me110s came in at low level. "Could see rear gunners smiling and looking out. Corporal Taylor was awarded a Military Medal for shooting one Me110 down, a very brave man. Sorry to say we lost a few personnel and aircraft. We certainly knew we were in the front line." He could have written much the same about squadron life in the desert now, a year later.

One of the recently arrived pilots in 73 Squadron was Sergeant (now Group Captain) David Green. With admirable Staff College lucidity he details the squadron's functions: "The night defence of our day air strips and other installations near the bomb line; protection of vital installations such as harbours; ground attacks on enemy installations on the far side of the bomb line; and intruder patrols of enemy airfields. The squadron was flying Hurricane IICs equipped with four 20mm cannons, and apart from blinkers over the exhaust pipes there was no special type of night flying equipment. The navigational arrangements were rudimentary. There was a VHF homer with the squadron, but as it was only worked by the Intelligence corporal, it was of very little use. However, it was not frequently needed, as we very quickly developed our own pilot nav techniques, which allowed us to fly in R/T silence throughout all of our trips."

They took off and landed on a flarepath that consisted of a single row of eight or ten glim lamps, an undershoot and an overshoot red light, and a Chance light with a top beacon that could be used if required, but "I can't recall the floodlight ever being called for or used. In fact we would have been in dead trouble with the C.O. had we done so" (because it would have drawn the attention of enemy aircraft from a great distance). "The whole control of night flying came under an Aerodrome Control Pilot, who was normally one of the junior pilots, such as myself, who undertook the task in rotation. It was his duty to get the flarepath laid in the afternoon and to man it with a couple of airmen throughout the night until flying ceased at dawn." The ACP had a schedule of activity and all movement was done by the clock. No R/T was used. A pilot going on a sortie would start up on time, not use his navigation lights at any time, but use his downwards identification light while taxiing, which gave a small amount of illumination. As the ground was normally flat and free of obstacles, he would taxi from dispersal straight for the Chance light. There he would stop, carry out his pre-take-off checks and flash the downward identification light when ready. The ACP would flash a green or red Aldis lamp pointed at the ground, whereupon – if it was a green – he would take the flarepath and go. Coming back one would never look for the flarepath, because it was never on unless there was a movement in progress. One would arrive over the airstrip, then signal with a series of flashes with the downwards identification light. The ACP would switch on the flarepath and one would land. As soon as one had cleared the flarepath it would be switched off."

A section, usually of two aircraft operating separately, was kept at readiness to be scrambled to intercept enemy aircraft reported to Group and Sector. They were positioned as close to the runway threshold as possible. When there was a scramble, they would move to the flarepath and take off without waiting for a green. Pilots on readiness or standby in day squadrons were relieved from time to time, but in night squadrons they stayed on all night. They rested on beds in the flight tent used by the ground crews. When the field telephone rang, the flight sergeant answered it. If he yelled "Scramble!" two airmen would hurl themselves out of the tent and sprint to the aircraft. "At the same time the pilot concerned would spring from his camp bed, and barging everyone and everything in his way aside, run as fast as he could through the darkness to his aircraft. It was a matter of moments between slumber and full power along the flarepath.

"Once airborne, with the aircraft 'cleaned up' (undercarriage raised etc) except for closing the canopy, which would have restricted visibility and caused distraction from reflected lights, the reflector sight was switched to 'dim', cockpit lighting kept as low as possible, the gun selector was set to 'fire', the four-channel VHF R/T was set to the Ops frequency and the sortie continued under the controller's directions. Eyeballing one's way about the desert night sky, even moonlight, was a fairly profitless experience. Throughout the whole of my tour, from

November, 1942, to December, 1943, I cannot recall anyone on the squadron actually making a visual interception from a scramble, leave alone claiming a victory. I think I came nearest to it on one occasion when, during a scramble, I reached the flarepath just as a Ju88 clearly seen from the ground, strafed it from a couple of hundred feet. He did no damage and by the time I accelerated along the flarepath he was long gone."

The second form of night defence was layer patrols. These might consist of up to five aircraft at 2,000 feet height intervals on patrol lines between the expected approach path of the attacker and his likely target, normally an important supply port. "The sortie was pre-briefed on the ground in detail. The entire operation was a timed one, which in important instances could have involved successive waves of aircraft. All aircraft flew totally blacked out and in R/T silence, unless being controlled by Sector or in an emergency. To achieve correct height separation, a standard altimeter setting was set before take-off – usually to the atmospheric pressure at base – and remained unaltered." If the atmospheric pressure in the operational area varied much from this, low-level attacks could be fraught with the risk of diving into the ground. On the other hand, pilots could rely on the accuracy of the height reading when they were landing back.

"Offensive sorties were of two types, recce/ground attack and intruders. Both were flown by single aircraft. On recce/ground attack, we might be given a specific area where targets could be expected, either through intelligence reports or observations by the day squadrons. If the latter were the source, we were given a more general area or line, such as the coastal road, along which to seek out targets of any sort, opportunity targets. It was entirely up to each pilot to decide how and when to attack. As one would expect, night attacks with cannon tended to be rather more thoughtful and deliberate than those in the daytime. There were enough dangers inherent in the exercise without the addition of undue panache. Some used two guns at a time, in order to conserve ammunition; others, including me, thought that if the target was worth the risk at all it was worth giving it the lot. If there was a moon or any other sort of lighter sector, such as dawn or dusk, the attack was always made from the darker sector. The approach had to be steady, in a 25- to 30-degree dive. Fire was usually opened at about 1,000 ft and continued to a bottom limit of about 500 ft. On breaking away, a climbing turn was made immediately, back towards the dark sector. It was, however, a very hit and miss affair, particularly where the height was concerned. There were times when, with the altimeter still reading a respectable altitude, I have suddenly become aware of

25 73 Squadron pilots and one of the Hurricanes in which they made blind take-offs at night (see p.114). *Left to right:* Jimmy Rawson, David Green, John Horne, Teddy Bennet and Eddie Karatau. (*D. Green*)

26 Flight Lieutenant Bamkin, RAAF, and crew, victims of a bizarre and fatal accident (see p.127) (*T. Davies*)

27 Pilots of 260 Squadron, Gabes, Tunisia, April, 1943: "Never was there a more good-natured, well-knit, friendly, easy-going gaggle" (p.128). *Left to right:* Brian Thomas (NZ), Bill Stewart (Canada), Peter Blomfield (UK), Lionel Shepherd (UK), Don Barber (Canada), "Snake" Rattle (Canada), Eddie Edwards (Canada), George Tuck (USA). (*P. Blomfield*)

28 "260 Squadron . . . by this time was flying Mustangs". (p.163) (*G. Brown*)

vehicles, tents etc. immediately beneath the belly of the aircraft. One wonders who was the more surprised, oneself or the enemy."

During the dark, moonless, period, on the fairly rare occasions when strafing was undertaken, another technique could be used. This entailed dropping the one parachute flare that was carried, picking a target and attacking below the flare as it descended. "The snag here was that, in order to illuminate a target and attack it, one was also illuminating oneself. Needless to say, this was not a universally popular form of attack."

Distant enemy airfields, probably used by transports or bombers, were the usual targets for intruders. "We kept R/T silence throughout the trip and took over and relieved on timing. We didn't even catch sight of each other. The Luftwaffe was not as discreet as we were about lighting when night flying was in progress. Their airfields used to display quite a number of lights and therefore it was fairly easy to stay in position once we were there. If we did an hour's patrol in the target area, these sorties usually stretched to maximum duration. In the vicinity of the airfield we normally patrolled about two miles downwind of the flarepath and maintained about 4,000 ft, a height that enabled us to attain a good speed in an attack. The enemy often used a double flarepath, with floodlights, and the Ju52s coming in and out had their navigation lights on and used their landing lights to touch down." One of the complications of the task was that the Hurricane's two drop tanks did not have a fuel gauge in the cockpit, so the pilot had to drop them after a certain time had expired.

The distance exacerbated the navigation problem, particularly on the return to base. Although the day fighter squadrons were usually based on or near the coast, the night-fighting No 73 was operating mostly from landing grounds 60 miles deep in the desert. The only means pilots had of finding their way home was to plot a course and distance from base to some landmark on the coast that they could discern even in dark periods, then, starting from there, fly back on the reciprocal. The air was clear, so, even without moonlight, surf and prominent coastal features were visible.

Even the brief illumination of an exiguous flarepath was sometimes denied to 73 Squadron. Maurice Smyth recalls that when they were defending Benghazi from frequent air raids, no light at all was provided at the two airstrips the squadron was using. The aircraft were parked "pointing in the right direction to avoid tents and vehicles", and pilots took off blindly, relying totally on their instruments.

On 8 December the Y Service reported that fifteen Ju88s were going to bomb the first convoy into Benghazi since its capture, consisting of fifteen ships whose cargoes were urgently needed. Even water had to come by sea, because the retreating Germans had polluted all the wells with animal carcasses. The Beaufighters of 252 Squadron had had a fight with Ju88s that attacked the convoy off the coast earlier in the day and shot one down. Pilot Officer Smyth was flying one of the Hurricanes that were sent up to cover the approaching convoy. At 5.30 pm the Ju88s appeared above cloud at about 6,000 feet and split up to attack from different directions. Smyth picked his victim, but it turned south. He followed it and every time it turned back towards Benghazi and spotted him, it veered southwards again.

"You couldn't catch a Ju88, even with a full bomb load, with a Hurricane. Anyway, this boy did a turn to starboard through the cloud – he was about a mile from me – and the cloud was about 600 ft thick. I estimated where he would come out the other side, set course accordingly and kept my height. I turned and dived where I assumed he'd come out, and got him. He was only about four or five hundred yards away, turning into the convoy. For once I had height on a German aircraft and was catching him. At 400 yds I'd got pinpoint harmonization on my cannons, so took very careful aim and hit him across the back of the crew's quarters and the starboard engine. The engine appeared to go right out. By this time he was turning inside me, so I had to break away to starboard and when I reversed my turn again he had disappeared, except that there was a boiling cloud of water in the sea. This was the squadron's three hundredth victory. I later heard that one of the crew had been picked up by the rescue ship. The rest of the squadron got a few then."

Once the convoy was in port, the Ju88s continued to attack it every night at low level, despite the barrage balloons and "a hell of a lot of ack-ack". On 13 December radar picked up a raid and Pilot Officer Maurice Smyth was put on to it. For the second time, he had height over a Ju88. "I caught sight of him and dived after him. He turned right across the aerodrome from which I had taken off, and all the flak opened up at me. He then went down to the road and railway bridge at Benghazi about five miles away, going like the clappers, I'd got full booster on and was slowly catching him, slowly losing height. He turned right across Benghazi harbour. The ack-ack gunners let him go and let me have the lot. I was almost blinded by the enormous amount of ack-ack coming up from the ships. I got out of it as quickly as I could, and by this time the Ju88 had gone."

During the next few days twelve Hurricanes of the squadron moved to Wadi Temet. "We were ahead of the Army and a column was to come up and supply us. A strip of sand had been scraped out. When we got there, there was only a Lysander on the strip. We had just taxied off the strip and got out of our aircraft when eighteen Fiat G50s came out of the sun and started dive bombing. Very accurate dive bombing, too. The Lysander took off and did a very steep turn at the end of the landing strip. The Italians set several Hurricanes on fire and came down strafing. We could only sit and watch. When the G50s had gone, we saw a 30cwt Army vehicle approaching us. It was only 100 yards off when it obviously went over a mine. The rear wing was blown off and it was flipped on its back. We discovered that we were in the middle of a mine-field, so we sat tight. The next day the same thing happened with ano-ther bunch of G50s, which got most of the rest of the Hurricanes. On the following two days two or three Ju88s attacked us. Fortunately most of us had double water bottles and we had emergency rations. We got water out of the seven-gallon tanks of some of the Hurricanes that weren't too badly damaged. On the night of the 15th a Stuka came down very low and we could see the rear gunner belting at anything that moved."

Squadron Leader Wedgewood was tour-expired and handed over 92 Squadron to Squadron Leader J. M. Morgan, DFC, who had shot down six hostiles, all in the desert. The Halifax in which Wedgewood was fly-ing home to England crashed at Malta and all aboard were killed. Mor-gan was destined to be shot down over Italy in 1944 and captured.

Eisenhower's attempt to take Tunis from the west had failed. It was now up to Montgomery to do so from the east.

On 14 December 7th Armoured attacked the Agheila line and the New Zealanders made an outflanking advance. On the 16th the Axis forces at Agheila split into small groups and began to retreat. On the 17th Rommel started withdrawing to Buerat, 240 miles west. The Eighth Army paused at Nofilia, 120 miles west of Agheila, while Mont-gomery prepared his next offensive.

No 92 Squadron had moved from Msus to Antelat, then to El Hassiat, 90 miles south-east of Agedabia. Neville Duke records that the squad-ron was at El Merduna for Christmas. A lorry from Cairo delivered the traditional fare and the members of the pilots' mess sat down to "an enormous meal of turkey, pork, Christmas pudding, wine and various trimmings."

Another who fed well that Christmas was Richard Roberts, of 459 RAAF Squadron. "The Aussies had pinched three piglets from some-where." When the Squadron moved, "they were put in sacks and we tied them on to the Hudsons' bombracks and shut the doors. They were fed on scraps from the cookhouse and the officers' and sergeants' messes, so they grew fat. The desert at Gambut was hard and stony, so we used 40-gallon fuel drums to cage the pigs in the sty." When the time came to slaughter them, "a shearlegs was put up over a pit. The pit was lined with tarpaulins and boiling water poured in to scald the pigs. Roy Tier enticed a pig over the side of the sty. With a small sledge hammer he clouted it on the head. The pig shook its head and jumped the 40 gallon drum and headed west towards the Jerry lines with 459 Squadron members in full cry. When we caught it, Roy shot it with a Service revolver. The Squadron had three Christmas dinners that year, 1942: one at Genaclis, one en route, one at Gambut."

The last great step forward in Libya, to take Tripoli, entailed moving 239 Wing to the aerodrome beside Marble Arch. The enemy had barely departed, but not before burying thousands of mines on the airfield and along all the approaches to it. The huge ostentatious marble pile on the Cyrenaica-Tripolitania border stood shining white amid a brown waste dotted with scrub, which faded to infinity on the south. The coastal road was a bituminous ribbon that disappeared in the distance to east and west: the sea offered glimpses of cobalt to the north.

Operation Chocolate had been a small-scale rehearsal for just such a cumbrous transportation of men and equipment as, with some added refinements, was now necessary. On 16 December, 1942, the Royal Engineers set about clearing 2,000 mines from the airfield, a task that cost them twenty lives but was finished in twenty-four hours. An R.A.F. Aerodrome Reconnaissance Officer, in touch by radio with Advanced HQ, accompanied the New Zealand Division that had gone around Rommel's southern flank. Simultaneously a supply column went as far forward as possible. The 239 Wing advance party, equipped with radar, R/T and W/T transmitters and receivers, field telephones and cables, and motorcycles, marked time at Belandah, where 216 Group's Hudsons would embark them. At El Adem, 316 USAAF Group's Dakotas were waiting and ready, loaded with enough petrol to meet 239 Wing's needs for one day of intensive operations. As soon as the airfield was reported safe, the wing's four Kittyhawk squadrons, 3 RAAF, 450 RAAF, 112 and 250, began landing. They carried out sixty sorties from Marble Arch that first day. This combined WDAF/Eighth Army performance was as much an abstract monument to air/ground concord as the vulgar erection from which the aerodrome got its name was a concrete one to Italy's misbegotten dominion, of which the Allies were making such a mockery.

Thus 1942 ended with Hitler, Mussolini and their instrument, Rommel, asking themselves, in the rhetoric of Wordsworth, "Whither is fled the visionary gleam? Where is it now, the glory and the dream?"; while Montgomery, with total victory on the near horizon, could gloat over the words of St Luke: "He hath shewed strength with his arm; he hath scattered the proud in the imagination of their hearts."

But without the gifts of Tedder and Coningham and the skill and bravery of their air forces, the rush to within reach of the Tunisian frontier could not have been achieved. For these two commanders the appropriate reflection would have been two lines from Byron: "For the Angel of Death spread his wings on the blast, And breathed in the face of the foe as he pass'd."

CHAPTER 8

Triumph in North Africa

"Desert Air Force" had crept into use, for brevity. In January, 1943, Montgomery, describing the recent battle, wrote that, in concert with Eighth Army's offensive, "The immediate consideration after El Agheila was the establishment of the Desert Air Force at Marble Arch and Mecuma, with forward squadrons at Nofilia. We also required to take Sirte and start work at once on the airfields there so that the Desert Air Force would be ready to give its customary scale of support."

The new year brought changes. Tedder was nominated Vice Chief of the Air Staff. Air Chief Marshal Sir W. Sholto Douglas, who had commanded 43 Squadron in the First World War and won the MC and DFC, replaced him as C-in-C RAF Middle East. A total reorganization of the air forces was soon to follow. But first the Libyan capital must fall.

Between 8 and 21 January Neville Duke, who had just turned 21, shot down three Macchis and an Italian Ju87. He was also promoted to Flight Lieutenant and made a Flight Commander. A few days later he was awarded a bar to his DFC. One of the Macchi pilots taken prisoner was a colonel commanding a *Gruppo,* who expressed a poor view of the German fighter pilots. They avoided combat, he said, unless numbers, height and sun were favourable. Naturally, he thought his compatriots fought much better. It was true that the Italian fighter pilots had been showing more doggedness and courage lately.

No 73 Squadron had an encounter, happily brief, with the exuberant inventiveness of one of the most popular and unorthodox characters in the annals of the R.A.F. Even those who had not served with Richard "Batchy" Atcherley or his twin brother, David, knew and talked about their lively aberrations and exploits. Both were also imbued with a deep love of, and pride in, their Service and with the sheer joy of flying. Air Commodore D.F.W. Atcherley was AOC 211 Group. It occurred to him, perhaps inspired by the Albacores' venture a few months before and the more recent Operation Chocolate, that there was a fresh opportunity to surprise the enemy, this time by night. He suggested to Squadron Leader Monty Ellis, DFM, the Squadron Commander, that his Hurricanes might take off at dusk one evening, each carrying a glim lamp aboard, and land behind enemy lines at a spot where cans of petrol had been dumped for the occasion. The pilots could lay a flarepath with their glim lamps, harry the enemy all night and return to base at dawn. The Squadron had a still better idea: they turned the proposition down.

Eighth Army began its new offensive on 15 January, 1943. The 17th of January witnessed another bold and brilliant feat of large-scale relocation when 239 Wing moved from Hamraiet to a landing ground prepared for it south-east of Sedada. The landing ground reconnaissance party reported at 8 am that day that it had found a suitable site. Protected by a screen of armoured cars and working well within earshot, and almost within view, of a local skirmish that was still being fought, the party fully prepared the new landing ground for the arrival at 11.30 am of the Wing's advanced reconnaissance party in four Hudsons and a Dakota of 216 Group. The main flying party of 196 officers and men, made up by each squadron to be a complete servicing echelon, landed in sixteen Hudsons at 1 pm. They were escorted by the Squadrons' own aircraft, for the armour was already moving on. Ten Me109 fighter-bombers attacked while the transport aircraft were landing, but inflicted no casualties. The Wing's sorties continued at once from this new airfield, which had been captured by the Army, opened up and put to operational use all in the same day.

The Allied ground and air forces quickly forced the Germans to abandon their Buerat positions. Rommel retired to a line Tarhuna-Homs, but Eighth Army drove on until he retreated to the Tunisian frontier. On 23 January, 1943, Eighth Army entered Tripoli. On the same date WDAF took over Castel Benito and a Sector Operations Room was established at Misurata. The air defence of the Libyan capital was of prime importance, for it was now the main supply port for the advance across Tunisia. Because the German long-range bombers based on Crete were expected to raid the port by night, one flight of night-fighting Beaufighters from 89 Squadron joined the Hurricanes and Kittyhawks at Castel Benito.

Almost the whole of the Italian Air Force in North Africa withdrew to Sicily and Italy, leaving sixty single-engine fighters in southern Tunisia. The Luftwaffe retired to the same area, adding about 160 aircraft to the 150 of *Fliegerkorps Tunis* that were already there.

This was an appropriate time to review the organization of the air forces. On 1st February, Air Vice Marshal Harry Broadhurst, DSO, DFC, AFC (later Air Chief Marshal Sir, with KCB, CBE to add to his honours) took command of WDAF. His was already a distinguished record. In 1931 he was mentioned in despatches for operations on the Indian North-West Frontier. In 1937, when commanding 19 Squadron, he and two other pilots won the air firing trophy. He also led a formation aerobatics threesome with the inner wingtips of the Nos 2 and 3 tied to his, in the annual R.A.F. Display at Hendon. When war broke out he was 33 years old and C.O. of 111 Squadron. Soon promoted to Wing Commander and then Group Captain, he continued flying frequently on operations over England and France. By the time he reached AVM's rank he had shot down twelve German aircraft in addition to many probables and damaged.

On 4th February Eighth Army crossed the Tunisian frontier.

Tedder's penetrating intellect had quickly analysed the defects in the structure of the RAF and USAAF in the Mediterranean. While Eastern Air Command and 12th Air Force were operating independently in Tunisia, Commonwealth and American medium and heavy bombers under HQ RAF Middle East were also attacking targets there and in Sicily and Italy. The work of the anti-shipping and reconnaissance squadrons based on Malta was aiding the Tunisian campaign. To Tedder it was clear that a single unified command was needed to cover the whole Mediterranean and North Africa and that the British and American air forces should be integrated. His appointment to be Vice CAS was postponed. Instead, on 17 February, he himself was duly appointed AOC-in-C Mediterranean Air Command and established his HQ in Algiers, beside that of General Eisenhower, Commander-in-Chief.

Eastern Air Command and 12th Air Force were combined to form Northwest African Air Force under General Carl Spaatz. Northwest African Strategic Air Force, under General Doolittle, Northwest African Coastal Air Force, under AVM Sir Hugh Pugh Lloyd, and *Northwest African Tactical Air Force, under Air Marshal Sir Arthur Coningham* were created. The last-named consisted of WDAF, 242 Group (light bombers and fighters from Eastern Air Command) and tactical squadrons of 12th Air Force, which were called 12th Air Support Command. RAF and USAAF maintenance facilities were united in Air Service Command, Tedder had an American Chief of Staff, Spaatz had a British deputy, and down the chain of command at HQ level each British or American Commander had a deputy of the other nationality.

This new organization bestowed on the air forces the great flexibility that is essential for air power to be used most effectively. No longer would air units and formations be allotted to the Army or Navy or to specific geographical areas. Under Tedder all the air strength in the Mediterranean could now be directed to the various decisive points as necessary: deep behind the enemy's front, his airfields near the front, transport on the roads, convoys along the coast, even targets in Sicily and Italy. The Allied land forces were integrated under General The Hon Sir Harold Alexander, Eisenhower's Deputy. Coningham immediately set up a joint Headquarters with him, thus keeping the same close grip on tactical land-air requirements as he had when commanding WDAF.

Montgomery handsomely acknowledged his reliance on the air arm by defining the doctrine he shared with Tedder and the latter's subordinate commanders. "Any officer who aspires to hold high command in war must understand clearly certain basic principles regarding the use of air power.

"The greatest asset of air power is its flexibility, and this enables it to be switched quickly from one objective to another in the theatre of operations. So long as this is realized, then the whole weight of the available air power can be used in selected areas in turn; this concentrated use of the air striking force is a battle-winning factor of first importance.

"It follows that control of the available air power must be centralized, and command must be exercised through R.A.F. channels.

"The commander of an army in the field should have an Air Headquarters with him to direct control, and command of such squadrons as may be allotted for operations in support of his army.

"Such air resources will be in support of his army, not under his command."

Triumph in Libya, after the bemused ferment of successive battles, brought stability, despite Eighth Army's natural desire to set foot in Tunis before First Army and the squadrons pressing hard from the west. In this jubilant interval, recreation took a prominent place. Station cinemas were opened at Castel Benito and Benina. The professional actors and actresses in ENSA (Entertainment National Service Association, reviled by the troops as Every Night Something Awful) had been doing their best to alleviate the monotony of Forces life. Now mobile cinemas and an R.A.F. concert party, "The Mirthmakers", also travelled around the units. The Welfare organization supplied musical instruments, gramophones, radios, indoor games, sports equipment, books and magazines. Certain establishments known to spread what are coyly termed "social diseases" were closed, leaving selected medically-supervised houses to remain in business, as in Cairo and Alexandria, with the usual separation of officers from other ranks.

No 459 RAAF Squadron, who were addicted to playing Australian Rules Football, even in the desert, concocted some further amusement for themselves by holding a sports day and the Western Desert's first dog show. The sports provided a turn up for the book that gave Sergeant Tier, the bookmaker-cook, a handsome return. The Australians, thinking little of the sporting prowess of the Britons on the squadron, confidently expected to win every event. One of Richard Roberts's tent mates, Morgan, "a short Yorkshire lad", was a long-distance runner, and, true to his county, canny and sparing with words. In the mile race he held back until the last 100 yards, then left the rest of the field far behind. "He made Roy Tier a millionaire, as all the bets were on the 'dinkum cobbers'." For the dog show, Sergeant Tier adorned Oscar, his pet duck, with a blue bow. The squadron mongrels, de-fleaed and spruced up, made a brave showing. The padre's entrant won the prize for Best Bitch on Heat. Her owner attained eminence in later life by becoming Bishop of Tasmania: one of three ex-members of the squadron to reach episcopal status.

Tom Davies, who was in the Signals Section of 454 RAAF Squadron, which flew first Blenheims and then Baltimores, recalls this period with less relish. The Squadron had moved "backwards" to mount air/sea rescue patrols for aircraft shot down in the sea during the Axis attempts to supply Rommel by both sea and air. While the Tripoli area was a land of plenty, those on desert airstrips were still on short commons. "Squadron rations were adequate but spartan, with few extras." This was different from Richard Roberts's experience on another RAAF squadron. "The beer ration was irregular. Men were hardly comforted by the knowledge that US forces were better organized with regular 'bus runs' to Cairo and Alexandria for supplies of 'goodies'.

"One afternoon a USAAF Mitchell returning from Cairo landed on our strip for an unknown reason. On take-off, the pilot, intending to raise the undercarriage, opened the bomb doors at about two hundred feet. The sky over our heads was suddenly black with the discharge of Lucky Strikes, Hershey bars, cartons of other half-forgotten luxuries, together with soap, razor blades and bottles — few of which bounced to our satisfaction. A generous quantity of the goods were returned to the crew when the Mitchell came back. But many an airman, with bulging cheeks, developed a taste for 'the American way of life!' "

He looks back on the Bedouin with little enthusiasm. "Whenever a squadron settled in position for any length of time, the local Bedouin tribe's encampment would prove a nuisance in neighbourly attention, particularly in nocturnal visiting. Despite the guards, anything of small value left outside a tent at night would be missing at daybreak. One night an airman was woken by a disturbance near his tent, challenged the obvious intruder and was killed by a single shot. At dawn, the C.O., Wing Commander Campbell, an Australian, led a party of air and ground crew to the nearby encampment to search for arms or Allied equipment of any kind. Men and women were separated and all tents were searched, yielding a few Enfield rifles. The liaison officer who accompanied our party suddenly rounded on the circle of womenfolk who stood keening in distress. He pulled up the voluminous skirts of an outsize vociferous lady to reveal, tied around her waist, bundles of NAAFI knives and forks, several pairs of boots, airmen, for the use of, and a variety of other purloined articles. We brought back an unwelcome gift in the form of fleas, which infested our clothes and bedding for weeks. But we never suffered further Bedouin visitations."

Later, the Squadron suffered the loss of a popular Australian pilot and his crew from an unexpected cause. A Flight took off at 4.45 am on a shipping strike, and while they circled at 500 feet before formating on their leader, Flight Lieutenant Bamkin's aircraft suddenly dived steeply into the ground, killing the whole crew. The official enquiry found that the dinghy on which the pilot sat had self-inflated, forcing him forward against the control column and rendering him helpless. Thereafter every pilot had to carry a knife in his stocking top, to puncture the dinghy-cushion if the same thing happened.

The enemy could not pause to enjoy any surcease from the demands of war. They were now holding a line anchored on Mareth, 80 miles west of the Tunisian/Libyan frontier. Rommel was not a man to sit and wait. Montgomery had been forced to draw breath while supplies caught up. To Rommel, inactivity by his tormentor must mean that another mighty effort to throw him out of Africa altogether was imminent. The Americans had come within striking distance south of the Mareth Line. Characteristically, Rommel pre-empted the strike. His supply line had been shortened as he pulled back westwards. His force had reached the numbers it had enjoyed at the time of Second Alamein. If he waited he would surely be attacked simultaneously from east and west. This was a classic situation for resorting to the strategists' interior lines theory and attacking one jaw of the enemy pincers before the other could snap at him. After he disposed of the first, he could use his entire resources against the second.

Early that February of 1943 Pilot Officer Peter Blomfield (later Squadron Leader, DSO, DFC) was posted to 239 (Kittyhawk) Wing at Castel Benito, with some twenty other pilots, mostly straight from operational training units. They were given the choice of squadron to join, provided, of course, that the squadron commander approved. The Australians naturally opted for 3 RAAF or 450 RAAF, Blomfield asked for 260, because it was a mixture of British, New Zealanders, Canadians, Rhodesians, South Africans "and any other good old nationalities that happened to crop up. It proved a good choice. Never was there a more good-natured, well-knit, friendly, easy-going gaggle. The ground crew were all RAF."

No 260 Squadron was commanded by Squadron Leader Osgood Villiers Hanbury, "known to all and sundry – even to his face – as 'Pedro'. Lean of jowl, sandy moustache, didn't suffer fools at all lightly, gave the impression of being as mad as the proverbial hatter on the ground; however, a cold, efficient leader and killer in the air. When I was asked to step into his trailer for acceptance/refusal, he glanced through my logbook, grunted something that mercifully didn't sound too disparaging and said, 'And how long d'you think you'll last, then?' All I could think of at the moment was a stuttering, 'Well, sir, at least as long as tomorrow morning, perhaps.' I was in. 'O.K.,' he said, 'come on and have a drink, there's only bloody awful Iti vermouth!' I flew as his Number Two for the next two months: what I learned in that short time probably enabled me to stay alive in spite of all the Me109s could do and to remember for always his oft-repeated adage 'He who fights and runs away lives to fight another day: the fool who stays and takes a chance gets took home in the ambulance!' No wonder that we all loved him."

When the Eighth Army moved up "we were ordered to set up shop in a dust-bowl known as Neffatia: the 'A' party left at crack of dawn to ensure that the aircraft detailed for that morning's show would find fuel, ammunition and perhaps tea ready for them on the new advanced landing ground. The 'B' party, bulk of the squadron personnel, reserve aircraft, M/T, everybody's kit etc. left the following day. There being a few more pilots than aircraft – for obvious reasons – some of us were transported in the 'tame' Heinkel 111 which had been donated to the squadron at Derna by the New Zealand sappers. Pedro's aircraft was unserviceable at the time, so he flew the He111 with all the gash pilots aboard: I recall Geoff Fallows (NZ flight commander), George 'Muscles' Tuck (a Yank from Detroit), Oscar Stohr, a Rhodesian Sergeant who was to be killed a week later when his engine cut on take-off. The flight, a mere 15 miles, was fraught: a sandstorm blew up in the sudden way they do: visibility marginal, port engine coughing occasionally, no option but to put it down somewhere. Pedro found a gap in the gloom and put the Heinkel down on another of the forward airstrips. Never had the time-honoured phrase then in vogue, 'Semper in excretum', been more applicable."

The Heinkel, which of course had British markings, was used to fetch Stella beer from Cairo in its long-range tanks. "The tanks had not as yet been used for fuel. It might have improved the taste of the beer if they had!"

While at Castel Benito, 'Nick' Nichol, a Canadian — "our tame scrounger par excellence" — found an Italian wine depot where there were some large vats of Chianti. "Out came the 60-gallon long-range tanks again. Nick filled five and brought them home. Shortly after this the Army closed the depot to the RAF. Rumour had it that in the very vat from which Nick had syphoned his haul was found the body of a New Zealand sapper. He was reported as being deep mauve and beautifully preserved! The only too obvious jest about the wine having plenty of body went the rounds."

All light-hearted enough, and typical of the wry flippancy that the R.A.F., with its Commonwealth sister Services, has always displayed, when the Germans are mawkish and more excitable nations become flatulent with bravado. But there was no break in operations against the enemy.

At Eisenhower's HQ and at General Anderson's 1st Army HQ it was expected that, if the Axis made an attack, it would be in the Fonduk area, 100 miles south of Tunis. On 14 February the assault came, but 40 miles south of Fonduk, when 10th Panzer Division roared through the Faid Pass to challenge the British First Army. At the same time, 70 miles further south, at Gafsa, another wing of the attack drove the Americans back. On the 17th the two wings joined at Kasserine. The situation was dire. Rommel's thrust seemed set to slash through the central Tunisian mountains, veer north and take the Allies in the rear.

Confusion spread during four days and nights, forcing 12th Air Force to abandon its forward airfields. With thick cloud over the operational area, 242 Group could make only one attack, but from 18 February Nos 13, 18, 114 and 614 Squadrons, flying Blenheim Vs — known as Bisleys — from Algerian bases, bombed every night, although the weather prevented accuracy. The new command system showed its worth. Coningham put the fighters of 242 Group and 12th Air Command on to offensive patrols — emulating the WDAF — instead of defensive sorties for the Army's protection. Spaatz placed most of his strategic bombers at Coningham's disposal. These moves greatly increased the effectiveness of the Anglo-American air force during this crisis. On 23 February the enemy began retiring to the coast. While the Allied air forces based in Tunisia bedevilled the retreating Axis troops, WDAF was wrecking Luftwaffe and Regia Aeronautica aerodromes near Mareth, El Hamma and Gabes, and blasting vehicle convoys and supply dumps behind the Mareth Line, all in preparation for Eighth Army's next offensive.

On 24 February Rommel was appointed to command Army Group Africa, which included von Arnim's Fifth Panzer Army and the First Italian Army of *Generale* Messe. Two days later elements of two of von Arnim's Panzer divisions put in an unsuccessful attack against British positions at Medjez el Bab. On 6 March Rommel had one last fling by mounting a massive assault near Medenine. Montgomery, fortified, as he always insisted on being, by photographic reconnaissance, was ready and the German attack failed. Throughout, 242 Group's strafing had played a great part in the enemy's failures to carry his objectives.

On the brink of being absorbed into Desert Air Force, 232 Squadron was heavily embroiled in the air fighting over Algeria and Tunisia. The Goldfish Club was not a body that aircrew deliberately sought to join: it was open only to those who had been forced to put their aircraft down in the sea. On 25 February Flight Sergeant Joseph Ekbery suddenly qualified willy-nilly in the customary unpleasant fashion. In action against Me109s, he found two of them on his tail, "one of which shot a hole through my starboard wing near the root. As my oil pressure was dropping alarmingly, I pulled into a dive, levelling out after dropping 5,000 ft. At this point I saw Red 2 shoot up an Me109 and break off combat when attacked from astern. When last seen, the e/a attacked by Red 2 was spinning down from 12,000 ft." He then made for land, "but was forced to ditch my aircraft 30 yards off shore".

In the context of current events this was trivial, but, to a young NCO pilot, no less important than the vicissitudes that beset a General officer on either side. Although the German Commander-in-Chief realized already that the Allies would soon defeat the Axis in Tunisia, he was no Tweedledum. "Let's fight till six, and then have dinner," was not his way, as 92 Squadron were well aware. Their Operational Record book shows the evidence: "1st March, 1943. We shall remember this day for a long time, although there was only one operational trip for us. Five aircraft were scrambled for a local interception patrol of the Hazbub area in the morning and were vectored onto 3 Macchi 202s, F/L Duke DFC and bar, shot down 2 of them, thus being able to avoid having the 13th score appearing on his aircraft. At 5 pm the enemy started to shell the L.G. from the hills S.W. of us and it wasn't long before he was able to get the range of the runways and dispersals. An order was received for all pilots to sit in the cockpit of their aircraft and in this we were fortunate in having 6 aircraft at standby and another 6 at readiness. Just after 6 pm, when the sun was going down, all aircraft were told to take off for L.Gs east of us. What a sight it was! Aircraft from three squadrons taking off from two runways missed each other by inches.

"Shelling was a very large gun on bearing 270 (probably a 17mm). Lasted 1725-1830. One airman killed, five injured. Shelling continued during the night, shortest interval between shells 40 seconds."

Next day, twenty-one Kittyhawks of 2 SAAF and 5 SAAF Squadrons, eighteen of them carrying bombs, attacked the gun position. They dropped eleven 250- and seven 500-pounders. There was no more gunfire from there. And J. S. Ekbery was in a predicament once more during a diversionary sweep near Bizerta to distract attention from USAAF Flying Fortresses bombing a convoy. "I saw a FW190 cross my path, but out of range. I turned to follow him, and while doing so, saw another FW190 below me and to my left. I chose this aircraft for my attack and as I dived he obviously spotted me as he turned his nose up to meet me. We both opened fire at the same time and I estimate that we were not more than 25 yards apart before he broke away. I saw strikes on his wings and turned to follow him, but he was spinning and had dropped some 4,000 ft, passing into cloud before I could press home my attack. He was still spinning when I last saw him. During this combat my windscreen was hit by a cannon shell and after I landed, it was found that my propeller had also been hit. I saw another e/a which I attempted to follow, but the squadron was now going home, and my visibility being considerably impaired, I returned to base in cloud. I claim 1 FW190 as probably destroyed."

Rommel, whose health had been poor for months, left on 9 March for sick leave in Germany. In northern Tunisia, General von Arnim took over, and, in the south, Generale Messe.

An Allied offensive was being planned, to converge on the Axis forces from east and west, unite the British Eighth and First Armies and cut off Messe's First Italian Army. On 20 March Montgomery attacked the 20-mile-long Mareth Line, whose southern flank rested on the Matmata Hills, beyond which lay the desert. General Patton's attempt to cut the coast road, as an aid to Eighth Army, did not succeed. Eighth Army, having gone round the southern flank of the Mareth Line, was squeezing the Axis forces into a rapidly contracting area, while Patton engaged them in the north. By 14 April the enemy was established in his last defensive positions, a ring of hills around Bizerta and Tunis.

Blomfield takes up his story: "On the occasion of the briefing for all the 239 Wing pilots, by none other than the AOC, Harry Broadhurst, to outline the part the RAF fighter-bombers were to play in support of the Eighth Army's left hook at El Hamma to outflank the Mareth line, we were told in no uncertain manner that we were expendable!

We were to be the Army's mobile artillery and casualties were expected to be high. The actual operation has been written up many times as the first and classic example of close support on a maximum scale. We were lucky: the Gremlins stayed home, the flak, though certainly intense, did not have the luck. The Army got through with comparatively light losses; our losses were negligible."

By night on 20 March Eighth Army attacked the Mareth Line. By 27 March Montgomery was able to send a congratulatory signal to Broadhurst that read: "I would like to convey to you my great appreciation of the superb support to the land battle that has been given by the Air Force under your command yesterday and in fact every day since the battle began. Such intimate and close support has never to my knowledge been achieved before and it has been an inspiration to all the troops. The results have been first class. I sincerely trust you have not suffered many losses. Please convey to the Commanders and all the pilots the grateful thanks of myself and the whole Army for their truly magnificent efforts."

This Broadhurst circulated to all ranks with his own added encomium: "From AOC. The following signal has been sent to me by General Montgomery as a result of the operations undertaken on the afternoon of 26 March. It is unnecessary for me to say how proud I am of the magnificent effort which was made by all units on that particular operation. There is no doubt that it was a major contribution to the success of the Army in their attack on the Mareth positions and I would like Commanders to convey to all their pilots my appreciation of their efforts, also the substance of General Montgomery's signal."

The Battle of El Hamma was just one more hard fight in the non-stop advance of the Allied Air Forces and Armies to both east and west of the final objective, Tunis.

The Northwest African Air Forces had sunk so many ships trying to reach Bizerta and Tunis that the Luftwaffe had been forced to try to supply the beleaguered Axis forces by air. During the first week of April the Germans flew 150 sorties a day on this task. On 5 April the Allies shot down twenty-seven transport aircraft and destroyed thirty-nine on the ground. On 10 April twenty four Ju52s and fourteen escorting fighters were sent down.

Pilot Officer Maurice Smyth's logbook entry for the night of 15 April is: "Anti-shipping strike. Shot down one Ju52 into sea". He amplifies it verbally: "Everybody knew that they were being supplied at night. We'd done our best to intrude on them and stop them. This night, myself and, I think, Sergeant Beard, went out at dusk and, a fighter pilot's dream, I saw six Ju52s in loose formation at about a thousand feet. Of course both of us had a go at them. Four 20mm cannon against a Ju52 was distinctly unkind and the first one just burst into flames and, like a burning torch, went into the ground. I did a corkscrew turn and was just curving in behind another when a whole belt of green tracer came past above me — I'd started hitting him by this time — and I took quick evasive action. It was a Ju88 with four cannon just above the cockpit. By the time I'd got rid of that bird everything else had vanished except for a couple of aircraft burning on the sea. When I reported this, I was told that Ju88s didn't carry four cannon above the cockpit. I learned only the other day, 47 years later, that they did at that time; so I was right."

On 18 April RAF Spitfires and USAAF Warhawks intercepted an estimated one hundred Ju52s near Cap Bon, of which fifty-two were claimed to have been shot down, for the loss of seven Allied fighters, in what became known as the Palm Sunday Massacre.

With the shrinking number of enemy aircraft in Tunisia, WDAF disported itself boisterously over inshore waters to the detriment of Axis shipping and, it appeared, of Royal Naval property. In order to polish their marksmanship, fighter pilots took to using buoys as practice targets. During April they had sunk eleven enemy vessels. If their aim improved, their tally of buoys threatened to exceed that respectable total, to the consternation of the nautics. Three RNVR lieutenants accordingly wrote jointly to the Mess Secretary No 244 Wing — betraying ignorance of the functions of the incumbent of such an RAF office — in admonition: "It has been observed by various individuals of unimpeachable character that Spitfires are making use of valuable dan buoys as targets.

"These dans, which mark the way through a minefield, have been laid at enormous expense and with great skill and daring in order to safeguard the shipping bringing you your bully, biscuits, pickles and booze (R) booze. Should the unlikely event occur of one of these buoys being sunk or damaged by your planes, no booze will be forthcoming. Calamity!!!!

"For a fee we could lay a very large-sized beacon for you to practise on and perhaps hit.

"Should this pernicious habit of buoy-strafing not cease, no further pennies will be contributed to buy you new Spitfires."

For the rest of April and into May the erosion of the enemy's tenure wore on. On 7 May Tunis fell to the British and Bizerta to the Americans, whereupon the German and Italian remnants tried to fall back on the coast at the Cap Bon peninsula. That day also saw the departure of all enemy fighters from North Africa. The only air support left to the

Axis was by bombers based in Sicily and Sardinia; and they made few sorties.

On 10 May, Maurice Smyth relates, "it was reported that a tough German battalion was holding out at Kilibia aerodrome, so 73 Squadron were given pamphlets to drop "urging them to give themselves up", which of course was hopeless. Having done this, I was banking round. I didn't see any tracer but a shot came through the side of the aircraft and burst on the instrument panel. The whole damn thing blew up and I got cut on my wrist and forehead and some splinters in my legs as well. I was a bit annoyed about this so I went down and strafed them. I thought, well, trying to be kind to the gentlemen, asking them to give up, and they shoot at you. I had to go to the hospital but I pulled out when I saw the terrible state of some of the injured soldiers and I felt ashamed of myself, I was getting bits and pieces out of my legs for years afterwards."

On 12 May General von Arnim surrendered the forces under his command. In the hope of inciting Messe to fight on with ardour, Mussolini promoted him to Field-Marshal, but on the following day he too gave in.

Tedder's Order of the Day summarized the indispensable contribution by Western Desert Air Force and the other air formations to victory in the campaign.

"By magnificent team work between nationalities, commands, units, officers and men from Teheran to Takoradi, from Morocco to the Indian Ocean, you have, together with your comrades on land and sea, thrown the enemy out of Africa. You have shown the world the unity and strength of air power. A grand job, well finished. We face our next job with the knowledge that we have thrashed the enemy, and the determination to thrash him again."

Ahead lay the conquest of Sicily and Italy. The title Desert Air Force came officially into being, a battle honour that the successors of Collishaw's small command were to bear to the end of the war, although the desert was behind them. Ahead lay strongly and bravely defended mountain peaks, deep valleys and broad rivers that the armies would have to climb and cross under an inexorable weight of fire, preceded, covered and backed up by aircraft constantly under the hammer of flak and the onslaught of fighters. It was like peering into the crater of a momentarily quiet volcano that everyone knew must soon erupt.

CHAPTER 9

Sicily Falls

Mixed with the feeling of triumph, and relief at a temporary respite from battle, was a touch of nostalgia, a word whose current usage usually denotes a yearning for the past, whereas its root meaning is homesickness. Those who had spent many months, perhaps two or three years, in the desert, did know a curious and unexpected sense of deprivation that was a kind of homesickness. They had made themselves at home in the wilderness. They had taken pride in making the best of a meagre supply of creature comforts. They had put up with the vicissitudes of a harsh climate whose sandstorms could blind and choke them, the scorching sun could stun them, the chilly nights could set their teeth chattering. They had been always exposed to the malevolence of the enemy, whichever Service they were in and whether they flew aeroplanes or serviced them. For the time being there was nothing to give them the satisfaction of knowing that they were being tested to the utmost and proving themselves able to overcome the worst of hardship and danger.

Eighth Army and Desert Air Force had their own special touch of panache, their distinctive slight swagger. They were the true desert veterans, looking with a measure of patronage on their comparatively white-kneed comrades of First Army and its accompanying air component. Despite the close and friendly co-operation between the Services, the R.A.F. told the story of the Army officer who was so stupid that even his brother officers noticed it. The fighter and bomber squadrons' traditional mutual ragging found expression on one side by the scurrilous allegation that there was a bomber pilot who did not know the difference between arson and incest: he kept setting fire to his sister. The bomber boys' riposte has faded from memory.

There was time to snatch some leave. Throughout the campaign Lebanon and Palestine had been popular places for rest and recreation. The coolness and beauty of the mountains and Beirut's veneer of Gal-

- MILAN
- St. Angelo
- Reggio nell Emilia
- BOLCGNA
- Rimini
- FLORENCE
- Ancona
- Jesi
- Assisi

I T A L Y

ADRIATIC SEA

- Tusciano
- ROME
- Guidonia
- Anzio
- Cassino
- Campobasso
- Vasto
- R. Sangro
- R. Trigno
- Agnone
- Termoli
- Gargano Peninsula
- FOGGIA
- Marcianise
- NAPLES
- BARI
- Gioia
- Salerno
- Ava
- Battipaglia
- Monte Corvino
- BRINDISI
- TARANTO

TYRRHENIAN SEA

- Trapani
- Palermo
- Messina
- Str. Messina
- Reggio di Calabri
- SICILY
- Catania
- Gerbini
- Augusta
- Siracusa
- Comsi
- Cassible
- Pachino

Scale of Miles
20 0   40   80   120

136

lic sophistication from over 20 years as a French Mandated Territory gave Lebanon a special charm in contrast with the crowded and uncompromisingly Arabic culture and atmosphere of Cairo, cosmopolitan though that city was. In Palestine there were other alluring features, apart from sight-seeing in the Holy Land. On Mount Carmel was an internment camp where ladies of enemy nationality were confined. Their liberty was not totally restricted, however. Allied officers were permitted to book them out for an evening's entertainment, usually dinner and dancing in the night club higher up the slope. It was taken for granted that the escort would receive a suitable expression of thanks from his partner. Those officers-and-gentlemen whose exposed portions of lumbar anatomy were pock-marked by vicious bites from the local insects by the end of the al fresco proceedings forebore from complaining.

On 19 May a victory parade and flypast at Tunis marked the end of a phase. For the time being the fighters' operational tasks would be convoy patrols, escorting bombers on daylight raids, sweeps over Sicily, and night intrusion; for the bombers, day and night attacks on Sicily and Italy.

The Joint Planners of the coming invasions were confident that the campaign in prospect would be less difficult than the one just concluded. "In Italy," they predicted, "the Army and the population will be sick of the war and only anxious to get back to normal conditions. They will generally be favourably disposed to us and bitterly resentful towards any Germans who may remain in the country."

To that a realistic American might have responded, "Oh yeah?" and a cynical Briton, "And pigs will fly." The Italians were not genuinely favourable towards anyone but themselves, and they hated their own Fascist officials more murderously than they hated Germans, who, after all, had integrated themselves with the natives by contributing vigorously to an increase in the population to compensate for Italian lives lost in action during the past three years.

The first landings on European soil were made with the capture of four small islands, on two of which Italian aircraft were based. Pantelleria, a mass of volcanic rock, 10 miles long and 4 wide, lay half-way between Cap Bon and Sicily. Underground it had workshops, living quarters, and a hangar 1,100 ft long. The Allies mistakenly thought it as impregnable as Gibraltar, so dropped over 6,000 tons of bombs there in five weeks. It was seized on 11 June. No 225 (Tactical Reconnaissance) Squadron, based on Cap Bon, flew constant sorties in their Hurricanes over the island, looking for the white cross of surrender on the airfield. As soon as it was seen, the pilot photographed it and returned to base. Fifteen minutes after he landed a print was delivered to the Army. On the 13th Lampedusa — which also boasted an airstrip — half the size of Pantelleria and 90 miles south, midway between Tunisia and Malta, was taken. So was Linosa, about 4 square miles in area, 35 miles to its north. On the 14th Lampione, another mere speck of land, 15 miles west of Lampedusa, was captured. All gave in without putting up any resistance.

Malta was the place to be nowadays. Largely in ruins after nearly three years' battering by enemy bombs, it was more than a British possession, it was a piece of Europe and had been the base of the Mediterranean Fleet for over a century. Its people were lively. Privation, bombardment, death and injury had not quelled their hot-blooded ebullience. It was the nearest point from which fighters could reach southern Sicily. DAF squadrons were tightly packed on its airfields. Soon there were 600 aircraft on the island. There were also scores of military nurses and hundreds of young civilian women. Every night saw parties and dances, each day those off duty made their way to the beaches to picnic and swim with girlfriends.

One pilot, whom no one had ever suspected of hankering after a clerical career or converting the heathen in the far corners of the earth, was, nonetheless, practising the missionary position one night with a co-operative nursing sister in a secluded cove, when he himself received a sharp prick — but in his bare buttock with a bayonet. A voice said, "Trespassing on out-of-bounds military property." The pilot couldn't deny that he was, in a manner of speaking. "Show me your identity card." He had to find his clothes first. The sentry was satisfied. "Have a good time, Sir . . . Miss."

At least one officer of Air rank did not have to depend on such passing favours. There was an English lady on Malta — attractive enough, but with legs that were six inches too short for her trunk — who was married to a lieutenant-commander. He, in a drunken brawl a couple of years before the war, had accidentally killed a brother naval officer. Court-martialled and sentenced to a few years in prison, he was escorted to England. His wife remained behind and, when the war began, became a Civilian Code and Cypher Officer. She was now hostess at this very senior officer's residence and his mistress. She accompanied him to Algiers when he was posted there and, later, to Italy: fulfilling throughout the three functions of "cypherine", official hostess and what Herrick called "a fine distraction".

In the intervals of enjoying the varied amenities of Malta, the day fighter pilots led a strenuous life in the air. The Spitfires flew daily over Sicily, escorting bombers and fighting off attacks by Messerschmitts,

Fiats and Macchis. Before leaving North Africa Pilot Officer Joseph Ekbery had destroyed a Me109 on 26 April. No 232 Squadron was now flying both Mk V and Mk IX Spitfires, and on 6 July he submitted the following Combat Report after an operation on which he flew a Mk IX. The Squadron had been on patrol to cover Liberators over Gerbini when "109s were reported and engaged by the Vs. During this engagement one 109 was seen climbing ahead, below Knockout Yellow section in which I was flying. Asking the remainder of the section to watch my tail, I dived on the aircraft, which half-rolled and dived. I started from 23,000 ft. The 109 pulled out of the dive and opened up during which time I closed range to 100 yds and gave him a long burst of four seconds with all guns. I saw strikes and the enemy aircraft flopped over to the left. His Glycol system burst and his starboard undercarriage dropped whilst making a tight orbit to ensure my own safety. I saw the 109 hit the deck and burst into flames. I came home by myself at zero feet."

Wing Commander "Cocky" Dundas had joined 324 Wing as Wing Commander Flying, leader of five Spitfire squadrons, 43, 72, 93, 111 and 243. Despite his decorations, record of air fighting from the Battle of Britain onwards, and manifest qualities of dash and courage, his situation as a newcomer was conformable with anyone's who arrived to take charge of seasoned pilots to whom he was a stranger. It took a life-or-death situation to give a commander the chance to prove himself, and these were not slow in occurring.

His came one morning when the wing had been on a sweep over southern Sicily and were, he describes, "heavily engaged by a large force of Me109s and had a long hard fight, in the course of which the wing was broken up into small formations". While he and his No 2 were returning to Malta they were set upon again and the latter's aircraft was damaged. Its cooling system had been punctured, it was emitting smoke and the pilot reported that his engine temperature was rising. They were at 16,000 ft, had crossed the Sicilian coast and Dundas thought there was a good chance of his No 2 making it to base. He throttled back and told him to follow closely.

They were half way home when Squadron Leader George Hill, "a rough, tough Canadian", commanding 111 Squadron, called on the R/T to say he was circling a dinghy with a man in it, gave his position and "asked for company". Dundas had only 15 gallons of petrol left. Hill said he had 25, but "some 109s had put in an appearance". By this time Malta was in sight. Dundas alerted Air Sea Rescue, then told his No 2 to carry on, but bale out if his temperature rose above 125 degrees. He then turned away to find Hill, around whom six 109s were circling and attacking in turns. Two minutes later he radioed to Hill "that I was now among those present", and "charged in and through the circle of Messerschmitts, taking a couple of snap shots as I went." Hill joined him in attacking the startled Germans, who quickly made off. Both were dangerously short of petrol, so steered towards Malta at minimum revolutions. They just managed to reach the airfield and by the time Dundas taxied to dispersals his tank had run dry.

Relieved for a while of the devouring excitement and crush of dread that had filled their days in North Africa, DAF's squadrons were refreshed and ready for Operation Husky, the invasion of Sicily. The date chosen was 10 July: the moon would be in its second quarter, giving enough light until midnight for an assault by paratroops and gliderborne infantry, and dark enough after the moon had set to allow the seaborne force to go in.

This was the largest-scale invasion ever attempted to date. At 4 am, on a 40-miles front at the south-east corner of Sicily, 250,000 British and Commonwealth troops went ashore from landing craft. Forty miles to their left, along a 40-mile stretch of the south coast, 228,000 Americans attacked simultaneously. Unpredicted strong winds blew the British and American glider-towing aircraft far off course. Of 137 gliders released, sixty-nine descended into rough sea, fifty-six came down widespread along the coast and a mere twelve in the ordained landing zone. Out of some 3,000 paratroops, only 250 dropped in their proper dropping zone. But the rest of the operation, in General Alexander's words, "went according to plan".

In the air the Allies were so much stronger than the enemy and their fighter patrols so effective that, in the fleet of 2,500 naval vessels of every sort, including landing craft, only twelve were sunk by bombs. From first light the sky over the beaches swarmed with aircraft. The brilliant reflected sunlight on their wings and the graceful paths they traced as they soared and dived and banked, the multicoloured tracer from their guns, presented spellbinding visual images among the barbaric noise of bombs and artillery fire, the rolling smoke from tons of high explosive.

For the invasion of Algeria, the R.A.F. had formed Servicing Commando Units, which went ashore in the second wave of the assault. One of these, No 3201, with 244 Wing H.Q. personnel and an R.A.F. Regiment anti-aircraft squadron, was set ashore by a tank landing craft on D-Day morning. In the evening a mobile radar ground-controlled interception unit hit the beach. The following morning the servicing commando was at work on Pachino airfield, with a detachment of Royal Engineers, restoring the surface of the runway that the departing enemy had ploughed up. Flying Officer D. N. Keith, a Canadian in 72 Squadron, who had just shot down a Macchi 200 and a Ju88, forced-landed in their midst, short of petrol. The S.C.U. refuelled his aircraft and pushed it to the nearby straight stretch of road, from which he took off.

On the 12th the rest of 244 Wing embarked at Malta and Air Vice Marshal Broadhurst set his Spitfire's wheels down on Pachino's new runway laid with pierced steel planking, to check progress. Next day Broadhurst and 244 Wing's aircraft landed at Pachino. Life was once again as makeshift as in the desert, sleeping and messing in tents, but not quite as spartan. Sometimes the mess was a large tarpaulin stretched between trees. Always, wine was available and tomatoes, melons and lemons were there for the picking.

On the 16th Ekbery made another claim. He was flying Yellow Three in a Spit IX, as top cover to other aircraft over the invasion area, when enemy aircraft were reported dead ahead. "The squadron climbed to engage, Yellow Section reaching the same level as the bandits which were recognized as 109s. Having driven off two attacks by sections of four e/a on the Spit Vs below, I followed the third section down. Choosing the most backward of the four 109s, I climbed to attack and fought for several minutes during which I fired short bursts with slight deflection. No strikes were seen until about the fifth burst, which hit his engine and wing. Glycol poured from the engine and the wingtip blew off. The 109 went straight down into the deck and burst into flames, the position of the crash being just east of Etna, the fight having started south-east of Catania. The bandits which had rejoined the fight cleared off and I was able to return to the squadron."

Flying Officer Keith, since making a forced landing on the unfinished Pachino strip, had sent down a Ju88 and a Me109, which brought his score to eight and a half and earned him a DFC. On the 18th he was hit by flak, baled out, hit the tail of his aircraft and was killed.

A few days later 244 Wing moved to Cassibile and 239 Wing replaced it at Pachino. Peter "Blom" Blomfield found that Pachino was ". . . sacrilege: they carved it out of a vineyard! The weather was hot, the devil thirst was upon us; there were dusty grapes in abundance. We partook copiously. No one told us that the season for picking was still some weeks away. The following day Montezuma had no small degree of vengeance: most of the wing were relieved in both senses."

A drastic change in take-off and landing procedure affected all the squadrons as soon as they began to operate from Sicily. In the desert's ample space they had been able to take off six or more at a time in staggered echelon, to avoid sand blown back by each aeroplane enveloping the ones behind. Using a PSP runway only 75 ft wide, they had to take off and land one at a time, which, when two or three squadrons operated together, made for much crowding in the circuit and torment for the air traffic controller.

No 239 Wing moved to Agnone, on the Catania plain, an airstrip built on reclaimed marsh, where "the mosquitoes could not be counted in any cubic foot of air space. Anyone outside his net after 7 pm could have been lifted and carried away." They soon shifted to high ground, which was not good news for one of "Nick" Nichol's "finds" that had travelled with 260 Squadron since they were on a landing ground near Sirte, and been smuggled first into Malta and then Sicily. From an old Italian settler in North Africa, he had acquired a piglet: "a small, black and white cuddly lump", says Blomfield. "It moved with us, fed well on bits from everyone's meals, liked the odd draught of vermouth or Chianti . . . and flourished . . . and grew." The sow's existence came to the notice of higher authority. "Word got around and the powers that be said a definite 'No' to any further progress to the Italian mainland." Pathos enters the tale. "She had grown into a large and not at all cuddly lump, but was everyone's friend. There was a lot of pork there! Nick had obviously to undertake the task of her demise. I shall never forget the look on his face as he led her away to a quiet corner of the camp with .38 Smith & Wesson in hand. The cooks did a splendid job, though."

On the ground, although the Germans were fighting with their usual stubbornness, the Italians showed little spirit. The inhabitants of mainland Italy and Sicily had always regarded each other as separate nations. The majority of the troops in the present defence were from the mainland and saw no reason to sacrifice themselves. Those who were Sicilian-born had an over-riding wish to shorten the fighting and limit the destruction of their farms, their homes and their towns.

The objective was to reach Messina, on the north-eastern tip of the island. Montgomery's Eighth Army was working its way there around the east coast and across the centre at its widest part. Patton's U.S. Seventh Army, also making a pincer movement, followed the west coast while some of its elements drove across in the centre. It was a race in which egotism, ruffled feelings, national pride, and the rivalry and dislike between two fractious generals of widely different character created an over-stimulated competitiveness.

Montgomery, classically educated, religious — although this did not temper his conceit or the sin of pride — constrained, austere except in his bonhomous manner with the rank and file, was the British public's great conquering hero and the object of worldwide admiration. His first consideration, that his men must suffer as few casualties as possible, made him cautious and, in comparison with other commanders, a trifle slow. He would not move until satisfied that his force was thoroughly trained for its task, that he had the necessary strength in troops, armour, artillery and equipment to avoid defeat, and all the information about the enemy that aerial reconnaissance could provide. He also, like everyone in the Eighth Army and Desert Air Force, felt superior to the generals, their armies and their air forces, who had fought the short campaign from the Torch landings to Tunis. In his dealings with Allied generals he was monumentally tactless.

Patton's immaturity was betrayed by the ostentatious display of two pearl-handled pistols on his belt, as though he pictured himself as the star in a Western film. The profanity with which he often expressed himself revealed a paucity of education. His slapping the faces of two private soldiers who were in hospital for psychiatric treatment, because he suspected them of cowardice, were monstrous acts that laid bare two appalling facets of his character. He was hysterical and unable to control himself. And to hit subordinates, who would be court-martialled and harshly sentenced if they struck back, is the vilest, most shameful deed that an officer or N.C.O. can commit. For any able-bodied man to strike someone who is lying in bed is sheer depravity. Add to that Patton's dislike of all foreigners, not least the British, and his jealousy of Montgomery, and one has a compendium of such unwholesome qualities that his squandering of his men's lives comes as no surprise. Despite their disparities, he and Montgomery did have some common ground in conceit, pride and tactlessness.

The character and ability of a general are relevant to air operations, because finally it is the infantry who win any war. It is they alone who can gain and hold ground. Artillery, armour, engineers are all ancillary to the primitive and basic business of close-range rifle and machine-gun fire, the throwing of grenades and the bayonet charge with blade and rifle butt. An air force can prepare the way, soften the opposition, give close support by strafing while the assault is being made; but if the general is no good and his infantry cannot beat the enemy back and retain the ground they have taken, then airmen's lives are made all the more precarious and their efforts wasted.

While Montgomery and Patton regarded each other askance, the commanders of the various RAF and USAAF forces continued to co-operate in harmony and remained aloof from the unsavoury resentments and contentiousness of their ground-gripping equals.

A week after the landings the Allies were established on four Sicilian airfields and five others were being abandoned by the enemy air forces. Both the Luftwaffe and Regia Aeronautica had been reduced to virtual ineffectiveness. The Luftwaffe's main job was to deliver reinforcements, ammunition, spare tank parts and other necessities to the battle line. The havoc wrought by DAF's fighters among the enemy's transport aircraft in North Africa repeated itself. On 25 July, thirty-three Spitfires of 322 Wing bounced some thirty Ju52s escorted by four Me109s. Within ten minutes twenty-one Ju52s were shot down. All the first twelve to be destroyed were carrying petrol and exploded in flames when hit.

The cauldron of revolt was bubbling in Italy. On 24 July the Grand Council voted to depose Mussolini. On the following day King Vittorio Emmanuele dismissed him and brought *Maresciallo* (Field-Marshal) Pietro Badoglio out of retirement to replace him as Prime Minister. On the 26th the Fascist Party was dissolved, Badoglio formed a new Cabinet and proclaimed martial law. While secretly intending to make peace with the Allies, he publicly declared his continuing loyalty to Germany.

By the end of July, forty Allied squadrons were flying from twenty-one airfields in Sicily. But the German Army was still holding out in a landscape that was ideal for a protracted rearguard battle to cover withdrawal. The steep narrow valleys and the mountain slopes gave cover for infantry, field artillery and flak. For the attacking infantrymen, ambush and every other form of surprise lay constantly in wait. For fighter-bombers and bombers, strafing and bombing in the face of light and heavy flak and machine guns, spotting enemy positions was more difficult than it had been in North Africa.

On 15 August Badoglio sent an emissary, *Generale* Castellano, to see the British Ambassador in Madrid, Sir Samuel Hoare. He offered unconditional surrender when the Allies landed in Italy, provided that Italy could join them. The Allied High Command, seeing the prospect of a quick defeat of the Germans in Italy, made a hasty plan to take advantage of the Italians' willingness to transfer allegiance to them. The capture of Rome beckoned. Airborne troops would land at the capital's four nearest aerodromes without fear of flak, where Italian Army units would receive them. The Italian divisions in the area would ensure the safety of the members of the Italian Government concerned with the armistice. Allied squadrons would be flown in for the defence of Rome and to support the main invasion.

On 17 August the fighting in Sicily ended. The Axis had lost 32,000 men killed or wounded and 162,000 taken prisoner, with 1,850 aircraft destroyed or captured. The Allies lost 23,000 men killed, wounded and missing, and some 400 aircraft. But 40,000 German troops, 50 tanks and 100 guns, and 62,000 Italian troops had managed to cross the Straits of Messina to the mainland.

CHAPTER 10

Victory

Italy's offer of surrender had become the crucial issue in determining not only the immediate actions of the Allies but also the duration of the whole campaign. Negotiations with Badoglio had introduced an atmosphere that was both tense with possibilities and massively inert as Italian emissaries went back and forth between Rome and Madrid, Lisbon – where the meetings were first transferred – and, finally, Cassibile in Sicily. The surrender terms lay in the hands of the Allied Chiefs of Staff, represented by Eisenhower, Allied C-in-C, advised by Alexander, C-in-C of the Allied Armies, and Tedder, all three of whose H.Qs were still in Algiers. Badoglio was told that the time and place of the invasion would not be revealed. A few hours before the main force landed, Eisenhower and Badoglio would simultaneously broadcast announcements of the armistice. The latter would instruct his nation to cooperate with the Allies against Germany. The fleet was to sail to specified ports, the air force to fly to Allied airfields in Sicily, Libya and Cyprus, and Allied POWs were to be released.

Meanwhile Northwest African Air Force bombed airfields and railways, to try to isolate the German divisions in southern Italy and expel or destroy the remnants of the Luftwaffe.

At 4 o'clock on the morning of 3 September, 600 artillery pieces on the Sicilian shore of the Straits of Messina and 120 naval guns began to bombard the toe of Italy. At dawn, units of 13 Corps in Eighth Army landed near Reggio di Calabria, where they met little resistance. DAF patrolled over them throughout the day while they made their rapid advance. At 5.15 that afternoon a document agreeing armistice terms between Italy and the Allies was signed at Cassibile. Preparations started for the American 82nd Airborne Division, based at Kairouan, to make the planned drop on four airfields around Rome to coincide with the main landing, Operation Avalanche, which was to be made at Salerno at dawn on 9 September.

Eisenhower had laid down that the announcement of Italy's surrender must be made on 8 September. Before U.S. 82nd Airborne could take off on its mission, it was essential to be sure that the Italian Army would honour its commitment to prepare the airfields for the paratroops' arrival. Eisenhower sent Brigadier General Maxwell D. Taylor in a Royal Navy motor torpedo boat to Ustica, whence he was taken by the Italian Navy to Rome, to find out what Badoglio really intended to do, then signal accordingly on the radio link between Rome and Allied H.Q. By the time Taylor arrived in Rome on the 8th, the force bound for Salerno had put to sea and the British 1st Airborne Division was waiting at Bizerta to set sail for Taranto.

Half an hour before the U.S. 82nd Airborne was due to set out, Eisenhower, Alexander, Tedder and Coningham, who had got together at Bizerta, received a signal from Taylor to say that the Rome operation should not be attempted. A message also arrived from Badoglio, confirming that the strength of the Germans in the area precluded the planned airborne assault. The 82nd's mission was cancelled at the last moment and it was too late to give them an alternative task. Eisenhower replied to Badoglio: "I intend to broadcast the existence of an armistice at the hour originally planned." At 6.30 pm he did so. At 7.45 pm Badoglio reluctantly made a similar announcement, then, with members of the Cabinet and the King, bolted for Brindisi. The Germans gave the Italians no chance to turn on them: they instantly disarmed any who had not laid down their arms voluntarily. The invasion forces received the news of Italy's capitulation with joy and the misplaced expectation of a weakened resistance to the landings.

Aerial reconnaissance had given Kesselring, the German C-in-C in Italy, warning that invasion was imminent. But rumour among the troops attributed the fanatical defence they encountered at Salerno to a more fanciful cause. The popular story was that as ships were leaving Oran, a Chinese merchant seaman was heard to shout across to a compatriot friend in another vessel, "See you at Salerno". "Apocryphal" is the verdict that suggests itself. It seems unlikely that two Chinese would have communicated in English or that a listening Axis spy of any nationality would have understood Chinese.

At 3.45 am on 9 September, 1943, the Anglo-American 5th Army stormed ashore, commanded by the American General Mark Clark, whom Field-Marshal Sir Alan Brooke, Churchill and Eisenhower held in the highest esteem. Kesselring had correctly worked out the most likely place for an invasion, and had positioned his defences accordingly. News of the Italian surrender had done more than raise the morale of the assault force, it had induced a false optimism. Any expectations of something akin to a crowd scene from an opera, with a horde of ecstatic peasantry celebrating release from the tyranny of dictatorship by assembling on the beaches to welcome the invaders, withered when the Allies were met by a tempest of accurate artillery and machine-gun fire.

The Salerno plain and its immediate hinterland were ideal terrain to defend. Beyond the orchards, fields, olive groves, vineyards and clumps of oak, the hills, fissured and clad with undergrowth, rose to 1,000 ft. For the attackers, there was always the discouraging knowledge of being under constant observation from high ground. Matthew Arnold's lines written a century earlier seemed prophetic: "And we are here as on a darkling plain / Swept with confused alarms of struggle and flight . . .", except that no one fled, for both sides were tenacious of the ground they held.

Another invasion fleet had sailed from North Africa. Bound for Taranto, on the inside of Italy's heel, it bore the British 1st Airborne Division, for whom there were not enough transport aircraft available to permit an aerial assault. This force also landed at dawn on 9 September and, like 13th Corps at Reggio on the 3rd — which by now had advanced nearly 75 miles — was unopposed.

One of the highest priority objectives of the Salerno force was to capture the only airfield in the area, Monte Corvino, near the small town of Battipaglia. For the time being air cover had to come from afar. The first friendly fighters to appear were twelve USAAF Mustangs to give low cover as the attack went in, while twenty-four USAAF P38 Lightnings and eight Fleet Air Arm Seafires from a carrier flew medium and high cover respectively. Carrier-borne Seafires kept up their patrols from dawn to 8.30 am and from 6.30 pm to dusk. In the interval, Spitfires from Sicily replaced them. These had to fly at least 175 miles to the battlefield, which meant using long-range drop-tanks and staying only 25 minutes on patrol. At night Beaufighters defended the beachhead. The intention was to establish two PSP airstrips there within 48 hours. The Royal Engineers had these ready in time, but the enemy was still within rifleshot, so they could not be used.

Mobile G.C.I. units and No 1 Mobile Operations Room Unit went ashore on the heels of the first troops to storm from their landing craft. According to No 1 MORU's Form 540, or Operations Record Book, "It was fortunate that the news coincided with a NAAFI issue of gin and whisky, the first for some weeks, as well as the purchase in the morning of 94 litres of vino bianco. It was accordingly possible to celebrate the news in due form and with proper ceremony."

Among the American pursuit (fighter) squadrons patrolling the battle zone was the first all-black outfit, the 99th (P40 Warhawks), whose unorthodox R/T procedure and wit were a joy to the R.A.F. One typical exchange recorded in the R/T logbooks occurred when the 99th flew into 88mm flak for the first time and, with good sense, took immediate evasive action that scattered them. Major Davis, their C.O. – a West Point graduate – called them back into formation, but one had a problem: "Say, Boss," he radioed, "this is yo' Red Fo'. Mah engine's runnin' real rough. Figure I'll RTB." (Return to base.)

The Major's reply was blunt. "Red Fo', this is yo' boss. You-all's jes' as shit scared as the rest of us, yo' get yo' ass back in fo'mation pronto."

Presently another voice called: "Say, Boss, this Blue One heah, One bandit, three-o'clock, low."

Plaintively, the alleged enemy contradicted him: "Hey, you guys, I ain't no bandit, I'se jes' lost."

Also heard on the radio was the running commentary from another of the squadron when he saw flak hit his wing man: "Hey, see that niggah burn . . . see that niggah jump . . ." And, as the unfortunate whose aeroplane was on fire didn't get around to pulling his ripcord until he had tumbled a couple of thousand feet, accelerating towards terminal velocity, "Man, see that niggah go!"

There were not many bandits (code word for enemy aircraft) about. The Luftwaffe put up some forty FW190s, of which the odd one would dart down at high speed to strafe now and again, but few penetrated the screen of Spitfires, Seafires, Mustangs, P38s and P40s. The worst destruction was wrought by Do17s carrying a new type of weapon beneath their wings: radio-controlled glider bombs. Two of these hit a battleship, H.M.S. *Warspite*, and put her out of action for six months. One hit an American battle cruiser, USS *Savannah*, and damaged her almost as badly. Another sank the Italian battleship *Roma*, when the Luftwaffe attacked some of the Italian warships that were on their way to be handed over to the Allies.

The Regia Aeronautica's contribution to Allied air strength was negligible. Most Italian aircrew ignored the order to surrender, as the table below shows. Those single-engine pilots who obeyed it did so with typically meretricious flamboyance by performing aerobatics over their destinations.

By the 12th there was still no airfield in use at the beachhead. In the interests of the Army's morale, as well as its protection, a more conspicuous air force presence was sought. Under Coningham's flexible, close-knit style of command, inherited from Collishaw, the fighter units of his Tactical Air Force were interchangeable, and he had put 322

First-Line Aircraft	Strength	Serviceability	Surrendered
Bombers	188	40%	30
Torpedo Bombers	57	23%	35
Dive Bombers	100	?	8
Ground Attack	36	70%	21
Fighters	535	50%	105
Army Co-op	228	?	16
Coastal	242	?	47
Transport	250	?	51
Total	*1,636*		*313*
Second-Line			
Stored Reserves	350		
Advanced OTU	250		
Old/Obsolescent	850		16
Total	*1,450*		*16*

and 324 Wings temporarily under the operational — but not administrative — control of 12th Air Support Command. The latter's commander was a redoubtable little man, Brigadier General "Shorty" Hawkins. Cigar-chewing, his facial skin like saddle leather and his voice as dulcet as chunks of rock being ground in a concrete mixer, he was the prototypical comic strip or B movie character of his rank and vocation. It was No 324 Wing, he decided, that must move to one of the two waiting landing grounds, Tusciano. This was hard by the ruins of the Greek city of Paestum, of which the visible remains were the Temple of Neptune that had stood there since 420 BC. At sunset every night the ancient marble glowed with golden and roseate beauty. But there was nothing lovely, romantic or holy about its surroundings just now.

The Germans were counter-attacking. The din of artillery, naval guns, tanks, small arms and the fighter-bombers' 500-pounders resounded among the craggy heights. Smoke from high explosive, burning buildings, undergrowth and trees mingled with the dust that shell-bursts hurled up from the plain. The runway, a mile inland beside the road and parallel with the beach, was well within range of the enemy gunners. Group Captain G. K. Gilroy, DSO, DFC — a pre-war Auxiliary, known as "Sheep" because he had been a sheep farmer — commanding the wing and Wing Commander Dundas, DFC, Wing Leader, pointed out that shelling would probably destroy and damage many aircraft. Hawkins was willing to run the risk.

No 93 Squadron, led by Squadron Leader K. Macdonald, was ordered to use the Tusciano landing ground for refuelling between patrols. Coming in to land the pilots found themselves under anti-aircraft, machine-gun and rifle fire: from their own side. They pulled away and asked the MORU to tell the soldiers to desist. When informed that it was safe, they tried again. This time an ack-ack shell shot Macdonald's Spitfire down and killed him.

That evening three of the wing's squadrons landed at Tusciano. Gilroy led the first and Dundas the second. Again there was gunfire to take the pilots by surprise: not ack-ack, but British field artillery deployed in an olive grove and shooting straight across the runway. Gilroy flew back to Malta to arrange the movement of his further two squadrons. Dundas called on the gunners' C.O., a lieutenant-colonel, to ask him to cease fire while aircraft were taking off and landing. The colonel replied that he had been ordered to fire "flat out round the clock" and that was that. The wing flew and the artillery blasted away, and, remarkably, a Spitfire and a shell never did arrive in the same few cubic feet of airspace at the same instant. Nor did the enemy do any serious damage; short of ammunition, they saved it for the ground troops and the ships at anchor.

The combined efforts of the German Army and Air Force were concentrated on forcing Fifth Army to withdraw. To this end the Luftwaffe's long-range bombers were brought in, in numbers unequalled since the raids on Malta eighteen months before. On the 13th they nearly succeeded: there came a moment when General Clark asked the American Rear Admiral H. Kent Hewitt to prepare to re-embark his American troops and either transfer them to the British sector or further south. This action was obviated by the hasty supply of reinforcements.

Eighth Army's progress along Italy's instep from Reggio and from Taranto, at the heel, had been quick and comparatively easy. The most important immediate objectives were the ports of Brindisi, which was taken on the 11th, and Bari. Next came the group of airfields around Foggia, 15 miles inland from the Gargano Peninsula, the spur on Italy's boot.

On the 12th it was decided that 239 and 244 Wings would move to the mainland, using the large-scale air transport expertise acquired in the desert. By the 15th they were at Grottaglie aerodrome near Taranto. At Salerno the enemy counter-attack had been frustrated. More airstrips had been built and Wing Commander G. Millington,

DFC, (later Air Commodore, CBE) C.O. of 225 (Fighter Recce) Squadron, which had replaced its Hurricane IICs with Spitfire Vs, took one flight with him to Asa, the most northerly of these. He sent the other flight, under his 2 i/c, Squadron Leader McCandlish, to Gioia, north of Taranto, where 244 and 255 Wings and 1437 Strategic Recce Flight were. Getting in and out of Asa was precarious. It was only 800 yards long, with a deep ditch at the end of the landing run to trap anyone who came in too fast. A balloon barrage to the west of it had to be avoided on the approach, and, on take-off, necessitated an immediate sharp left turn to dodge the cables. On the site there was also a battery of medium artillery. The domestic site, separate from the airstrip, was no less uncomfortable. Shells from the British battery and from the enemy in the hills whistled overhead. Millington ordered all ranks to dig slit trenches and sleep in them. "The largest mosquitoes I have ever seen," he adds, "leapt into activity at dusk. The first thing to do on arrival was to put on long trousers and roll our sleeves down for protection. There was a threat of malaria, but the doctors loaded us up with bottles of pills."

On the 23rd 239 Wing set up at Bari. Four days later Foggia was in Allied hands. Bombing of the airfields there during the past fortnight had destroyed 300 German aircraft.

The first week's fighting at Salerno had cost the Luftwaffe 221 aircraft and the Allies eighty-nine. The air-sea rescue squadrons and high speed launches had not been idle. Brigadier General Hawkins, on a visit to 324 Wing from Sicily, found his aircraft unserviceable when it was time to leave. Wing Commander Dundas lent him a Spitfire which, regrettably, had not been refuelled. Half way back it ran out of petrol. The ASR centre, hearing "Hawkins here, Mayday, Mayday, Mayday, baling out," did not know Hawkins from Adam, so the crew of the Walrus amphibian that fished him out half an hour later were astonished to find a dripping wet one-star general aboard. On reaching dry land he signalled his regret to Dundas for losing a Spit and admiration for ASR's efficiency. This was exemplary graciousness and sang froid.

A more junior British pilot who baled out was less courteous but is equally memorable for his sense of humour. While descending under his parachute, he had seen an HSL that happened already to be at sea speeding towards the spot where he should hit the water. Within a minute of his immersion, he was hauled aboard. The weatherbeaten coxswain's look of satisfaction at the swiftest rescue on record turned to bafflement on the young man's mock-indignant first words: "Where've you been?"

Fifth Army was making ground up the west side of the Appenines, aiming for Naples, and Eighth Army was steadily gaining ground on the east. The Neapolitans are generally associated in the public mind with chicanery, perfidy, thievery, corruption, and, when they emigrate to America, gangsterism, rather than with bravery. Their valiant, if brief, display of courage at this juncture seems to have been totally forgotten. On 27 September the inhabitants of Naples, foreshadowing the fortitude of the Partisan guerrilla bands in the twenty months ahead, rose against the Germans. For three days and nights they fought them in the streets at the cost of a huge number of casualties. It was only when advanced units of the British 10th Corps reached the outskirts of the city that the civilians stopped fighting. On 1 October Fifth Army was in possession of this great prize with its port that was essential to the further advance of the Allies.

For the air forces, the emphasis was on interdiction, prohibiting the enemy's movements by road or rail, thus cutting off his supplies and reinforcements. No 239 Wing's Kittyhawks were eminent where, in W. B. Yeats's phrase, "The blood-dimmed tide is loosed". Peter Blomfield describes an operation by 260 Squadron when the wing was at Termoli. "Eighth Army in the vicinity of Campobasso was being nightly 'inconvenienced' by a large long-range gun mounted on a railway flat. It spent all the daylight hours inside a railway tunnel near a place called Boiano." Four aircraft were detailed to liquidate this pest. The pilots were briefed "to 'skip' bomb at low level and place our two 500-pounders with delayed action fuses into the tunnel mouth. The hillside above the tunnel was about 150 feet high. The first trip that I led was aborted after ten minutes in the area, because the cloud was down to almost deck level." They went again next morning. "Again low cloud, but this time enough ceiling to be able to see the target. All four aircraft bombed from about 100 feet. Some bombs were seen to enter the mouth, some buried themselves in the embankment alongside. There was intense, but mercifully inaccurate, light flak and no one was badly hit. Later the Army sent a message that they were having no more sleepless nights. Later still, when the area was overrun, they found that the tunnel mouth was blocked and there was a huge hole above in the hill. The gun was there and a small tank loco had been blown off the rails, and a large section of the roof had been blown in." For this fine attack "Blom" was awarded the DFC.

A recently arrived pilot in the wing, A.W. McDougall, of 250 (Sudan) Squadron, also flying Kittyhawks, mentions bridges as another of the close-support squadrons' frequent targets. Bombing them from high or medium altitude was profligate on account of their small size; far better results could be obtained with the same weight of bombs against other targets. Bridges averaged 300 feet in length and 30 feet in width. The US 15th Air Force had been hitting one in every 190 sorties, but not always leaving them unusable. Hence the handing of the task to fighter-bombers, which could go in low. With the change, bridges began to figure in the proliferation of wrecked tanks, pillboxes and vehicles along the main roads that bore a notice stating simply "By courtesy of DAF."

No 250 Squadron published a newspaper, *The Sudan Sun* (With which is incorporated *The Desert Hard Times*), under the editorship of Leading Aircraftman Andrews. Humour was predominant. "PERSONAL. Can you play the saxophone? If so, will you PLEASE teach Cpl. Edwards." Evidently there was at some period a dearth of supplies in the Equipment Section. "Have you any old clothes? Unwashed towels, vests, pants etc wanted. The Stores have nothing. Help them."

The USAAF follow-my-leader attitude to navigation was conspicuously less demanding than the RAF's painstaking attention to the matter. It was usually left to the leading aircraft in each section of the formation, with the result that when a "lead ship" was shot down, its flock was set a severe problem in finding the way home. This didn't help the accuracy of high-level bombing, either: when father drops his bombs, we all drop ours. The C.O. of a certain Beaufighter squadron, a young wing commander who happened to be married to a lovely American girl, returned to camp one evening a trifle bemused. "Been talking to an American pilot. Asked him if he'd been working lately, and he said 'Yep, yesterday.' Asked him what it was like. 'Hell,' he said. Fighters? 'Swarms of 'em.' Flak? 'So thick, you could've walked on it.' Sounds frightful, I said. Where did you go? 'I dunno.' You . . . don't . . . *know?*. 'Hell, no, I was late for briefin'.' ". If the Wingco had noticed a slight impediment in the American's speech, it was possibly because he had his tongue in his cheek. Maybe not, though.

In October the weather began to deteriorate. Life in Sicily and in the early days on the mainland had been similar in one way to the old days in the desert — living under canvas and moving frequently. Now it was often possible to accommodate a unit partly in buildings. Amenities were closer at hand than they had been in North Africa. In the villages and small towns, with their bars and cafes, scrawled placards were soon offering "Eggsychips". Salerno even had an opera house. One did not need money, the Italians preferred to barter anything, from food to silk stockings, for cigarettes. All ranks received a free issue of fifty a week, in addition to the abundance that they could buy in their messes or the NAAFI. As each large town was occupied, an hotel would be requisitioned for an officers' club. An orchestra played in the evening in return for a square meal, and military nurses and female ENSA artistes could be entertained and danced with. Suitable premises were requisitioned by the NAAFI to cater for the other ranks' relaxation.

Italians captured in North Africa and not yet released appeared in increasing numbers as mess cooks, waiters and batmen. Pidgin Italian became the means of communication, often with ludicrous effect. One pompous officer desirous of toast consulted his pocket dictionary and demanded "Brindisi," with the accent on the second syllable. The mess waiter looked puzzled. "Brindisi, Signore Maggiore?" he ventured, putting emphasis correctly on the first syllable. "Si, si, brindisi, and be quick." The waiter began to giggle. Someone who did know the language intervened. "You're asking him to drink a toast, sir. What you want is pane tostato." The waiter looked relieved and darted off to fetch it. Mess secretaries were able to supplement the rations by local purchase of vegetables and fruit, eggs, poultry and fish that had been impossible in the desert.

It was no existence of ease, however. The pace of air operations never slackened unless weather kept aircraft grounded. Although the Luftwaffe was greatly depleted in this theatre by the demands of the Russian Front and the defence of Germany and occupied Europe, there were still fighters about to harass the Allies. And ground attack had become more dangerous than encounters with enemy fighters or flying through 88mm flak. The 37mm and 20mm, particularly the Flakvierling 38 with its quadruple barrels and rate of fire of 900 rounds per minute, were thicker on the ground than the heavy guns had ever been. Flying through the dense curtain of shells they put up was like playing Russian roulette with three bullets in a six-chamber revolver instead of one.

Then there was the mud. The memory of romantic and beautiful Italy that comes first to the mind of those who were in the field is not of ardent complaisant girls, mandolins, tenor voices and prolific heavily-scented flowers, glorious seascapes or the wonders of Rome's historic buildings, but of mud from October to March. Guns sank up to their axles in it, infantrymen plodded through it and were plastered with it. On airfields aircraft would often be bogged in it and everyone had to pick his way about with lumps of the glutinous stuff clinging to his boots or shoes. Those who had fought in France in the First World War said that conditions were as hard as in the trenches. Waterlogged or snow-clogged foxholes, rain, thunderstorms and ice made the autumns and winters dire. In the springtimes and summers the heat and glare reflected from the bare rocks of the mountainsides were as fierce as on desert sand.

The slow arduous advance up the narrow length of this country, whose inhabitants were so friendly and easygoing, but whose landscape was so unwelcoming and rugged, induced the same attitude of humorous embitterment and frustration that had been engendered by the rigours of trench warfare a quarter-century before. Ahead lay obstacles and trials of doggedness and bravery unencountered in warfare on flat ground. As one mountain peak was wrested from the Germans, another came in view across the wide steep valley; at longer intervals the fast current of a river, whose bare banks gave no shelter, had to be crossed in canvas boats by night under a sweeping scythe of machine-gun bullets, a rain of stick grenades and the thunderclap of shells.

Eighth Army's first river crossing was over the Biferno, near Termoli, on 3 October. Its second was at the Trigno, 12 miles north, on the 27th. The Germans pulled back to the Sangro, 17 miles further north. It was now that an ingenious new system of close support, Rover Control, was introduced. This was thought up by David Heysham, a South African fighter-bomber pilot who was now Group Captain Operations at DAF HQ. He devised it to suit the terrain over which Desert Air Force was operating and to reduce the time taken in meeting Eighth Army's requests for close-support attacks on specified targets.

It entailed keeping six, eight or twelve fighter-bombers, known as a cab rank, orbiting a fixed point near the forward ground control party's position. This party comprised an RAF controller — initially David Heysham himself, using the callsign "Rover David" — an Army liaison officer and an RAF radio mechanic and two R/T operators, one RAF, one Army. At first these were transported in an armoured car, and a tank was also experimented with, but eventually the vehicles chosen were a lorry, a jeep and a trailer.

The procedure developed in North Africa for dealing with the Army's requests for named targets to be knocked out has been described in an earlier chapter. The final step in this was now for No 1 MORU to allot the task to a wing, one of whose squadrons would provide the cab rank. Each pilot carried large scale maps (1:100,000) divided into rectangles of 400 × 500 metres, numbered from south to north and lettered from west to east. Each block of 26 × 26 rectangles formed a larger rectangle that was itself identified by a single letter. During the long Battle of Cassino, these were supplemented by aerial photographs of the target area, with the grid superimposed on them.

When the cab rank leader reported in position, the Rover controller would brief him, starting by telling him which map sheet he needed. Then, for instance: "Target in square B4." The leader would reply, "Understand target in B4." "See the main road running south-east to north-west?" "Yes." "About a third of the way down the road, from the north-west, there is a bridge where the road crosses a stream that runs roughly east to west." "Got it." "Follow the stream eastwards to a wood." "Found it." "Your target is three Tiger tanks hiding in the wood." "Roger, three Tigers in the wood."

There was nowhere in a fighter's cramped cockpit to stow maps in an easily accessible place, so fighter pilots habitually stuffed them into the tops of their flying boots. Finding the right one was a fumbly business.

The leader would brief the other aircraft he needed for the attack, giving it or them details visible from the air and the direction of attack. He might first swoop down and make a quick pass over the target to verify his observations and tactics. Next, he would lead the attack. By this means, a succession of aircraft could keep a cab rank going all day. To operate the system, a considerable degree of air superiority was, of course, essential. Had the Luftwaffe been at strength, it would repeatedly have attacked the cab ranks and these would themselves have needed protection.

At first, the system was known as "Rover David" and each controller used that also as his callsign. Gradually the names "Rover Control" or "Cab Rank" became general and controllers began to append their own first names to "Rover" as their callsign. This simple and most effective method of providing immediate close support was taught to the Americans and used by the R.A.F. and U.S.A.A.F. throughout the operations in Europe that followed the Normandy Landings in June, 1944.

November saw a hardening of the line as winter set in with snowfalls. The first snow on low ground fell at Foggia on 1 December. The advance on Rome stagnated.

On 1 January, 1944, Eisenhower, Montgomery and Tedder, who were going to England to prepare for the invasion of France, handed over to General Sir H. Maitland Wilson, Lieutenant-General Sir Oliver Leese and General Ira Eaker respectively.

The first important move on the ground in 1944 was Eighth Army's 10th Corps assault crossing of the Garigliano River. By this time 324 Wing was back in the DAF fold and Dundas, who had just finished a tour of operations, was on the DAF HQ. Staff, at Vasto. Squadron Leader Duke, who had been on rest since June, was instructing at 73 OTU, Abu Sueir, Flight Lieutenant Ekbery, who had finished a tour at the end of October, with an entry in his logbook by the squadron commander that read: "I have had considerable fighting experience with this pilot and he is an Above Average pilot and leader," was commanding the 244 Wing Training Flight at Bari.

Fifth Army launched an offensive on 20 January, but failed to drive the enemy back. On 22 January, in an attempt to take a short cut to

Rome, the Allies landed at Anzio and by the 23rd had 50,000 men ashore commanded by an American, Major-General John P. Lucas. He, unfortunately, did not exploit the surprise this sprung on the Germans. Instead of being in Rome within a few days, his force was still within the Anzio perimeter, enduring ferocious attacks, under the command of General Lucian K. Truscott, until 30 May.

At the end of February Squadron Leader Duke was posted to command 145 Squadron in 244 Wing (Group Captain Brian Kingcombe), stationed at Marcianise, north of Naples. On 16 April Joe Ekbery joined the same squadron as a flight commander.

Vile weather persisted through February and March. At the end of March Broadhurst, the youngest air vice marshal in the Service, went home to take command of 83 Group and Coningham to form and command Second Tactical Air Force, both preparatory to the invasion of France. Air Vice Marshal W.F. Dickson (later Marshal of the RAF Sir William, GCB, KBE, DSO, AFC) took "Broadie's" place.

The assault on 1,700 feet-high Monte Cassino, on top of which stood the monastery built by St Benedict in 529 AD, had begun in February. The hill, at whose foot stood the town of Cassino, was the most massive barrier on the path to Rome. The huge building, walls thirty feet thick, was an object of veneration. Around it, the Germans built strong defensive positions. General Wilson, and Lieutenant-General Sir Bernard Freyburg, VC, commanding the New Zealand Corps, consisting of 2nd NZ and 4th Indian Divisions, were among those who had no doubt that the Germans had established themselves also in the abbey and were at least using it as an observation post. On 13 February leaflets were dropped on it threatening to bomb it if the Germans did not withdraw. On the 15th 427 tons of high explosive and 166 tons of incendiary bombs were dropped on the monastery, while 314 shells were fired at it. The ruins at once provided further shelter and the Germans accordingly moved into what was left of the building. From then on repeated assaults were made on it, in what became one of the hardest-fought and most famous battles in history. Rover made a contribution, particularly on one day when it wiped out mortar positions on the mountain.

No 285 Wing, of which 225 Squadron was a part, was at Trigno airfield. By this stage of the war, no pilot should have failed to recognize which side of the line he was on. On the enemy side, nobody and no vehicle stirred by day, for fear of being spotted from the air. On the Allied side, aircraft were abundant on the airfields and there was considerable movement on the roads. Millington recalls a day when he and two other officers, leaving their dispersals for tea in the mess, saw six

Warhawks go in low to strafe 239 Wing's airfield nearby. Dispersed Kittyhawks and astonished men pelting for slit trenches at the last moment were blasted off the ground, riddled by bullets, set ablaze. A few days later the colonel commanding the American group from which the Warhawks came called to apologize to 239's C.O., a tough South African, Colonel Laurie Wilmot. While the visitor was engaged, some of the wing's airmen got busy with paintbrushes. When he emerged from Wilmot's tent he found several RAF roundels added to the row of swastikas on his aeroplane denoting the aircraft he had destroyed.

The versatile 225 Squadron's duties demanded perfect accuracy of flying, skill in the use of cameras, spotting for the gunners and directing counter-battery fire, dive — and low-level — bombing, and air combat, so that its pilots, who flew alone or in pairs, could defend themselves. Over Cassino it was daily engaged on photographic reconnaissance. A popular character on the Squadron was the only Chinese pilot in the RAF, Flying Officer Kai Hai Tan, from Malaya, known, after the well-known fictional detective of many novels and films, as Charlie Chan. "Charlie" was flying in the Cassino area one day when his wing man lost visual contact and called on the R/T to ask his position so that he could re-formate. "Can you see the flak near Cassino?" Charlie asked. "Yes," his No 2 replied. "Well, fly towards that: I'm in it," said his leader calmly. Could oriental inscrutability and acquired British imperturbability be better exemplified?

May was a notable month for 145 Squadron. During eight days in the middle of the month, the Squadron destroyed sixteen enemy aircraft, of which Duke accounted for two Me109s and two FW190s, which were much used as fighter-bombers. Ekbery's logbook entry for 19 May is: "1 FW190 destroyed."

On the 21st he flew five sorties, on the last of which he took off at 6.20 pm in a formation of eight, to escort Boston bombers, and landed at 7.30 pm.

The Squadron Intelligence Officer's Mission Report gave the following account. "Just airborne and orbiting for rendezvous when 20 e/a reported east of Rome coming south. After two minutes saw ten FW190s at 15,000 ft, ten at 17,000 ft abreast, four Me109s at 20,000 ft. Our aircraft between 15-17,000 ft. Bombers had not arrived so engaged the FW190s head-on. Chased to north. Most 190s jettisoned bombs. Lt J.M.G. Anderson chased a 190 in a shallow dive to north, fired from 250 yds astern, strikes on tail. Another burst from 150-200 yds followed by white flash from engine. The 190 was at deck level when pilot pulled up and turned. Saw e/a hit a hill at F9999 and blow up.

"F/L J.S. Ekbery chased a lagging 190 at 3,000 ft, fired from 200 yds, hitting fuselage and port wing. Black smoke came from 190 and it went down like a falling leaf. Last seen going down at 2,000 ft near G0647. Claims a probable. He then turned into another 190 and fired from 200 yds with hits on fuselage and wing. Hood jettisoned and pilot baled out at G0162. Saw another 190 east of Rome, overtook 500 yds, two bursts from 200 yds, bits flew off. E/a went in at F9159. Claims two FW190 dest. F/S S.C. Sterling chased a 190 north of Rome and at deck level fired from 100 yds astern. Bits flew off, cockpit in flames. E/a tried to pull up, went in in flames at F77596. Sterling fired at others, but no results seen. Claims one FW190 dest. S/L N.F. Duke fired on 190 from 150 yds. Saw flashes and strikes on near starboard side of fuselage, raked it again and e/a went in at G0961. Chased another 190 and fired from 250 yds, and while e/a turned on back going down, got hits with long bursts. Pilot baled out from 14,000 ft at G0765 but chute did not open. S/L Duke turned south and saw bombers and escorted by himself to target where lot of heavy AA. Claims two FW190 destroyed."

These two kills brought Ekbery's total to six and won him the immediate award of a DFC.

At the end of May 244 Wing acquired a new Wing Leader, Wing Commander Hugh Dundas. (In November, 1944, he was promoted to group captain and took command from Brian Kingcombe, another magnificently brave and brilliant pilot and leader of men.) A week later, on the usual low-level strafe, Neville Duke was shot down behind enemy lines, baled out and landed in a lake. While he was swimming to shore Italian Partisans rowed out and rescued him. They were in contact with American troops who took him over and got him back to his squadron.

The campaign in Italy was not one of frequent strokes by the R.A.F. of such brilliance that they echoed around the globe, such as the Blenheims' destruction of Amiens gaol, the Mosquitoes' wrecking of the Gestapo HQ in Copenhagen, the Lancasters' dam-busting attack, the first 1,000-bomber raid, the laying waste of Dresden and Hamburg, a Beaufighter dropping a union flag on the Arc de Triomphe in the middle of a bright day, the sweeps over France by three or more massed wings of Spitfires. This was a business mostly of close-support fighters slogging away day after day ahead of the land force; of air superiority fighters ranging the sky in search of scarce and elusive enemy aircraft; of anti-shipping strikes by Beaufighters scouring the Jugoslav Archipelago at 50 feet and weaving their way among the islands through a crossfire of flak; of light and medium bombers dropping their loads where they would be of most benefit to the painfully advancing army. All this was punctuated by massive set-piece episodes like the battles at the Anzio beachhead and for possession of Monte Cassino.

Pilot Officer Gordon Brown, a new arrival on 260 Squadron, spent his first ten days at the 239 Wing Training Flight at Termoli. His introduction to Italy was pastoral rather than warlike, a reminder of Marvell's "Thrice happy he who, not mistook / Hath read in Nature's mystic book." "We lived under canvas and I remember watching some horses which were grazing in the same field and saw one drop a foal. As a very young city boy I was amazed." He flew his first solo in a Mustang on 29 May and his first operation on 1 June.

On 18 May Cassino had fallen and on the 31st the Allied force fighting in the Anzio sector took its final objectives. On 4 June the Allies entered Rome.

Brown continues: "My log book shows a flight from San Angelo to Guidonia on 10 June, ferrying bombs. Guidonia was a peacetime Italian Air Force station and it had been destroyed by the Germans. As the army was moving rapidly and air operations were non-stop, we had to fly bombs up to the new landing ground." The Squadron moved twice more and then again, to Jesi. "All this time we lived in tents, but on about 1 October, 1944, we moved into a villa for winter quarters. Food was mainly of the dried type — powdered eggs, milk, even dried meat, plus tins of all kinds. The Squadron used to organise 'yaffle runs' consisting of two pilots, a driver and a cook. Latterly we had an Italian civilian cook who also helped with the language problem. We used to barter some of our stores for fresh food. The locals were desperate for salt, tins of sardines and the odd gallon of petrol for their tractors; also cigarettes. We obtained a beautiful goose, a calf, eggs, potatoes, vegetables etc. One of the finest meals I had at this period was a brew up on a petrol fire (à la 8th Army) consisting of tins of M and V (meat and vegetable stew) and baked beans all mixed together.

"When we were at Jesi, swimming parties were organized to the nearest Adriatic beach — no swimming costumes, just all boys together."

One SAAF pilot, whose name he forgets ("Capt Jack ?") was hit and baled out on 2 August. "The five remaining aircraft of his flight (including me) saw his aircraft blow up on hitting the ground and he was seen to land safely by parachute. The story has it that he was immediately captured by a German detachment and put in the back of a small truck with an elderly soldier. Jack was wearing Nuffield flying boots, which had a knife in a little pocket, with which to cut off the top of the boot and made them look like ordinary civilian boots which would not give away the identity of the wearer. Jack apparently stabbed the soldier with the knife, rolled out of the truck and took to the hills, from where the partisans passed him through our lines."

The capture of Naples and Rome added a faintly surrealistic facet to the life of regiments and squadrons in the front line. From the forward foxholes and landing grounds, it was a journey of only two or three hours to all the comforts of civilization. Within this short time of leaving the general discomfort and the mud, the shells and bullets behind, a man could be seated comfortably in a bar, restaurant, opera house or cinema. The next day he might be back under fire again. A week's leave in Sorrento put the war far out of mind for a while.

The enemy was being noticeably ground down at last. On 19 July Mediterranean Tactical Air Force moved to Corsica, and DAF alone remained to give close support to both the Eighth and Fifth Armies.

It was more than a year since Desert Air Force had left the desert, but the tradition it had founded there and the spirit that made it unique remained. Even in these totally different surroundings, there was often a precedent to recall when a problem was met. This happened at Fortunata Ridge, a strongly defended hill that barred the road to Rimini and beyond. How could Eighth Army successfully assault the forward slope and avoid being stopped on the long crest, or cut to bits on the assault down the reverse slope? DAF had the solution: El Hamma, the battle that to fighter-bomber operations was what Agincourt had been to English archers against infantry and cavalry, had not faded from memory. On this September day, in a very different setting and 600 miles away from the place that had inspired it, DAF cleared the way once more for their old partners from North Africa. Three-quarters of an hour of unflinching and frenzied deck-level bombing and strafing flailed the ridge and the infantry and artillery positions on the far side. Eighth Army climbed and fought its way to the top and down the far side with minimum casualties.

October saw an offensive on Bologna, but the enemy's doughty resistance and the worsening weather brought it to a stop. Winter fell upon a front line which, although it was 200 miles further north than it had been a year ago, was still a formidable impediment to final victory.

In December Air Vice Marshal Dickson handed DAF over to Air Vice Marshal "Pussy" Foster.

Air fighting in any form can never be monotonous, but it can become heavy-gaited. Any unusual event sparkled against the background of routine and tedium. Two German hospital ships, the *Tubingen* and the *Gradisca,* plied between Trieste and Piraeus, taking wounded and sick German soldiers from Italy to Greece for treatment. Both were stopped now and then by the Royal Navy and boarded. On occasion they were found to be carrying perfectly fit troops to the battle front, with their weapons, and these were promptly imprisoned. Their passage had to be made in accordance with international rules. White overall, with a large red cross on either side of the hull, and showing lights by night, they were required to give 48 hours' notice before setting sail. All RAF and USAAF formations were warned of the ships' movements. On one occasion no signal giving *Gradisca*'s departure time and date from Piraeus was received. Aircraft from a Mediterranean Allied Coastal Air Force Wing on the Adriatic coast spotted and reported her late one evening. Telephone consultation with higher authority followed. The initiative was left to the Commanding Officer of the wing who now had on his strength a Beaufighter squadron that had won renown with DAF.

Off went twelve Beaus, each armed with eight 60lb rockets. They found the ship at last light, when identification in the gloom was difficult. There is no time for doubt, in war. Decisions must be made and action taken quickly. The rockets fizzed away, sheets of flame leaped as they struck and *Gradisca* went down. There wasn't much of a stir: she was probably chock full of armed fighting troops on their way to reinforce Kesselring. Not long after, the Germans tried to slip the *Rex*, the largest Italian liner afloat, laden to the scuppers with war materials, across the northern Adriatic. The same Beaufighter squadron put on a repeat performance and left the pride of Italy's merchant fleet, looking like a colander, settled deep in the water on a sandbank.

January, 1945, brought thick snow all over the country. Airfields were cleared in the usual R.A.F. way: all ranks out with shovels, a slow and wearying chore. Progress on both sides of the line was clogged but not halted. Rover patrolling went on whenever aircraft could take off, and many times the aircraft in the cab ranks were directed on to targets only two or three hundred yards in front of Eighth Army's most forward tanks. It was not until March that the weather allowed large-scale interdiction to be resumed.

For light bombers and fighter-bombers alike, the last few weeks of the war were the busiest since the Salerno landing. The enemy's anti-aircraft defences were as plentiful and terrifying as they had ever been. The bomber crews, flying straight and level on the run up to the target were hurled about by the blast from 88mm shells spread so thickly across the sky that it seemed impossible to get through without being hit. For many, it was. Ahead, astern and on both sides, a red glow would suddenly blossom and out of it fragments of an aeroplane and men's bodies would be flung as though tossed on the jets of a giant fountain. The explosion of a bomb load could not only blow up the aeroplane that carried it but also hurl the ones nearest to it upside down like feathers in a gale. Fighter-bomber pilots diving almost vertically could not deviate from their flight paths. They had to hold steady and unflinching as the medium and light flak flashed up close all around them and the rising smoke from the bombs of those who had gone before turned the deep valleys into a replica of Dante's Inferno: *"Lasciate ogni speranza voi ch'entrate . . .* Abandon all hope, you who enter." Not the politest form of Italian, but true to those numbing moments when racing down at the target with flames licking out of the barrels of the Flakvierling.

There were lighter moments, Squadron Leader Peter Blomfield, who was by then commanding 260 Squadron, which by this time was flying Mustangs, recalls a South African, 2nd Lieutenant Raymond Veitch "known affectionately as Drongie". He was given this nickname on the same principle by which bald men are called "Curly": drongie is Afrikaans for a drunkard, and Veitch was a teetotaller. "Blom" goes on: "He was flying at the end of the war as my number 2. In April '45 we were mostly involved in interdiction, rockets and strafing. Twice in the first week in April and again on the 30th he was hit by flak — a few feet ahead and it could have been me! — managed to make it to the north Adriatic coast and baled out into a minefield near Trieste. Each time either the RAF or the Yanks' sea-rescue service dropped him an airborne lifeboat. As his C.O. and No 1 I felt obliged to lead a section of Mustangs to cover the operations. I've never ceased to wonder why these prolonged and obvious rescue operations so close to the enemy shore went completely unopposed; but whether from lack of petrol or skin-saving now that their war was obviously nearly over, they never came to molest us." After the third episode, the AOC sent young Veitch a signal: "Personal from Foster to Veitch, I have appointed you Honorary Commodore of the Desert Air Force Yacht Club when it is formed."

To some, the reward for their gallantry over many long years came late. The citation for Maurice Smyth's Distinguished Flying Cross was gazetted on 23 February, 1945, and could be cited as a tribute to all Desert Air Force pilots and the spirit of the whole force. "This officer has participated in a large number of operational sorties against mechanical transport concentrations, locomotives and land installations. On one occasion he took part in an attack against a large mechanical transport park in which 257 vehicles were destroyed or damaged. Another time following a sortie over Dalmatia, he was forced to leave his aircraft and spent 16 hours in his dinghy and improvised a sail out of the dinghy canvas, before reaching safety. Despite this hazardous experience, this officer's enthusiasm for operational flying has remained undiminished and subsequently he has destroyed at least two enemy aircraft. At all times Flight Lieutenant Smyth has displayed a fine fighting spirit and pressed home his attacks with vigour and determination."

DAF continued to destroy German transport of all kinds until the last day. During the concluding weeks of the war no enemy vehicle could move between first light and full darkness without being spotted and strafed or bombed within two minutes. On 7 May, 1945, the Germans signed an instrument of unconditional surrender. An order was issued that all Allied aircraft in Italy would be grounded from the 8th, V.E. (Victory in Europe) Day. There were those who remembered the celebrations on Armistice Day 1918, when some pilots took to the air and performed celebratory aerobatics that were often more lethal than skilful.

The Western Desert lay 1,500 miles to the south. From DAF's new airfields in the far north of Italy the snowy Alpine peaks were in sight and only a few minutes' flying time away.

Desert Air Force maintained its identity longer than any other air formation overseas throughout the war. During five years of fighting over a variety of difficult terrain and in unfavourable climates, it maintained a cohesion, efficiency and fierce pride that touched everyone from its Air Officers Commanding to the most recently joined young aircraftmen, and was unmatched in the entire six years of conflict. Professionally, it evolved a system of co-ordinating its functions with those of the ground and sea forces that shortened every campaign fought from June, 1940, to the day when Japan acknowledged defeat on 15 August, 1945. This extraordinary amalgam of divers nationalities achieved a unity and harmony and attained a record of success that is an object lesson for every fighting air force that will ever be.

pp 166-167
Propaganda pamphlet in German
and Italian dropped by the RAF
over enemy lines and airfields.

pp 168-169
Two pages from the log book
of Squadron Leader Maurice Smyth DFC.

Distrutti dalla R.A.F.

**Dall'inizio dell'offensiva sino al 7 dicembre la R.A.F.
ha distrutto i seguenti aeroplani dell'Asse :**

JU. 87 - 61	ME. 110 - 20	SAV. 79 - 12
G. 50 - 38	MAOOHI-200 - 15	JU. 52 - 11
ME. 109 - 36	OR. 42 - 14	JU. 88 - 10

Gli altri apparecchi distrutti ammontano a 44. Le perdite britanniche nello stesso periodo
sono state di 98 aerei. **TOTALE DELLE PERDITE DELL'ASSE : 261.**

LA SUPREMAZIA DELLA R.A.F.

Le cifre che vi diamo su que-·
sta pagina vi dimostrano esat-
tamente l'andamento dei com-
battimenti aerei dall'inizio del-
l'offensiva. Non facciamo affer-
mazioni stravaganti: enumeria-
mo soltanto gli aerei che sono
stati sicuramente distrutti.

1. La vostra aviazione non può
operare in appoggio alle forze
terrestri, come, ad esempio, fece
a Candia l'aviazione tedesca.

2. D'altra parte gli apparecchi
britannici possono appoggiare
ed appoggiano le loro truppe terrestri bombardando e mitra-
gliando le truppe dell'Asse ovun-
que le trovano.

3. I vostri rifornimenti — spe-
cialmente il carburante — sono
metodicamente distrutti con at-
tacchi a bassa quota lungo le
strade che vanno dalle vostre
basi al campo di battaglia.

4. I vostri aerodromi, e gli aeroplani che vi si trovano, sono
martellati dai nuovi bombardieri
medi e pesanti britannici ed a-
mericani, fra cui si trova la fa-
·mosa "Fortezza volante."

5. I vostri porti in Cirenaica
ed Italia sono bombardati rego-
larmente, e così le vostre navi
che sfuggono alla Marina bri-
tannica — e non sono molte —
non possono sfuggire alla R.A.F.

Che cosa si deve dedurre da
tutto questo? Significa, anzitu-·
to, che non potete combattere
come potreste perchè non avete
i dominio del cielo sul campo di
battaglia, ed inoltre non sarete
**in grado di resistere a lungo
perchè si stanno distruggendo·i
vostri rifornimenti.**

**In altre parole questi cinque
punti si sommano in una sola co-·
sa: sconfitta per l'Asse!**

Von der RAF vernichtet

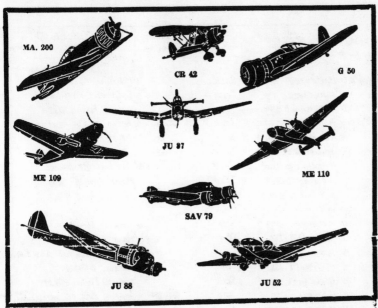

MA. 200   CR 42   G 50   JU 87   ME 109   ME 110   SAV 79   JU 88   JU 52

Seit Beginn der Offensive bis zum 7. Dezember vernichteten britische Luftstreitkräfte folgende Achsenflugzeuge:

JU. 87 - 61	ME. 110 - 20	SAV. 79 - 12
G. 50 - 39	MACCHI-200 - 15	JU. 52 - 11
ME. 108 - 36	CR. 42 - 14	JU. 88 - 13

Andere zerstörte Flugzeuge : 44. Britische Verluste im selben Zeitabschnitt : 98.
Gesamtverluste der Achsenluftstreitkräfte : 281.

NACH JAPANS UEBERFALL

1. Nach dem nicht provozierten Ueberfall Japans erklärten gestern die Regierungen London und Washingtons im Namen ihrer Staaten, dass sie sich offiziell im Kriegszustand mit Tokio befinden.

2. Der britische Premierminister Churchill gab gestern im Unterhaus und der Präsident der Vereinigten Staaten von Amerika, Roosevelt, vor dem amerikanischen Kongress, Erklärungen von weltgeschichtlicher Bedeutung ab, in denen der tückische Verrat und hinterlistige Ueberfall Japans im Stillen Ozean als ohne Gleichen in der Geschichte dastehende Aggression gebrandmarkt und der Wille der von Japan überfallenen Staaten zum Kampf und zur Endgetan wurden.

3. Im neuen Weltkrieg stehen vier Fünftel der Gesamtbevölkerung der Erde auf Seiten Grossbritanniens, Amerikas und ihrer Verbündeten, gegen ein Fünftel des schon durch die langjährigen, erschöpfenden Vorbereitungen und blutigen Kämpfe schwer in Mitleidenschaft gezogenen Einwohnerschaft der Achsenstaaten.

4. Amerika verfügt über die bestausgerüstete Wehrmacht der Welt. Ein Landheer von über 12,000,000 Mann Stärke mit vielen Panzer-Stosstrupp-Armeen, die modernste Luftwaffe aller Zeiten mit vielen Fallschirm-Flak- und Luftlandeverbänden und eine überaus mächtige Kriegsmarine

werden im Verein mit den Verbündeten und ihren unerschöpflichen Reservoiren ihrer Heimatsfronten mit den Welttyranneigelüsten der Diktatoren endgültig aufräumen und den Hitlerismus, Faschismus und die "Gelbe Gefahr" ausrotten.

5. Berlin bekennt jetzt offen die enormen Schwierigkeiten, die der angezettelte Russenfeldzug mit sich gebracht hat und gibt, nachdem Hitler vor 2 Monaten die Existenz von Russenheeren überhaupt ausgelöscht hatte, jetzt zu, dass der Widerstand der russischen Armee unbiegsam und die Winterschwierigkeiten für die deutsche Heeresleitung schier unüberwindbar sind.

6. Die englische Offensive in der lybischen Wüste geht bei klarer Luft-und Landüberlegenheit der Briten planmässig weiter.

YEAR 1942 DECEMBER		AIRCRAFT		PILOT, OR 1ST PILOT	2ND PILOT, PUPIL OR PASSENGER	DUTY (INCLUDING RESULTS AND REMARKS)
MONTH	DATE	Type	No.			
—	—	—	—	—	—	—— Totals Brought Forward
DECEMBER	4	HURRICANE II	707	SELF		MAGRUN TO BENINA
"	5	HURRICANE II	707	SELF		* SCRAMBLE BENGHASI
"	6	HURRICANE II	299	SELF		NIGHT FLYING TEST
"	7	HURRICANE II	299	SELF	🚚	* INTRUDER EL AGHEILA
"	8	HURRICANE II	299	SELF	卍	NIGHT FLYING TEST
"	8	HURRICANE II	299	SELF	卍	* DUSK CONVOY PATROL
"	9	HURRICANE II	299	SELF		* PATROL BENGHASI
"	9	HURRICANE II	299	SELF		NIGHT FLYING TEST
"	10	HURRICANE II	299	SELF		NIGHT FLYING TEST
"	10	HURRICANE II	299	SELF		TO BENINA
"	11	HURRICANE II	299	SELF		* PATROL BENGHASI 10,000 FT.
"	13	HURRICANE II	288	SELF		NIGHT FLYING TEST
"	13	HURRICANE II	288	SELF		* SCRAMBLE BENGASI AND BENINA
"	14	HURRICANE II	288	SELF		* PATROL BENGASI.
"	15	HURRICANE II	299	SELF		NIGHT FLYING TEST
"	15	HURRICANE II	299	SELF	🚚	* STRAFING EAST OF SIRTE (DISTANCE 30m FROM)
"	16	HURRICANE II	299	SELF		AIR TEST A/C. U/S.
"	17	HURRICANE II	299	SELF		AIR TEST A/C. U/S.
"	18	HURRICANE II	299	SELF		AIR TEST A/C. U/S
"	19	HURRICANE II	299	SELF		AIR TEST O.K
"	21	HURRICANE II	299	SELF		NIGHT FLYING TEST
"	22	HURRICANE II	299	SELF		* PATROL BENGASI
"	22	HURRICANE II	299	SELF		MAGRUN TO MADUNA No 1
"	23	HURRICANE II	299	SELF		NIGHT FLYING TEST

GRAND TOTAL [Cols. (1) to (10)]

......46.4....Hrs......30.40....Mins.

TOTALS CARRIED FORWARD

SINGLE-ENGINE AIRCRAFT				MULTI-ENGINE AIRCRAFT						PASS-ENGER	INSTR/CLOUD FLYING [Incl. in cols. (1) to (10)]	
DAY		NIGHT		DAY			NIGHT					
DUAL	PILOT	DUAL	PILOT	DUAL	1st PILOT	2nd PILOT	DUAL	1st PILOT	2nd PILOT		DUAL	PILOT
(1)	(2)	(3)	(4)	(5)	(6)	(7)	(8)	(9)	(10)	(11)	(12)	(13)
53.35	317.40	3.20	63.10							26.50	13.15	32.35
	.30	⊘	1.35	{No Luck Again. Couldn't See Wingtips !!! {Take Off With No Flare Path								
	.20	⊘	2.00	Straffed Headlights. Started 1 Fire. Innacurate Breda								.10
	.35	⊘		73. Sqdn No. 299 aircraft shot down (Ju88)								.20
		⊘	1.40	Bags of Fun. Shot Down 1 Ju88 into Sea								
		⊘	2.00	Flares Dropped Nothing Seen. Weather Duff.								.10
	.15											.15
	.20											
	.30											
		⊘	2.35	Plotting Good E/A's About.								
	.35			{Bags of 88's No Visuals No Heights Given.								.20
		⊘	2.00	{Ideal Conditions. Caught in In Begasi Barrage Very								
		⊘	2.00	{Shaking !! Caught in Benina Barrage at 1000ft !!!								
	.30	⊘		{Sighted Ju88. Engine Failed Over Sea. Crash Landed. 15								.15
		⊘	2.55	Straffed Headlights Put Them Out. Accurate Heavy Flak.								
	.40			300 Miles Over The Sea Heavy Raincloud Over Target.								
	.45											
	.30											
	1.00											
	.30											.20
		O	1.40	Nothing Doing								
	1.00											
	.30											.20
53.35	326.10	3.20	81.35							26.50	13.15	34.35
(1)	(2)	(3)	(4)	(5)	(6)	(7)	(8)	(9)	(10)	(11)	(12)	(13)

APPENDIX A

REGIA AERONAUTICA ORDER OF BATTLE IN LIBYA 10 JUNE 1940

Air Headquarters, Tripoli

Eastern Sector, H.Q. Tobruk

Bombers

Gruppo	Squadriglia	Type	Strength	Location
		14th Stormo		
44th	6	S79		El Adem
	7	S79		El Adem
45th	2	S81		El Adem
	22	S81		El Adem
		10th Stormo		
30th	55	S79		Benina
	56	S79		Benina
32nd	57	S79		Benina
	58	S79		Benina
10th Autonomous Group				
	84	CR42		Castel Benito
	90	CR42		Castel Benito
	91	CR42		Castel Benito

Western Sector, H.Q. Tripoli

Fighters

		2nd Stormo		
8th	92	CR32		
	93	CR32		
	94	CR32		
13th	77	CR42		
	78	CR42		
	82	CR42		

Bombers

		33rd Stormo		
35th	43	S79		Bir El Beda
	44	S79		Bir El Beda
36th	45	S79		Bir El Beda
	46	S79		Bir El Beda

15th Stormo

46th	20	S79	Bir El Ghnem
	21	S79	Bir El Ghnem
47th	53	S79	Bir El Ghnem
	54	S79	Bir El Ghnem

50th Stormo

12th	159	CA310	Sorman
	160	CA310	Sorman
		BA65	Sorman
Nucleus 16th	167	CA310	Sorman
	168	CA310	Sorman
	169	CA310	Sorman

Army Co-operation Squadrons

5th Army

64th	122	Ro37	Tripoli
	136	Ro37	Tripoli

10th Army

73rd	127	Ro37	El Adem
	137	Ro37	El Adem

26th Army Corps

	120	Ro37	Tirana

APPENDIX B

LUFTWAFFE STRENGTH AND SERVICEABILITY IN ITALY, CORSICA, SARDINIA, S. FRANCE, GREECE, CRETE, RHODES, AEGEAN, ALBANIA, JUGOSLAVIA

Luftflotte 2 Order of Battle 1st September 1943

	Strength	Serviceable
Long-Range and Torpedo Bombers	276	110
Bomber Recce	20	13
Dive Bombers	0	0
Ground Attack	28	10
Single-Engine Fighters	181	91
Fighter-Bombers	27	16
Twin-Engine Fighters	0	0
Night Fighters	0	0
Tac Recce	20	10
Coastal	6	6
Total	558	256

South-East Command Order of Battle

Long-Range and Torpedo Bombers	15	5
Bomber Recce	23	14
Dive Bombers	197	147
Ground Attack	0	0
Single-Engine Fighters	80	60
Fighter-Bombers	0	0
Twin-Engine Fighters	13	9
Night Fighters	20	15
Tac Recce	47	27
Coastal	46	35
Total	441	312

APPENDIX C

DESERT AIR FORCE ORDER OF BATTLE 3 SEPTEMBER 1943
D.A.F. H.Q. Lentini

Squadron	Role	Aircraft	Location
5 SAAF	Fighter	Kittyhawk	Ben Gardane
60 SAAF	Photo Survey	Baltimore, Mosquito	Sorman
225	Tac Recce	Spitfire Mustang	Bon Ficha
241	Fighter-Bomber	Hurricane IIE	Bon Ficha
6	Fighter Recce	Hurricane IV	Ben Gardane

324 USAAF Group

314, 315, 316		Warhawk	Haouria

211 Group (H.Q. Lentini)

7 SAAF Wing (H.Q. Pachino)

2 SAAF	Fighter	Spitfire V	Pachino
4 SAAF	Fighter	Spitfire V	Pachino

57 USAAF Group (H.Q. Scordia)

64, 65, 66	Fighter	Warhawk	Scordia

79 USAAF Group (H.Q. Palagonia)

85, 86, 87	Fighter	Warhawk	Palagonia

285 Wing (H.Q. Sorman)

40 SAAF	Tac Recce	Spitfire V	Francesco
1437 Flt.	Tac Recce	Mustang	Francesco

322 Wing (H.Q. Pachino)

81, 1252, 154, 232, 242	Fighter	Spitfire IX	Lentini

324 Wing (H.Q. Pachino)

43	Fighter	Spitfire V	Pachino
72, 93, 111, 243	Fighter	Spitfire V	Pachino
600	Night Fighter	Beaufighter	Cassibile

244 Wing (H.Q. Lentini)

1 SAAF	Fighter	Spitfire V	Lentini
92	Fighter	Spitfire V & IX	Lentini
145	Fighter	Spitfire V & IX	Lentini
417 RCAF	Fighter	Spitfire V & IX	Lentini
601	Fighter	Spitfire V & IX	Lentini

APPENDIX D

ORGANIZATION

R.A.F.

Basic unit: squadron.
Battle strength: 12 aircraft.
Establishment: 16 aircraft and 16 pilots.
Wing: three or four squadrons.
Group: no fixed number of wings.

U.S.A.A.F.

Basic unit: squadron.
Battle strength: 12 aircraft.
Group: three squadrons.
Wing: no fixed number of groups.

LUFTWAFFE

Basic unit: Staffel.
Strength: 12-16 aircraft, 20-25 pilots.
Gruppe: three Staffeln.
Geschwader: three Gruppen.

REGIA AERONAUTICA

Basic unit: squadriglia.
Fighters: flexible, about 15 aircraft. Bombers: 5 aircraft.
Gruppo: three squadriglie.
Stormo: three Gruppi.

L'ARMÉE DE L'AIR

Basic unit: groupe, comprising 2 escadrilles, each of 3 patrouilles of 3 aircraft.
Groupe establishment was 25-30 pilots and 25 or 30 aircraft, according to type.
Escadre: 2 or 3 groupes.
Groupement: several groupes, no fixed number.

INDEX

Ranks and titles given are the highest relevant to the text, not necessarily the highest attained during the entire war.

178

Eastern Air Command, 112; combined with 12th Air Force to form N.W. African Air Force, 124

Egypt. Strategic importance of, 14: British and Commonwealth forces' strength in on 10 June, 1940, 15. Political situation in, 35.

Egyptian Armoured Brigade, 35

Eighth Army, 3, 13, 69, 74, 77, 79, 81, 82, 90, 91-93 passim; 107, 119, 123; crosses Tunisian frontier, 124, 125, 131, 132, 142, 150, 152; first river crossing, 155, 156, 161

Eisenhower, Lieutenant-General Dwight D., allied C-in-C, 112, 119, 124, 129, 145

Ekbery, Sergeant Brian, 85, 99, 102, 113

Ekbery, Flight Lieutenant J.S. 112, 113, 130, 131, 139, 141; wins DFC, 156-159 passim

Ellis, Squadron Leader R.W. "Monty", 56, 95, 123

E.N.S.A., 125, 153

Eritrea, Italian threat to Sedan from, 14; surrender of Italian forces in, 62

Ethiopia, Italian threat to Kenya from, 14; surrender of Italian forces in, 62

Faid Pass, 129

Fallows, Flight Lieutenant Geoff, 128, 129

Fasher, El, 27

Fifth Army, 152, 156

Finlayson, Wing Commander Gordon, 75

First Sea Lord, 59

First Army, 125, 131

Fleet Air Arm, 98, 106

Fliegerführer Afrika, 50, 92

Fliegerkorps, 10, 50

Fliegerkorps Tunis, 123

Foggia, 150, 151, 156

Fortunata Ridge, 161

Fonduk, 129

Ford, Squadron Leader, 114

Fort Capuzzo, 23, 24, 31, 32, 59, 61

Fort Maddalena, 24

Foster, Air Vice Marshal: takes Command of DAF, 161, 163

France: British expectations of in North Africa, 15; reneges on promise to help Greece, 43

Franzisket, Oberleutnant, 60

Free French Brigade, 89

Freeman, Air Marshal Sir Wilfred, 65

French: familiarity with desert, 12; place in British plans for attack on Libya, 20

Free French Flight No 2, 32, 38, 39, 43

Freyburg, Lieutenant-General Sir Bernard, 157

Friedenthal, Major-General, 111

Fuka, 16, 17, 23, 67, 68, 71, 99, 104, 107

Gabes, 129

Gabr Saleh, 74

Gafsa, 129

Galland, Generalleutnant Adolf, 7

Gambut, 72, 82, 83, 86, 87, 90, 108, 119, 120

Gargano Peninsula, 150

Garigliano River, 156

Garrod, Sergeant, 6

Gavotti, Sotto Tenente Giulio, 11

Gazala, 39, 43, 56, 60, 66, 72, 76; Rommel establishes Gazala Line, 78; 81, 82, 86, 87, 89, 90, 97

G.C.I. Mobile Units, 147

Geiseler, Generalmajor Hans, 50

Genaclis, 120

Geneina, El, 27

George VI, H.M. King, 72

Germans: attitude to the desert, 12; Britain's plans for probable war with in North Africa, 15.

Gibraltar, 15, 27, 44, 84, 85, 112

Gilroy, Group Captain G.K., 149, 150

Gioia, 151

Goldfish Club, The, 130

Goodman, Flying Officer George, 60

Gott, General "Straffer", 97

Gradisca, German Hospital Ship. Sunk, 161

Graziani, Marshal, 22, 31, 37, 39, 40, 43, 45, 47

Great Sand Sea, 48, 79, 108

Greece, 3; Italy invades, 43; folly of British strategic policy, 55; German invasion of, 58; German bombers operating over desert from, 82, 89, 161, 162

Green, Sergeant, 26

Green, Flight Lieutenant David, 114 et seq

Grottaglie, 150

R.A.F.GROUPS

No201: Order of Battle, 11 June, 1940, 17, 54; becomes A.H.Q. Egypt, 62; 69, 105

No202: Order of Battle, 11 June, 1940, 17; use of Control and Reporting System, 19, 22; tasks on declaration of war with Italy, 21, 33, 37, 43, 54; becomes AHQ Egypt, 62, 69

No203, 105

New Zealanders; attitude to desert, 12
Nichol, Flying Officer "Nick", 129, 142
Nofilia, 119, 122
Norrie, Lieutenant-General C.W.M., 74, 75
North West African Coastal Air Force: formed, 124
North West African Air Force: formed, 124
North West African Strategic Air Force: formed, 124

O'Connor, Major-General Richard, 45-47 passim; 48, 49, 55
Olver, Squadron Leader, 108

Pachino, 140, 141
Paestum, 149
Pantelleria, 85, 89, 137, 138
Papagos, General, Greek Commander-in-Chief, 50
Pattle, Squadron Leader M.T. St J., 31, 37, 38, 48, 49
Patton, Major-General, 111, 131, 142, 143
Paulus, General von, 58
Peacock, Leading Aircraftman Doug, 51
Peronne, Lieutenant, 31
Photographic Reconnaissance Unit, No. 2, 105
Piazza, Capitano Carlo: first pilot in history to drop an aerial bomb, 11
Piraeus, 162
Plenderleith, Warrant Officer, 95
Poli, Sergeant Lido: wins Italian Gold Medal for Military Valour, 38
Polish Brigade, 58
Pond, Aircraftman Fred, 75, 76, 78
Porro, Generale Squadra Aerea Felice, 16, 28
Port Said, 14, 19
Portal, Air Chief Marshal Sir Charles, 59, 65, 81
Potter, Sergeant, 6

Qasaba, 16, 17, 35, 40, 107
Qattara Depression, 92, 104, 107

Radar, 18; Germans in North Africa, 73; in Crusader, 80, 86
Radio Direction Finding, 18
Reggio di Calabria, 145, 147, 150
R.A.F. Regiment, 76, 82
Rex, Italy's biggest liner: sunk, 162

Rew, Sergeant, 37
Rimini, 161
Ritchie, Lieutenant-General Neil, 77, 79, 81, 89
Roberts, Corporal Richard, 113, 119, 126
Roma, Italian Battle Cruiser: sunk, 148
Romagnoli, Maggiore Carlo, 19
Rome, 144
Rommel, Generalmajor Irwin, 3; visits Sicily en route to North Africa, 50, 55, 58, 59, 60, 73, 74, 78, 79, 81, 82, 89, 90, 92, 94, 95, 97-99 passim; 106-108 passim; 126, 127, 129, 130.
Ross, Flight Sergeant, 6
Rover Control System, 155, 156, 162
Rustom, Wing Commander, 97
Ryde, Major-General, 119

Salerno: landings, 145-147 passim; 150, 151, 153
Salvation Army Mobile Canteen, 104
San Angelo, 160
Sangro River, 155
Saunders, Flying Officer: shoots down the first German aircraft in combat over North Africa, 54, 55
Savannah, US Battle Cruiser, 148
Schultz, Oberfeldwebel, 83
Sector Operations Rooms, 18
Sedad, 123
Selby, Flight Lieutenant John, 95
Senussi, 12
7th Army, U.S., 142
Servicing Commando Units. No 3201, 140, 141
Shallufa, 54
Shegga, 24
Sicily, 15, 45; Rommel visits. 50; 89, 90, 123, 124, 134, 137, 139; invasion of, 140; fighting in ends, 144; 147, 153
Sidi Azeiz, 24, 30, 31
Sidi Barrani, 10, 16, 22, 23, 25, 28, 32, 33, 36, 37, 40, 46, 67
Sidi Haneish, 76, 78, 108
Sidi Rezegh, 77, 78
Sing, Wing Commander J.E.J., 112
Sirte, 54, 70, 122, 142
Smith, Flight Lieutenant J.P. "Smudger", 56
Smuts, General, 59
Smyth, Squadron Leader Maurice, 12, 95, 103, 104, 106-108 passim; 117, 118, 132, 134. DFC gazetted 163, 164.
Sollum, 2, 10, 24, 26, 43, 47, 70
Somaliland, 15, 62, 69

Spaatz, General Carl, 124, 129
Spanish Civil War, Italian Air Force in, 17, 19
Spence, Pilot Officer, 57
Springorum, Hauptmann, 60
Stanfield, Aircraftman Richard, 109
Stohr, Sergeant Oscar, 128
Straight, Air Commodore Whitney, 110
Strategic Reconnaissance Flight, No 1437, 105

SQUADRONS

R.A.F.

No6, 40, 54, 56, 61, 70, 92
No11, 43, 48, 68
No13, 129
No14, 60
No18, 129
No30, 17, 25, 40, 43, 60, 82
No33, 1, 17, 22, 24-26 passim; 30-33 passim; 35-37 passim; 39, 40, 46-48 passim; 66, 83, 105
No37, 40, 106
No38, 40
No39, 43, 48, 60
No40, 106
No43, 129
No45, 40, 56, 60, 105
No46, 105
No55, 30, 54, 56, 60, 67, 105
No70, 40, 106
No72, 139, 141
No73, 40, 54-56 passim; 60, 83, 93, 95, 104-106 passim; 108, 112, 117, 123, 134
No80, 30, 31, 33, 36-40 passim; 43, 46, 73, 75, 83, 105
No81, 112
No84, 43
No89, 105, 123
No92, 4, 105, 113, 119, 130
No93, 139, 150
No94, 83, 105, 108
No104, 106
No108, 75, 106
No109, 74
No111, 139
No112, 31-33 passim; 35, 37, 43, 48, 77, 79-83 passim; 104, 105, 120
No113, 30, 33, 36, 114
No114, 129
No117, 97,110
No127, 105
No145, 91, 105, 112, 113, 157, 158
No152, 112
No208, 33, 36, 38, 40, 55, 105
No211, 22, 23, 43

No213, 5, 105, 108
No216, 17, 24, 40, 53, 91, 97, 98
No217, 110
No223, 83, 85, 105
No225, 137, 151, 157, 158
No228, 17
No229, 66, 81
No230, 17, 29
No232, 130, 139
No238, 4, 76, 105, 108
No243, 139
No250, 60, 66, 81, 83, 90, 104, 105, 120, 152, 153
No252, 98, 106, 118
No260, 83, 105, 108, 128, 142, 152, 163
No261, 49
No267, 97
No272, 72, 74, 98, 106
No274, 39, 40, 46, 47, 57, 60, 81, 83, 93, 96, 105
No275, 39, 40, 46, 47
No332, 112
No335, 105
No601, 105, 111
No614, 129
No1437 Strategic Reconnaissance Flight, 105, 151
No2 Photographic Reconnaissance Unit, 105

Fleet Air Arm

No889, 105

R. Australian A.F.

No3, 4, 39, 40, 46, 47, 54-56 passim; 66, 77, 81-83 passim; 90, 104, 105, 120, 128
No450, 83, 104, 105, 120, 128
No451, 66
No454, 126
No459, 113, 119, 126

R. Canadian A.F.

No417, 105

South African A.F.

No1, 4, 60, 66, 75, 94, 105
No2, 60, 66, 83, 90, 105, 107, 131
No4, 83, 105
No5, 105, 131
No6, 106
No7, 106
No12, 105
No24, 60, 66, 105
No40, 105
No60, 105

R. Egyptian A.F.

No1, 17
No5, 17, 35